Table of Contents

Module 1 1
Module 2 14
Module 3 29
Module 4 46
Module 5 61
Module 6 73
Module 7 86
Module 8 97
Module 9 109
Module 10 123
Module 11 133
Module 12 142
Module 13 158
Module 14 172
Module 15 181
Module 16 189
Module 17 197
Module 18 217
Cutout Worksheets 238
Extra Resources 336

This workbook contains all of the worksheets found in the Math 2 Semester A course. To see the worksheet in color, view it online within the lessons. For any worksheets containing cutting activities, they can be found in the "Cutout Worksheets" section. The "Extra Resources" contain helpful tools that students are learning to use.

© 2021 by Accelerate Education
Visit us on the Web at www.accelerate.education

Name: _____   Date: _____

Extra Practice:
Doubles

Find the sum for each of the doubles addition sentences below.

```
  1        2        3
 +1       +2       +3
____     ____     ____

  4        5        6
 +4       +5       +6
____     ____     ____

  7        8        9       10
 +7       +8       +9      +10
____     ____     ____    ____
```

1

1.3 Doubles and Near Doubles

Next page

Near Doubles Addition

Find the sum of each of the near doubles addition facts by drawing counters in the boxes and circling the doubles facts to help you add.

Example: 5 + 6 = 11

      5   +   5   + 1

1. 6 + 7 = ____

2. 3 + 4 = ____

3. 2 + 1 = ____

4. 8 + 9 = ____

5. 4 + 6 = ____

1.3 Doubles and Near Doubles

Name: _____ Date: _____

Extra Practice: Ten Frame

Use your red and white counters to fill the ten frame as many different ways as you can. The red counters will represent the first addend, and the white counters will represent the second addend. For each way you make 10, draw a picture on the ten frames given on the next pages and write your addition sentence to make 10.

1.4 Make a 10

Record your addition sentences and draw a picture of your ten frame. Remember, the red counters will represent the first addend, and the white counters will represent your second addend.

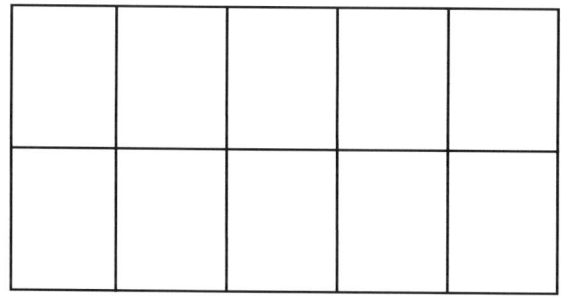

___ + ___ = ___

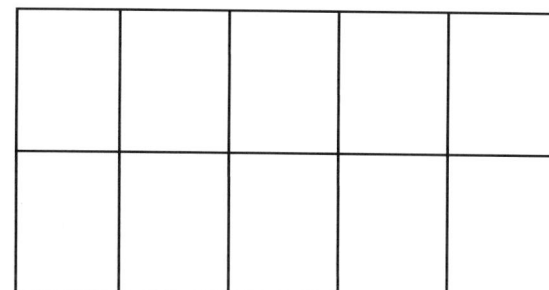

___ + ___ = ___

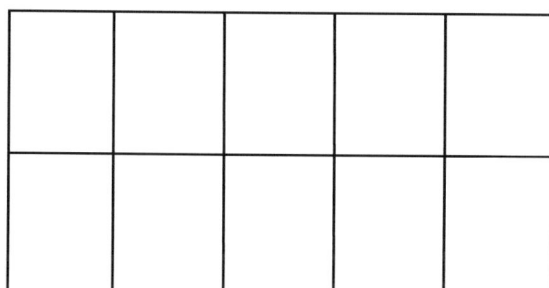

___ + ___ = ___

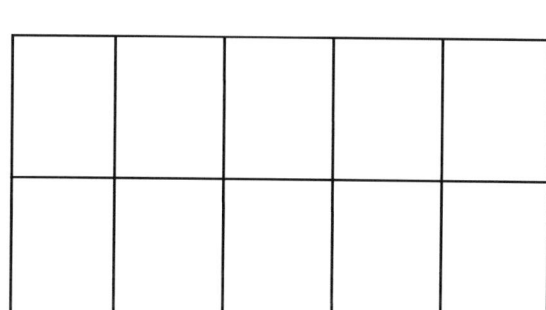

___ + ___ = ___

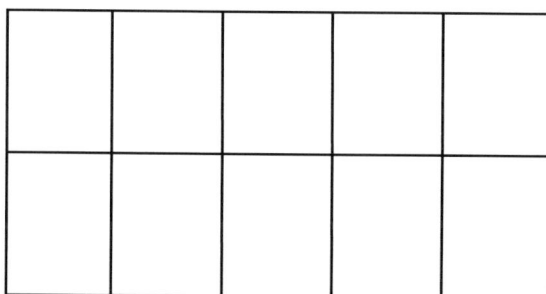

___ + ___ = ___

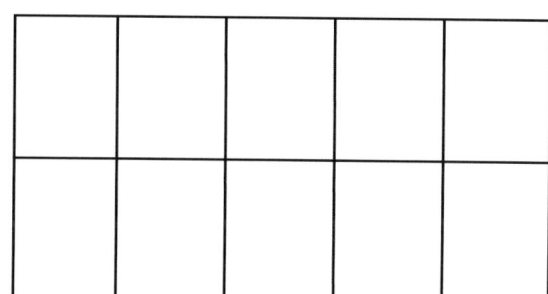

___ + ___ = ___

1.4 Make a 10

Next page

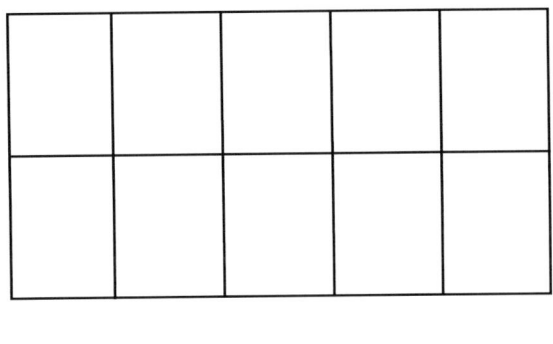

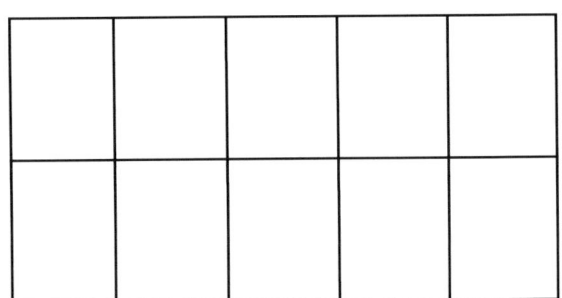

___ + ___ = ___   ___ + ___ = ___

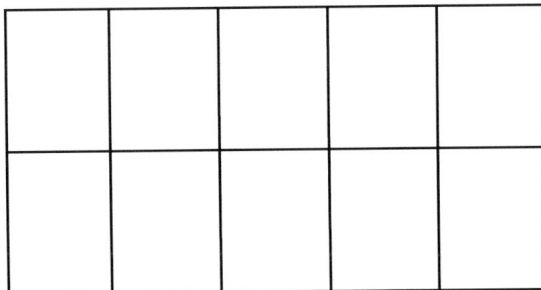

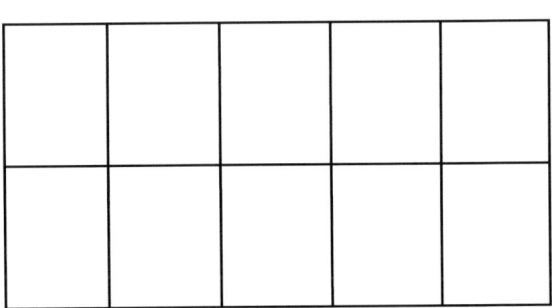

___ + ___ = ___   ___ + ___ = ___

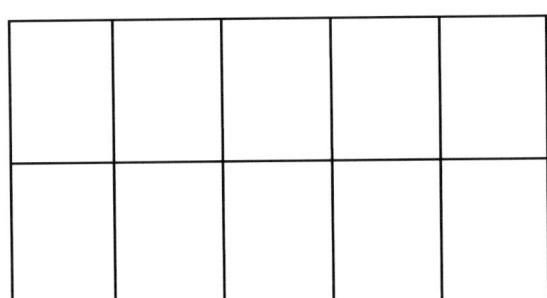

___ + ___ = ___

1.4 Make a 10

Name: _____ Date: _____

Adding on Two Ten Frames

Use pennies and dimes to create each addition sentence in the ten frames.

The pennies will represent the first addend, and the dimes will represent the second addend. Show your work by removing the coins and drawing brown and grey dots with crayons or colored pencils.

The brown dots will represent the pennies, and the grey dots will represent the dimes. Don't forget to record the sum on the empty line!

Example: 10 + 7 = 17

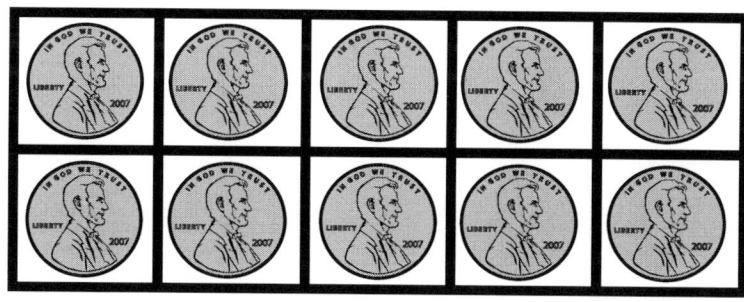

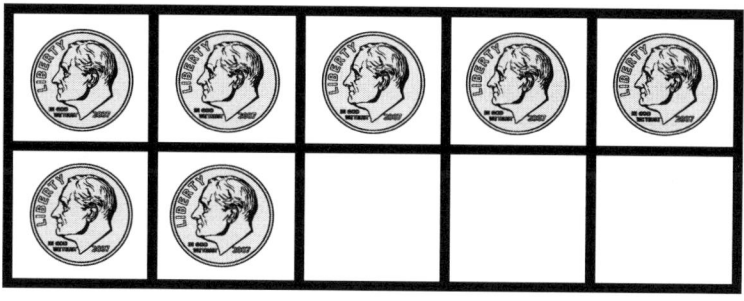

1.5 Practice Making Ten and Adding to Ten

6

Next page

1. 10 + 8 = ___

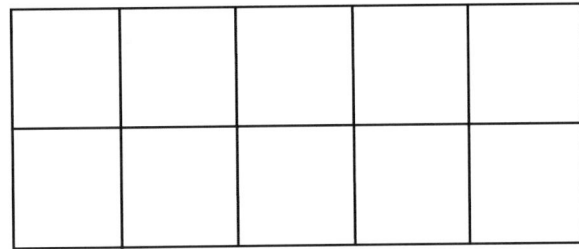

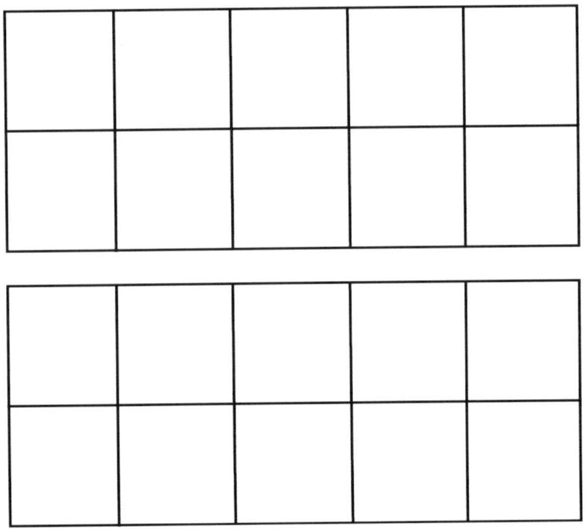

2. 10 + 3 = ___

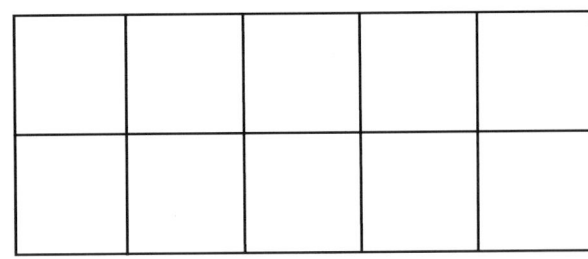

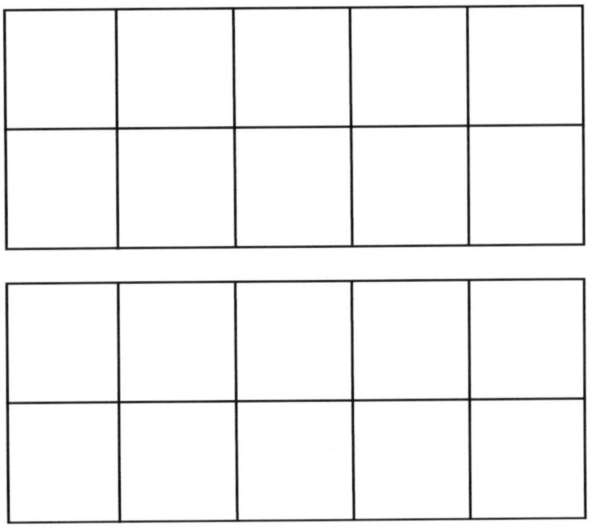

3. 10 + 6 = ___

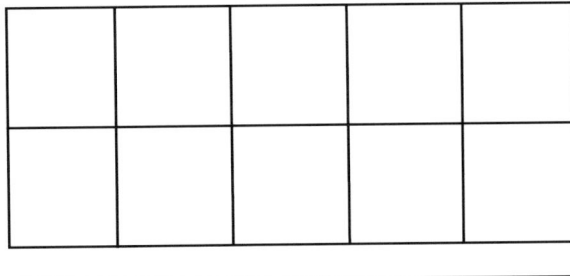

4. 10 + 2 = ___

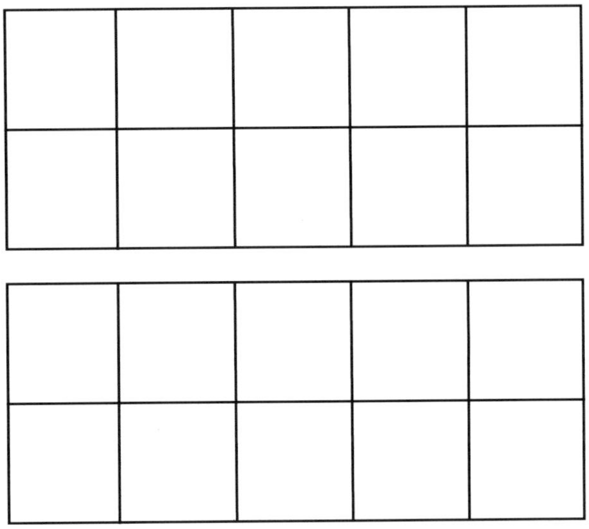

1.5 Practice Making Ten and Adding to Ten

5. 10 + 1 = ___

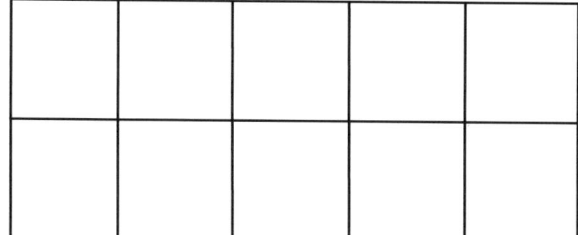

6. 10 + 4 = ___

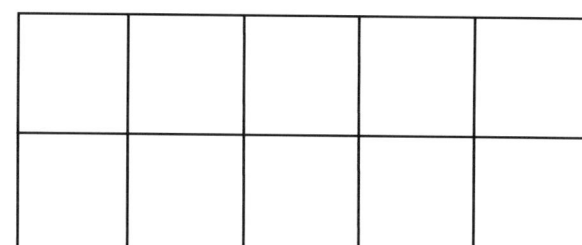

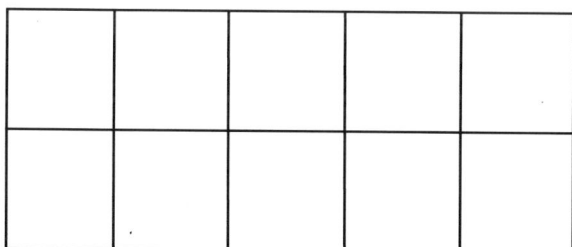

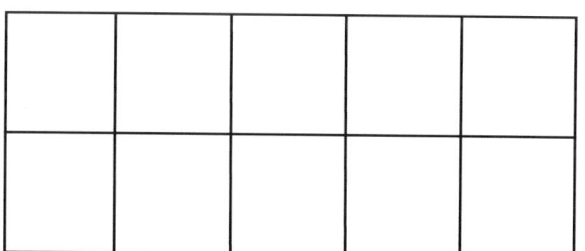

7. 10 + 0 = ___

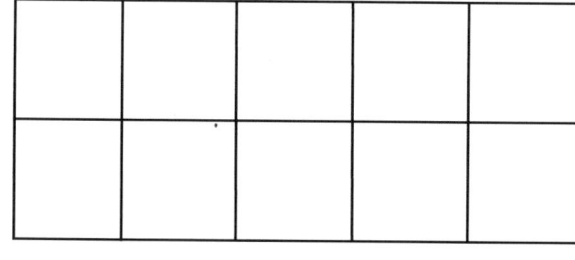

8. 10 + 9 = ___

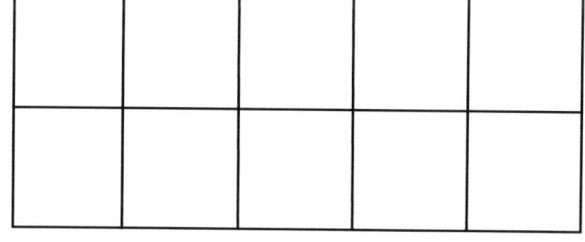

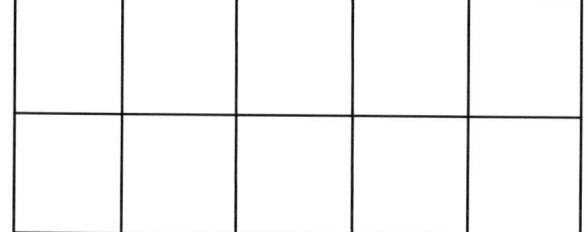

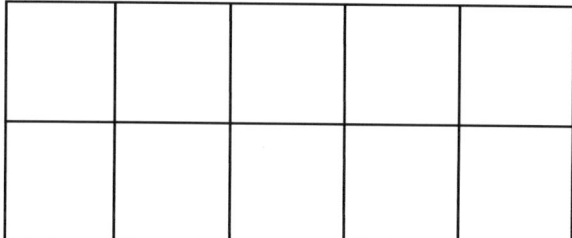

1.5 Practice Making Ten and Adding to Ten

9. 10 + 5 = ___

10. 10 + 10 = ___

1.5 Practice Making Ten and Adding to Ten

Name: _____ Date: _____

Practice: Adding to Ten Addition Sentences

Use the ten frames below to write addition sentences and put them in order. Remember, the first addend is made with red dots, and the second addend is made with yellow dots.

For each addition sentence, write the first addend in the first box, the second addend in the second box, and the sum in the last box. When you have found every sum, put the problems in order from the smallest sum (1) to the biggest sum (10).

Example:

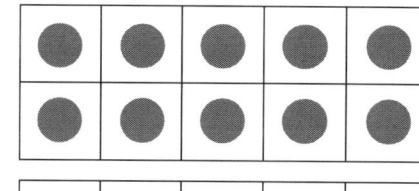

_3_

$\boxed{10} + \boxed{3} = \boxed{13}$

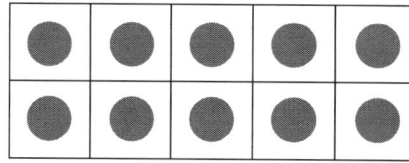

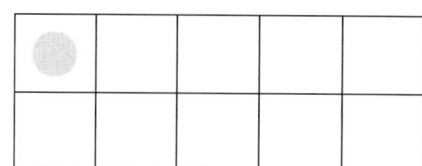

___

$\boxed{} + \boxed{} = \boxed{}$

1.5 Practice Making Ten and Adding to Ten

10

Next page

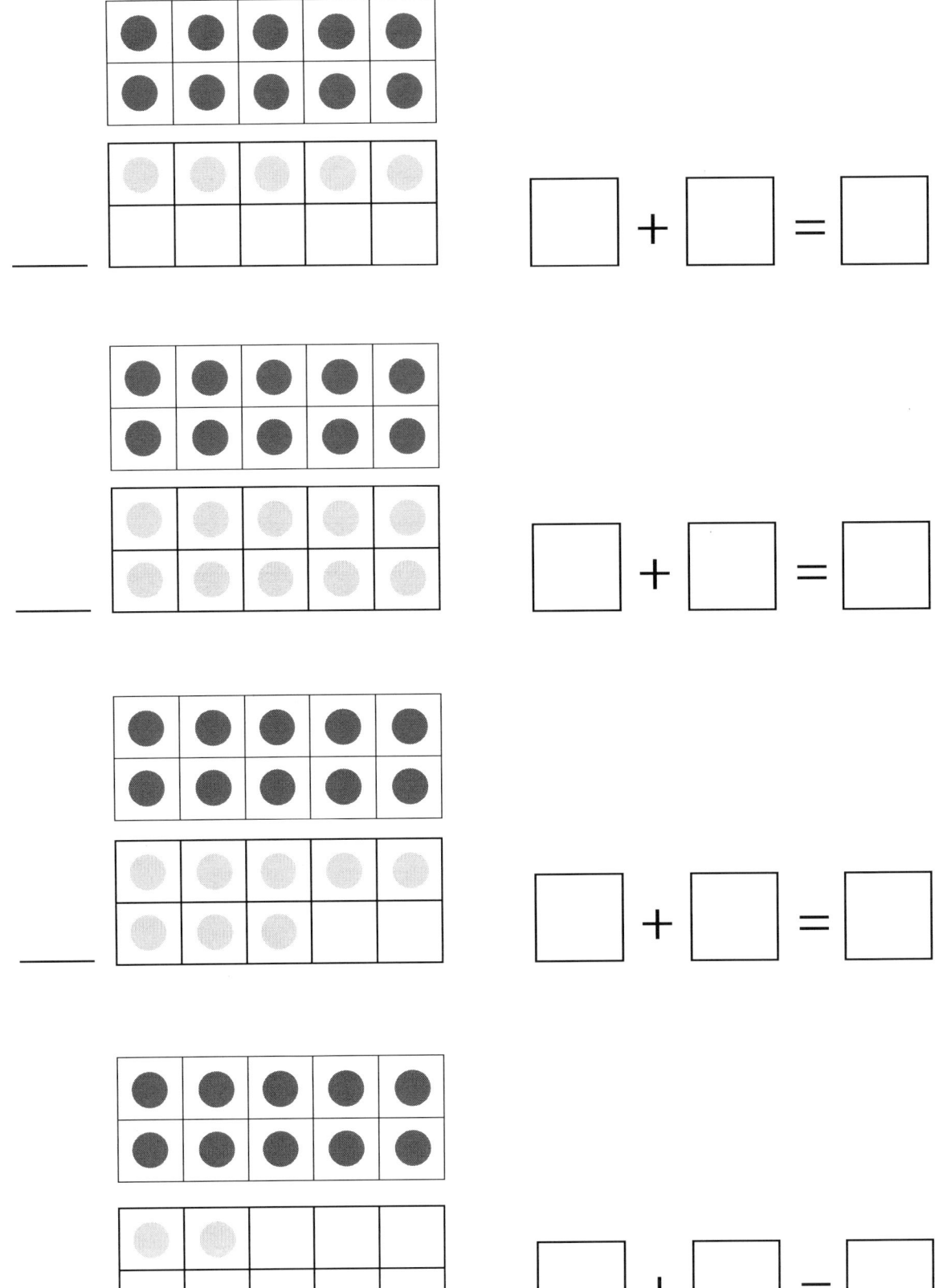

1.5 Practice Making Ten and Adding to Ten

1.5 Practice Making Ten and Adding to Ten

___ □ + □ = □

___ □ + □ = □

___ □ + □ = □

___ □ + □ = □

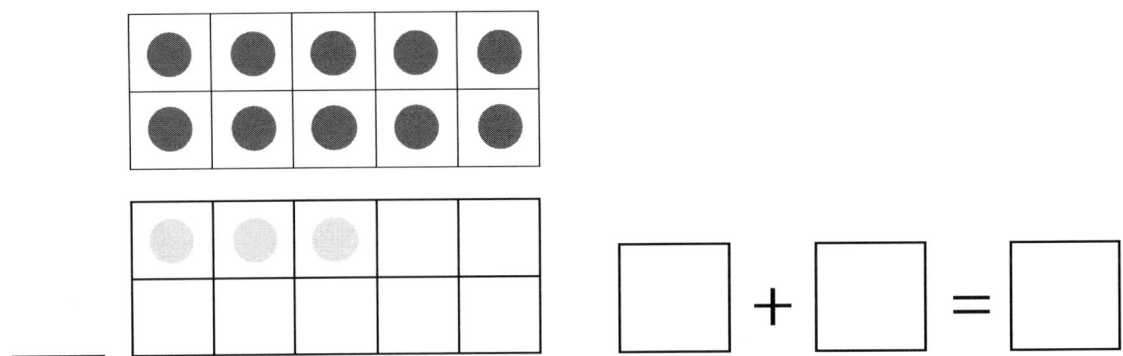

___ ☐ + ☐ = ☐

Name: _____ Date: _____

Practice: Finding the Difference

Find the difference of each of the subtraction sentences by using your colored candies or counters. For each subtraction sentence, draw the number of candies/counters that represent the whole. Then, draw x's over the ones that are being taken away. Count up your sum and write it on the line.

Example: 7 - 2 =   5

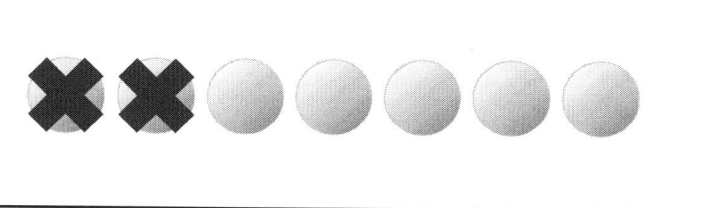

1. 5 - 3 = ___

2. 4 - 1 = ___

2.1 Subtraction Properties

14

Next page

3. 7 - 5 = ___

4. 6 - 2 = ___

5. 8 - 3 = ___

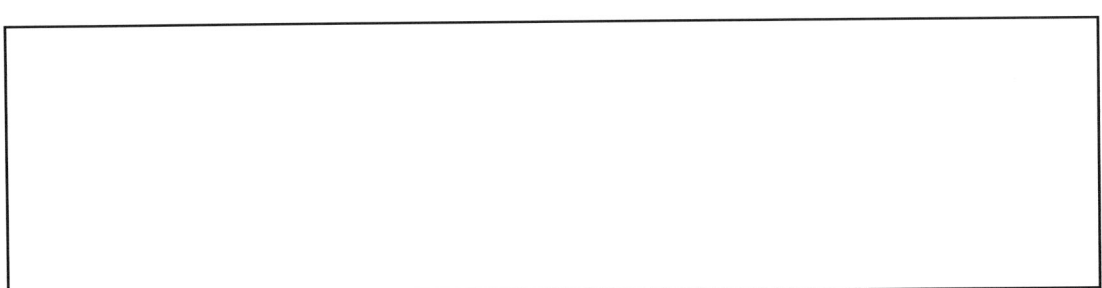

Extra Practice: Can you show the parts of a subtraction sentence? For each problem, put a W under the whole and P under each part. Be sure to circle the part that represents the difference.

Name: _____ Date: _____

Practice: Counting Back with Counters

Use the boxes below to count back with your counters! Find the difference to each subtraction sentence. Then, draw the counters in the box. Show that you are "taking away" by putting x's on the drawings of the counters you took away.

Example:

9 - 5 = <u>4</u>  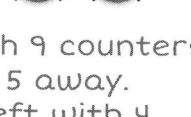 Start with 9 counters and take 5 away. You are left with 4 counters!	6 - 5 = ___	7 - 2 = ___
8 - 4 = ___	9 - 6 = ___	10 - 3 = ___

Extra Practice: Think About It- What is the difference of 9 - 5? How do you know? Use the box above to write and/or draw your thoughts.

Helpful Hint: Look at the example at the top of the page to use the counters!

2.2 Count Back to Subtract

16

Name: _____ Date: _____

Practice: Counting Back

Find the difference of each subtraction sentence by counting back. As you count back, label each of the pictures with the number you say aloud. Record your answer in the blank provided.

Example:

8 − 2 = __6__

1. 9 − 1 = ____

2. 7 − 4 = ____

3. 10 − 5 = ____

4. 6 − 2 = ____

17

2.2 Count Back to Subtract

5. 5 − 4 = ____

6. 8 − 3 = ____

7. 9 − 6 = ____

8. 5 − 1 = ____

9. 7 − 6 = ____

10. 10 − 1 = ____

2.2 Count Back to Subtract

Name: _____ Date: _____

Practice: Domino Subtraction

Gather dominoes with equal sides totalling 4, 6, 8, 10, and 12. Choose a domino and draw the dots on each side in the space provided. Write the subtraction sentence that matches each domino.

Example:

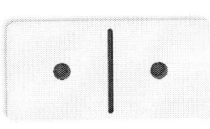 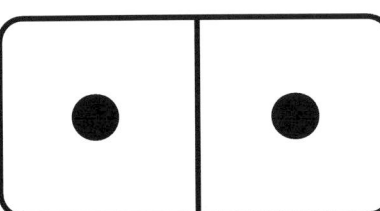 2 - 1 = 1

1.

___ - ___ = ___

2.

___ - ___ = ___

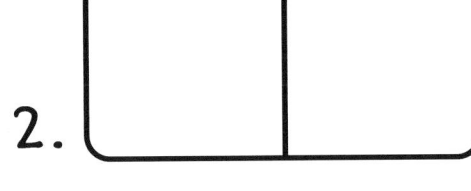

3.

___ - ___ = ___

4.

___ - ___ = ___

5.

___ - ___ = ___

19

2.3 Use Doubles to Subtract

Name: _____ Date: _____

Part-Part-Whole Chart

Use the chart below with your counters and walk through the steps given in the lesson.

Part	Part
Whole	

2.4 Relate Addition and Subtraction

20

Name: _____ Date: _____

Relating Addition and Subtraction

Complete the part-part-whole charts using circles to represent counters for each subtraction problem. Put the first part you see in the first part box. Put the second part in the second box. You can color the counters or just draw empty circles. Then, write the number of counters you drew in each box.

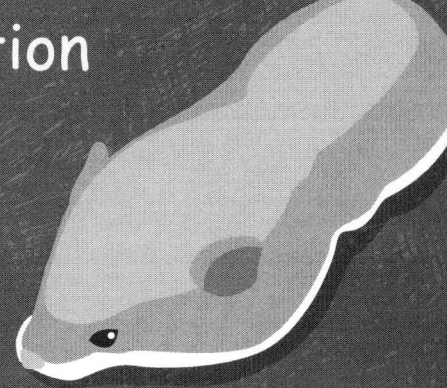

Example: 8 - 5 = 3

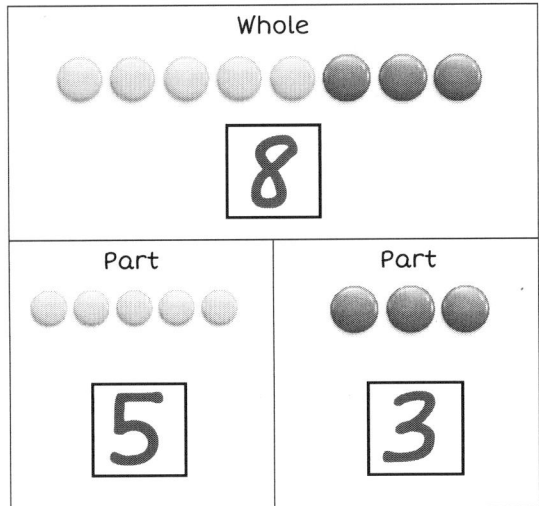

1. 6 - 2 = 4

Whole

Part Part

2. 7 - 5 = 2

Whole

Part Part

21

2.4 Relate Addition and Subtraction

3. 8 - 3 = 5

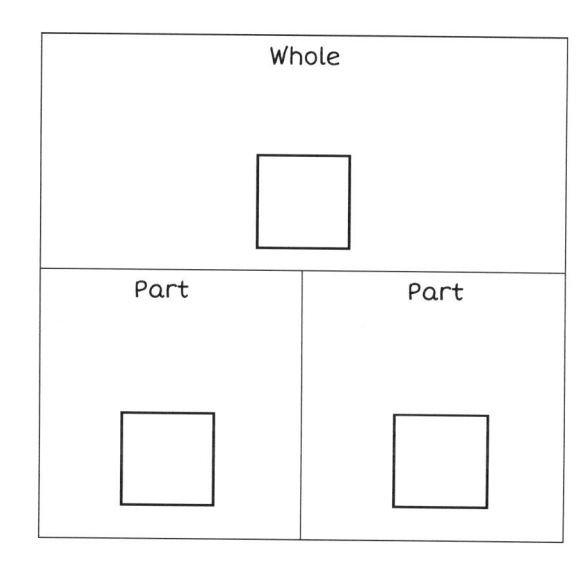

Whole
□

Part	Part
□	□

4. 9 - 6 = 3

Whole
□

Part	Part
□	□

5. 10 - 4 = 6

Whole
□

Part	Part
□	□

Extra Practice: Can you write the other subtraction sentence in the fact family for each of the subtraction sentences above? Remember, subtraction sentences should be written as **Whole - Part = Part**.

1. □ - □ = □

2. □ - □ = □

3. □ - □ = □

4. □ - □ = □

5. □ - □ = □

2.4 Relate Addition and Subtraction

Name: _____ Date: _____

Practice: Write Subtraction Sentences

Help feed the fish by looking at the row of counters in each problem. This row of counters represents your **subtraction sentence**. Count your **whole** number of counters. Then move the number of "x" counters into the fish to feed it. These "x" counters represent the **part** being taken away from the whole. Count the remaining counters outside of the fish to find the **difference**. Once you know your answer, replace your counters by drawing circles with your crayons. Don't forget to write your subtraction sentence in the blanks provided below.

Example:

[ ] - [3] = [4]

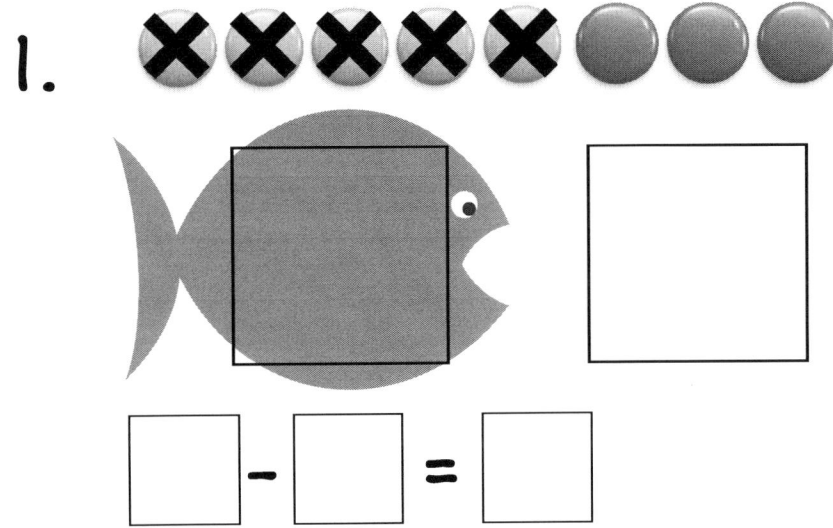

23

2.5 Write Subtraction Sentences

2.

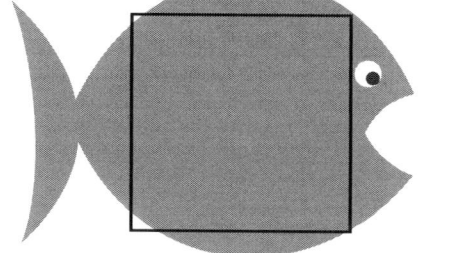

3.

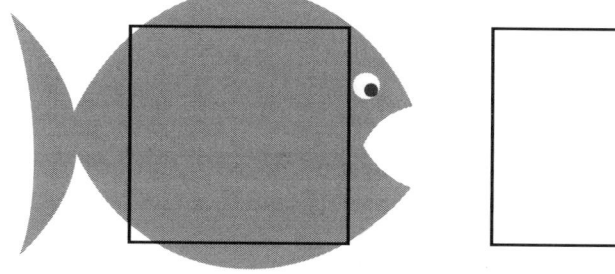

4.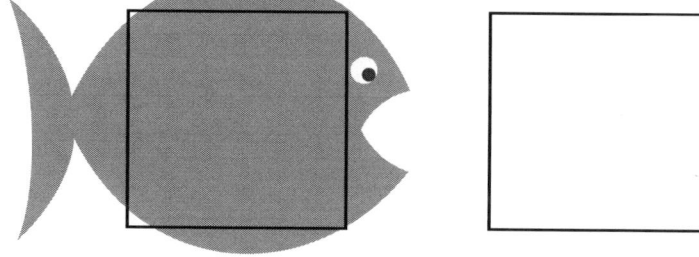

2.5 Write Subtraction Sentences

5.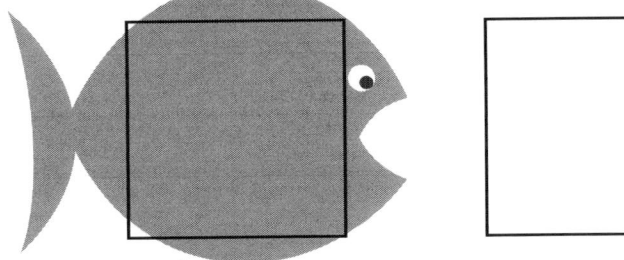

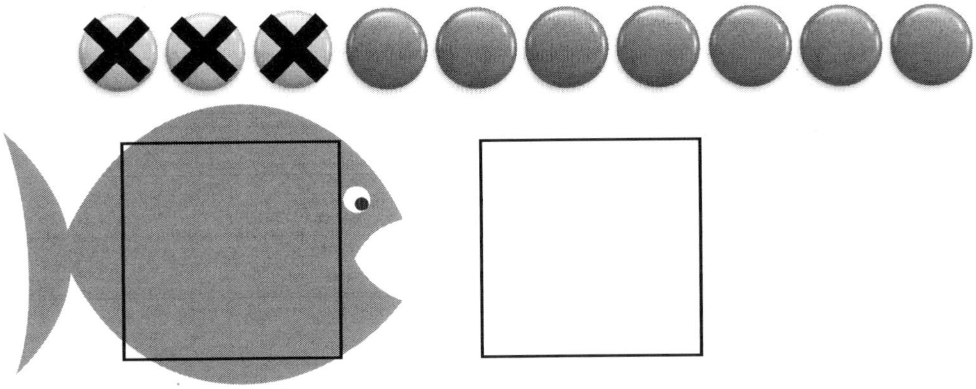

☐ - ☐ = ☐

6.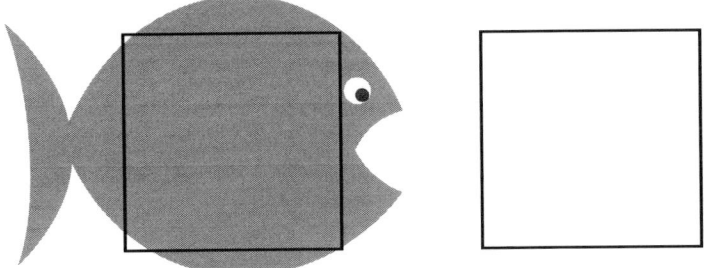

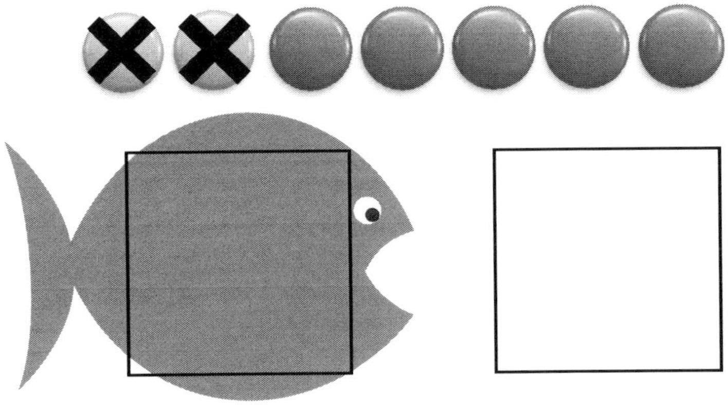

☐ - ☐ = ☐

7.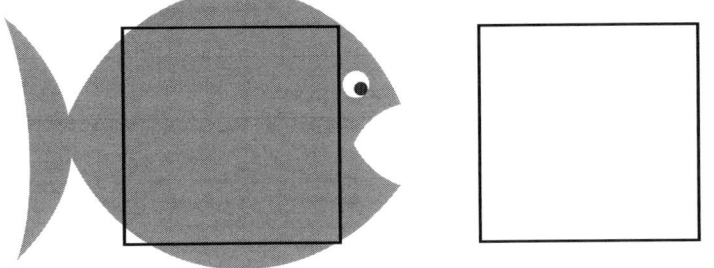

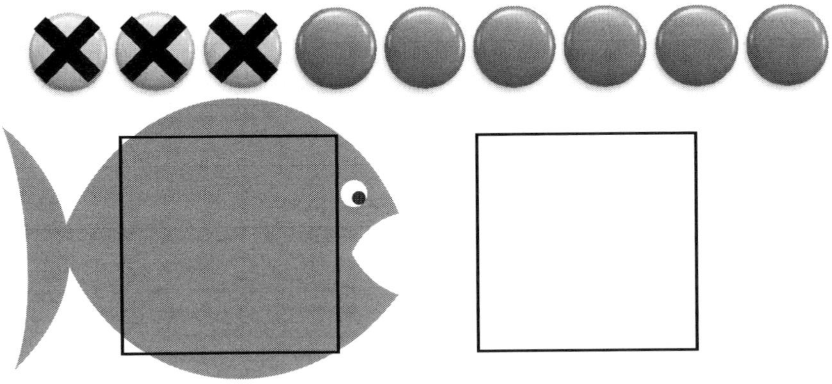

☐ - ☐ = ☐

2.5 Write Subtraction Sentences

8.

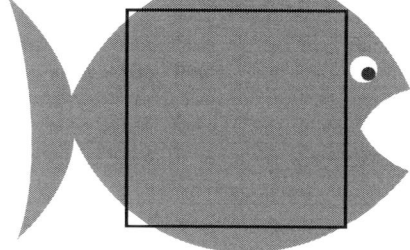 

☐ - ☐ = ☐

9.

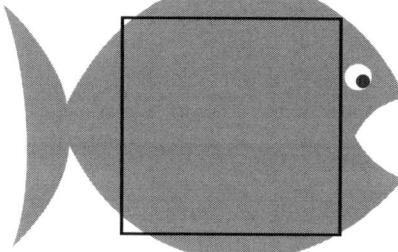 

☐ - ☐ = ☐

10.

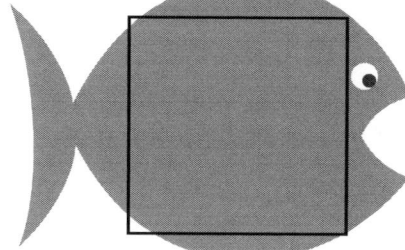 

☐ - ☐ = ☐

2.5 Write Subtraction Sentences

Name: _____ Date: _____

Write Subtraction Sentences

Reuben was very hungry when he got home from school. There were 8 cookies in the cookie jar. Reuben ate 6 of them. How many cookies are **left**? Write your **subtraction sentence** in the space provided. **Show your work** by drawing the cookies in the cookie jar. Draw an "x" over the cookies that Reuben ate. Then answer the questions in complete sentences.

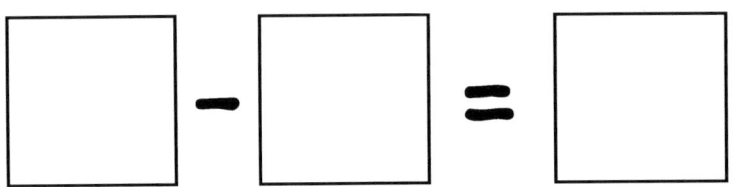

2.5 Write Subtraction Sentences

1. Looking at your subtraction sentence, which number is the whole?

2. How do you know that number is the whole?

3. Which number is the difference?

4. How do you know that number is the difference?

2.5 Write Subtraction Sentences

Name: _____ Date: _____

Addition Toolbox
Below are the strategies and manipulatives you have used in this lesson to help yourself add. Now you can use them whenever it works for you and the addition problem you are solving!

Counting On   Ten Frames

Doubles   Near Doubles

 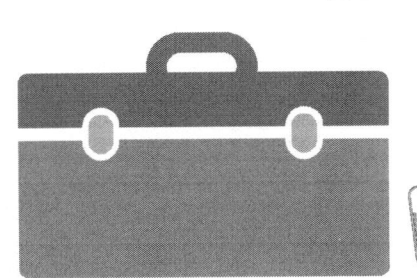 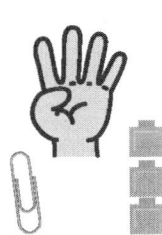

Strategies   Manipulatives

Counting On - Example: 12 + 3 = _____   - fingers

Doubles - Example: 6 + 6 = _____   - counters/coins

Near Doubles - Example: 5 + 6 = _____   - stacking cubes

Ten Frames - Example: 5 + 6 = _____   - paper clips

3.1 Add To (Up to 20)

Name: _____ Date: _____

Practice: Add to 20

Use an addition strategy to help you find the sum. Record the sum in the blank. Then color in the square with the color that matches the addition strategy you chose.

Counting On	● Red
Ten Frames	● Orange
Doubles	● Yellow
Near Doubles	● Green

10 + 6 ____	8 + 2 = ____	8 + 9 = ____	12 + 4 ____	1 + 1 = ____
5 + 6 = ____	8 + 8 = ____	9 + 5 = ____	1 + 2 = ____	4 + 1 = ____

3.1 Add To (Up to 20)

Name: _____ Date: _____

Brainstorm: Adding Three Numbers

How would you add the three numbers to help Lady Amelia figure out how many dragons she found on her quest? Write any words that come to mind and any steps or manipulatives you would use. You can also draw pictures of the dragons, manipulatives, or anything that shows your thinking!

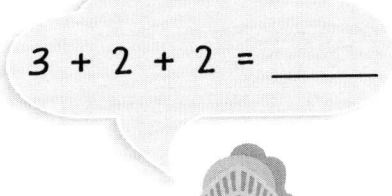

3 + 2 + 2 = _____

If you are feeling stuck, try answering these questions:
- What pictures would help you find the sum?
- Would you use counters or cubes to help you add?
- Can you add three numbers at once?
- Which numbers look like they are easy to add?

31

3.3 Add Three Numbers

Challenge: What do you think the sum is? How do you know?

3.3 Add Three Numbers

Name: _____ Date: _____

Adding Three Numbers

Can you find the sum of three adddends using your stacking cubes? First, make three separate stacks of stacking cubes. Each stack should represent each addend, just like this:

6 + 6 + 2 = _____

Next, circle the friendly numbers and combine those stacking cube stacks. Remember, friendly numbers are addends that are doubles or add up to 10. Add the friendly numbers together and write the sum under them, just like this:

(6)+(6)+ 2 = _____
12

Last, add the sum of the friendly numbers with the remaining addend:

(6)+(6)+ 2 = __14__
12

Directions: Make three stacks for each of your addends. Circle the friendly numbers and combine their stacking cube stacks to show you are putting your addends together. Write their sum underneath the circles. Then add the last number to find the total sum!

1. 2 + 8 + 7 = _____

2. 3 + 4 + 6 = _____

3. 1 + 2 + 2 = _____

4. 3 + 7 + 1 = _____

5. 3 + 3 + 6 = _____

3.3 Add Three Numbers

Name: _____ Date: _____

Adding Three Numbers

Danny the dragon needs help! Color the doubles fact, then find the sum. Each sum represents a color that you can use to color in Danny. If you can't find a sum in the color key, check your work and try again!

Example:
⑥+⑥+②= __14__

1. ①+④+④= ____
2. ①+⑥+①= ____
3. ④+⑥+⑤= ____
4. ⑧+③+⑧= ____
5. ⑤+④+⑤= ____
6. ②+①+⑧= ____
7. ⑥+⑧+④= ____
8. ⑤+⑥+⑤= ____
9. ①+③+①= ____
10. ⑦+②+③= ____

Sum	Color
5	Red
8	Orange
9	Green
11	Yellow
12	Purple
14	Grey
15	Black
16	Light Green
18	Pink
19	Light Blue

3.3 Add Three Numbers

Next page

3.3 Add Three Numbers

Name: _____ Date: _____

Add on a Number Line

Gather your base-ten blocks and set aside unit blocks to complete this activity below! Find the sum by circling the larger addend in each addition sentence, and then circling that same addend on each number line. Use unit blocks to represent the remaining addend by placing them in the spaces to the right of the larger addend on the number line. Draw your jumps over the unit blocks, and then record your sum!

Example:

4 + ⑤ = 9

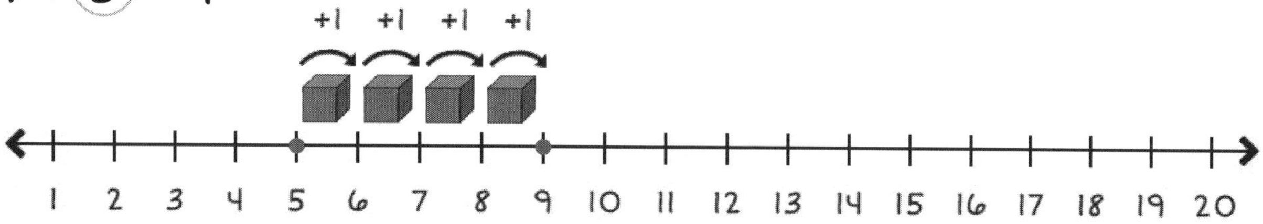

1) 3 + 10 = ____

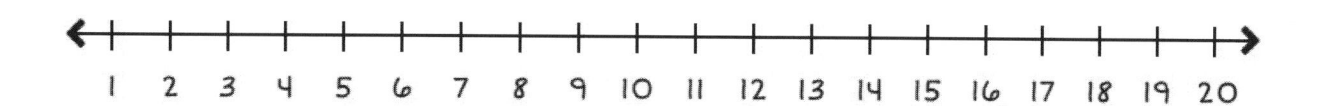

2) 6 + 4 = ____

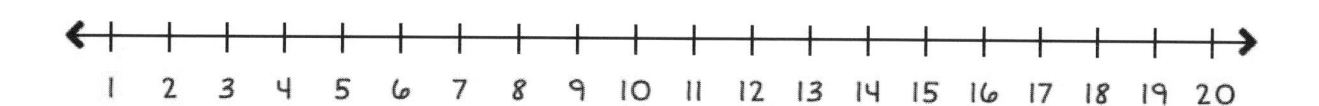

3.4 Add on a Number Line

36

Next page

3) 2 + 3 = ____

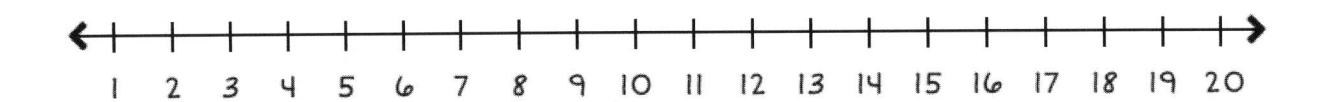

←|—|—|—|—|—|—|—|—|—|—|—|—|—|—|—|—|—|—|—|—|→
 1 2 3 4 5 6 7 8 9 10 11 12 13 14 15 16 17 18 19 20

4) 9 + 8 = ____

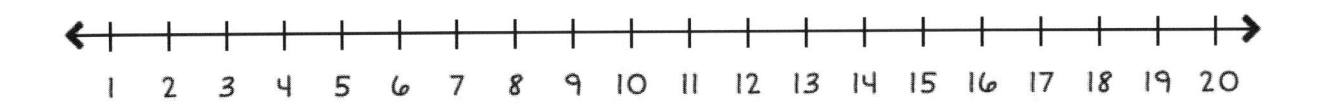

←|—|—|—|—|—|—|—|—|—|—|—|—|—|—|—|—|—|—|—|—|→
 1 2 3 4 5 6 7 8 9 10 11 12 13 14 15 16 17 18 19 20

5) 11 + 4 = ____

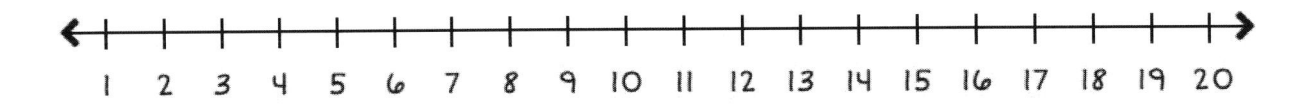

←|—|—|—|—|—|—|—|—|—|—|—|—|—|—|—|—|—|—|—|—|→
 1 2 3 4 5 6 7 8 9 10 11 12 13 14 15 16 17 18 19 20

6) 7 + 5 = ____

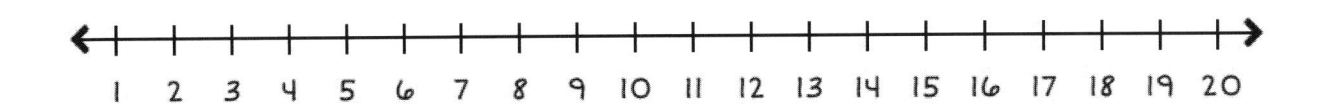

←|—|—|—|—|—|—|—|—|—|—|—|—|—|—|—|—|—|—|—|—|→
 1 2 3 4 5 6 7 8 9 10 11 12 13 14 15 16 17 18 19 20

7) 1 + 8 = ____

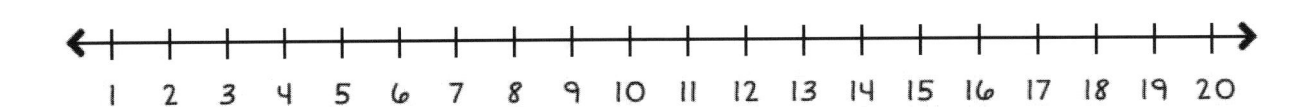

←|—|—|—|—|—|—|—|—|—|—|—|—|—|—|—|—|—|—|—|—|→
 1 2 3 4 5 6 7 8 9 10 11 12 13 14 15 16 17 18 19 20

3.4 Add on a Number Line

8) 8 + 6 = ____

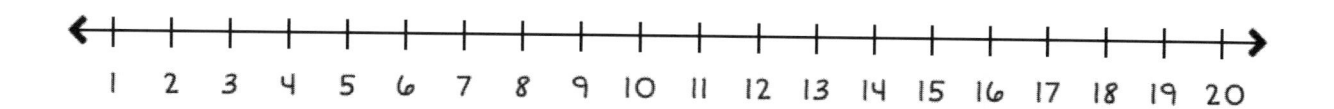

```
←—|——|——|——|——|——|——|——|——|——|——|——|——|——|——|——|——|——|——|——|——→
   1  2  3  4  5  6  7  8  9  10 11 12 13 14 15 16 17 18 19 20
```

9) 10 + 9 = ____

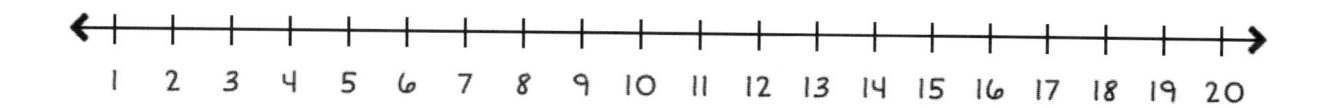

```
←—|——|——|——|——|——|——|——|——|——|——|——|——|——|——|——|——|——|——|——|——→
   1  2  3  4  5  6  7  8  9  10 11 12 13 14 15 16 17 18 19 20
```

10) 4 + 9 = ____

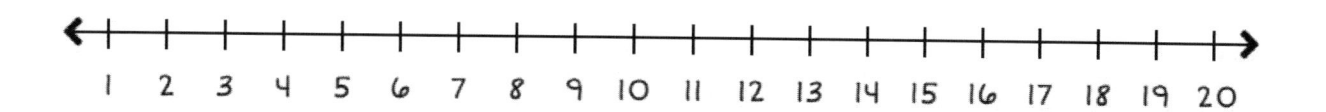

```
←—|——|——|——|——|——|——|——|——|——|——|——|——|——|——|——|——|——|——|——|——→
   1  2  3  4  5  6  7  8  9  10 11 12 13 14 15 16 17 18 19 20
```

3.4 Add on a Number Line

Name: _____ Date: _____

Add on a Number Line - Part 2

Practice adding on a number line! Circle the larger addend in the addition sentence and place a dot above that number on the number line. Then, jump the number of times the smaller addend tells you to. Don't forget to record the sum on the line provided!

Example:

1 + ⓘ⑰ = 18

←|—|—|—|—|—|—|—|—|—|—|—|—|—|—|—|—|•—|—|—|→
  1 2 3 4 5 6 7 8 9 10 11 12 13 14 15 16 17 18 19 20

1) 7 + 4 = ____

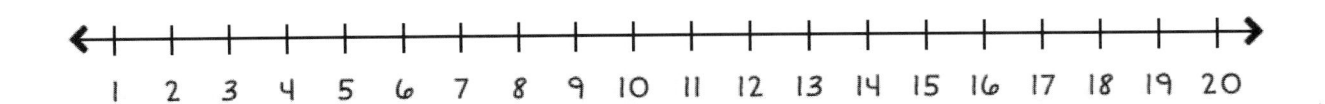

←|—|—|—|—|—|—|—|—|—|—|—|—|—|—|—|—|—|—|—|→
  1 2 3 4 5 6 7 8 9 10 11 12 13 14 15 16 17 18 19 20

2) 2 + 14 = ____

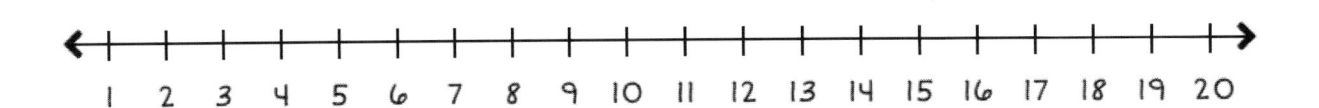

←|—|—|—|—|—|—|—|—|—|—|—|—|—|—|—|—|—|—|—|→
  1 2 3 4 5 6 7 8 9 10 11 12 13 14 15 16 17 18 19 20

3) 13 + 4 = ____

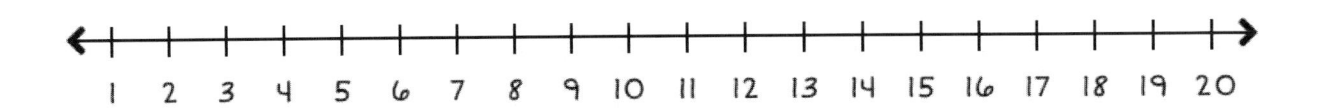

←|—|—|—|—|—|—|—|—|—|—|—|—|—|—|—|—|—|—|—|→
  1 2 3 4 5 6 7 8 9 10 11 12 13 14 15 16 17 18 19 20

4) 3 + 15 = ___

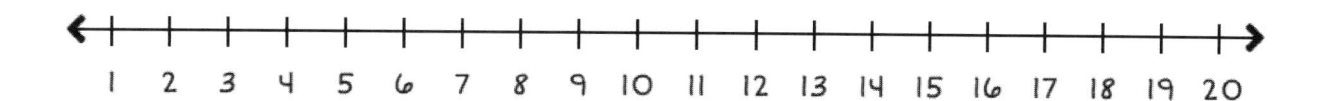

```
←―|――|――|――|――|――|――|――|――|――|――|――|――|――|――|――|――|――|――|――|→
   1  2  3  4  5  6  7  8  9  10 11 12 13 14 15 16 17 18 19 20
```

5) 8 + 12 = ___

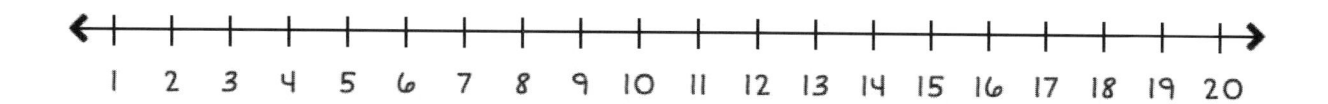

```
←―|――|――|――|――|――|――|――|――|――|――|――|――|――|――|――|――|――|――|――|→
   1  2  3  4  5  6  7  8  9  10 11 12 13 14 15 16 17 18 19 20
```

6) 11 + 4 = ___

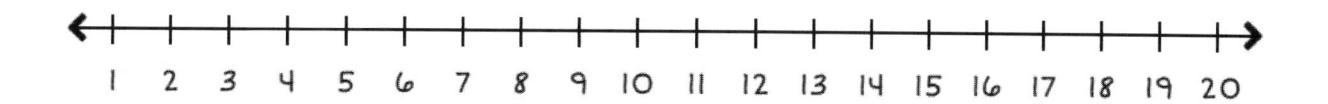

```
←―|――|――|――|――|――|――|――|――|――|――|――|――|――|――|――|――|――|――|――|→
   1  2  3  4  5  6  7  8  9  10 11 12 13 14 15 16 17 18 19 20
```

7) 3 + 10 = ___

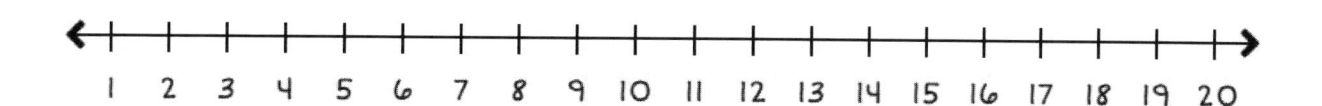

```
←―|――|――|――|――|――|――|――|――|――|――|――|――|――|――|――|――|――|――|――|→
   1  2  3  4  5  6  7  8  9  10 11 12 13 14 15 16 17 18 19 20
```

8) 9 + 3 = ___

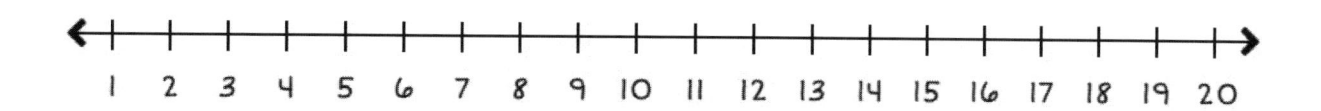

```
←―|――|――|――|――|――|――|――|――|――|――|――|――|――|――|――|――|――|――|――|→
   1  2  3  4  5  6  7  8  9  10 11 12 13 14 15 16 17 18 19 20
```

3.4 Add on a Number Line

Next page

9) 5 + 8 = ____

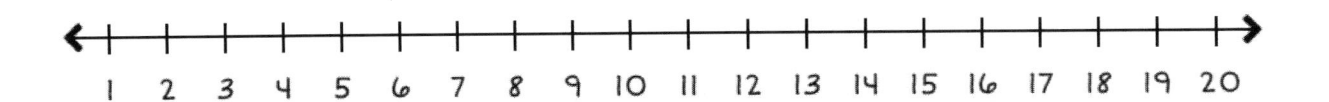

````
←―+―+―+―+―+―+―+―+―+―+―+―+―+―+―+―+―+―+―+―+→
  1  2  3  4  5  6  7  8  9  10 11 12 13 14 15 16 17 18 19 20
````

10) 7 + 9 = ____

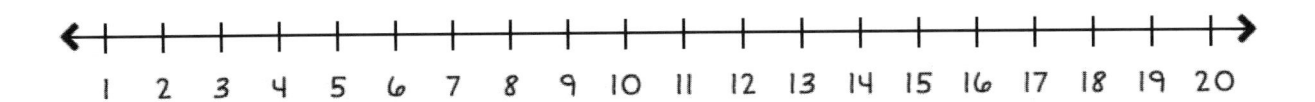

````
←―+―+―+―+―+―+―+―+―+―+―+―+―+―+―+―+―+―+―+―+→
  1  2  3  4  5  6  7  8  9  10 11 12 13 14 15 16 17 18 19 20
````

Name: _____   Date: _____

Missing Addends

1. Fill in the part-part-whole chart.
2. Record the missing addend in the addition sentence.
3. Use your crayons to draw dots in 1 or 2 of the ten frames.
4. Write the missing addend on the blank in the addition sentence.

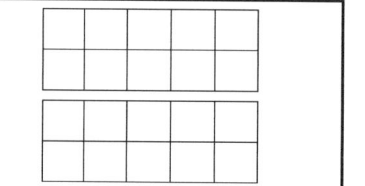

Example: 8 + <u>12</u> = 20	8 | ? 20	(ten frame with 8 filled, 12 lightly shaded)
1. 4 + ___ = 10	?	
2. ___ + 5 = 20	?	
3. 16 + ___ = 20	?	
4. ___ + 7 = 10	?	
5. 6 + ___ = 10	?	

3.5 Missing Addends

42

Next page

6. 11 + ___ = 20

7. ___ + 3 = 10

8. ___ + 6 = 20

9. 13 + ___ = 20

10. 2 + ___ = 10

3.5 Missing Addends

Name: _____ Date: _____

Practice: Missing Addends

Find the missing addends using a number line.
1. Draw a dot on the addend you know and another dot on the sum.
2. Draw your jumps from the addend to the sum.
3. Count your jumps and fill in the missing addend!
4. Match the addend with a code to solve the riddle below.

What do elves learn in school?

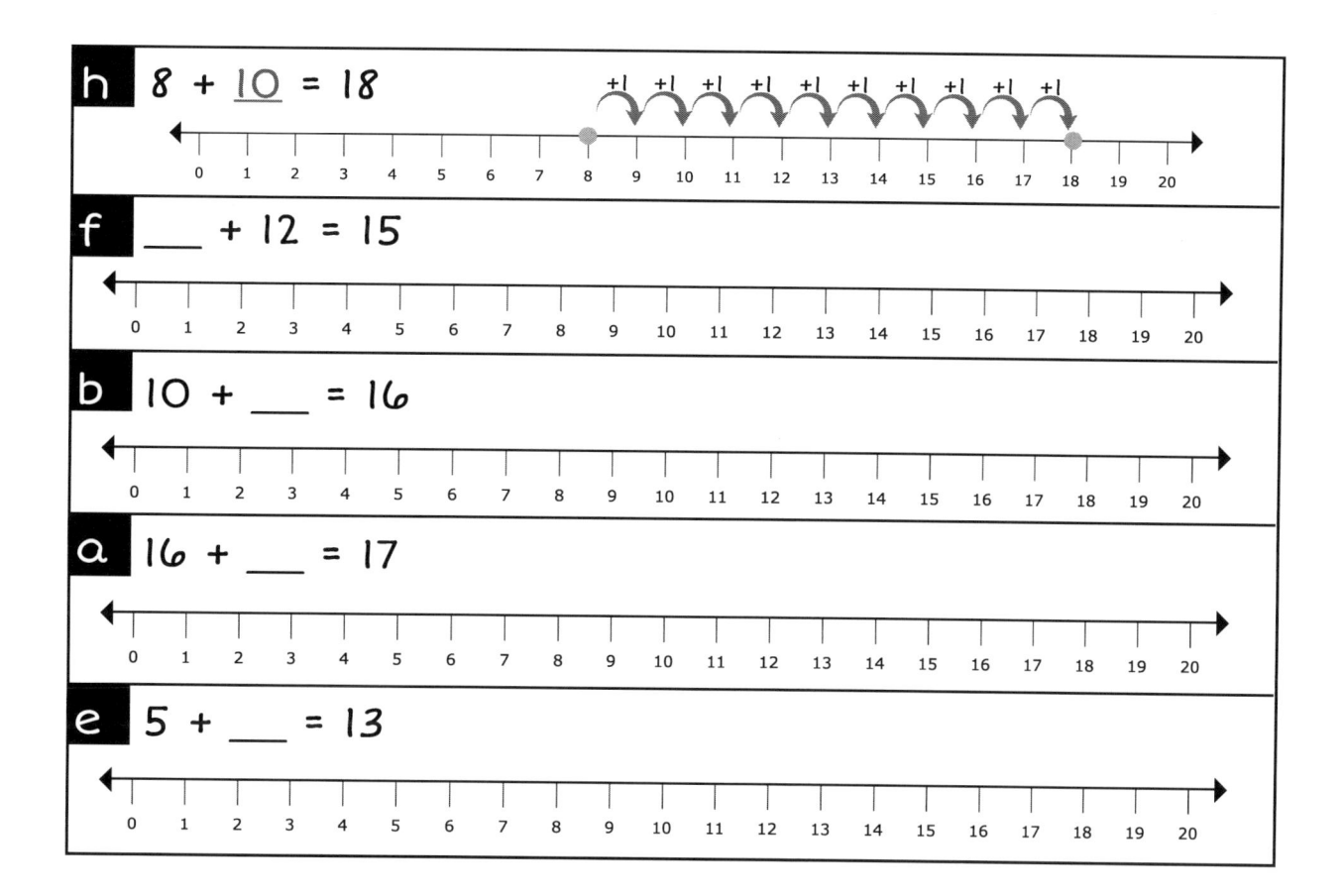

___ h   ___   ___ ___ ___   ___ ___ ___ ___
 7   10   5   8   9   3   1   6   2   15

h 8 + <u>10</u> = 18

f ___ + 12 = 15

b 10 + ___ = 16

a 16 + ___ = 17

e 5 + ___ = 13

3.5 Missing Addends

44

Next page

T ___ + 4 = 11

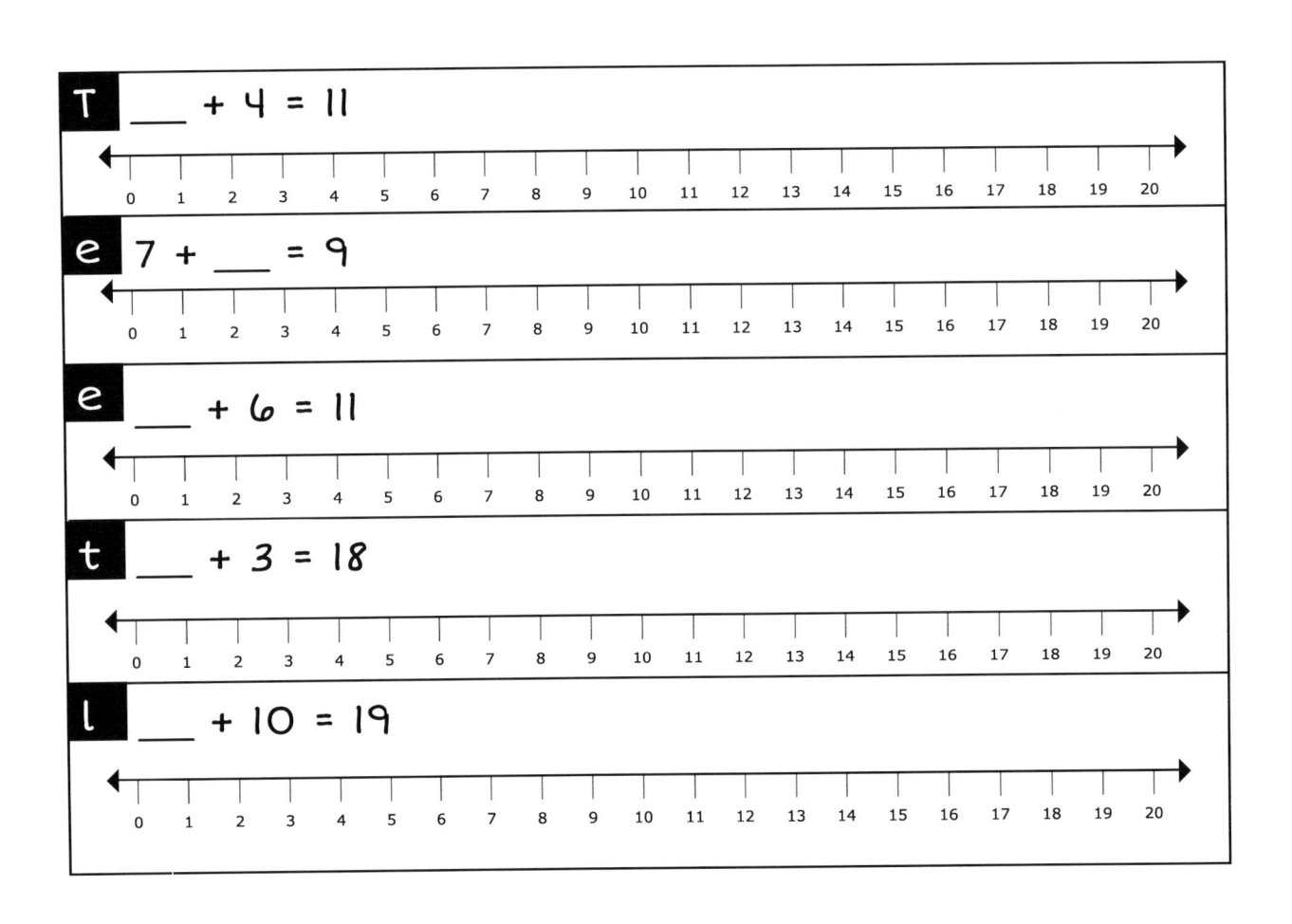

e 7 + ___ = 9

e ___ + 6 = 11

t ___ + 3 = 18

l ___ + 10 = 19

3.5 Missing Addends

Name: _____ Date: _____

Subtraction Picture Matching

The aliens need to get home for dinner! Match the subtraction sentence on the left to the correct picture on the right by drawing a line to connect the dots.

Example:

8 - 3 = _____ •————• ✗✗✗🛸🛸🛸🛸🛸

10 - 3 = _____ •   • ✗✗🛸🛸🛸🛸🛸🛸

9 - 4 = _____ •   • ✗✗✗✗✗🛸🛸🛸🛸🛸🛸🛸🛸

15 - 6 = _____ •   • ✗✗✗✗✗🛸🛸🛸🛸🛸🛸🛸🛸

8 - 2 = _____ •   • ✗✗✗🛸🛸🛸🛸🛸

12 - 5 = _____ •   • ✗✗✗✗✗✗✗🛸🛸

10 - 8 = _____ •   • ✗✗✗✗✗✗✗✗🛸🛸🛸🛸🛸

14 - 8 = _____ •   • ✗✗✗✗🛸🛸

13 - 5 = _____ •   • ✗✗✗✗✗🛸🛸🛸🛸🛸🛸🛸🛸

7 - 4 = _____ •   • ✗✗✗✗🛸🛸🛸🛸🛸🛸

15 - 5 = _____ •   • ✗✗✗🛸🛸🛸🛸🛸🛸🛸

Extra Practice: Can you find the difference as well? Write the difference in the blank of each subtraction sentence.

4.1 Take From (Up to 20)

Name: _____ Date: _____

Write About It!

What other strategies can you use to help you subtract?
Use the subtraction sentence 5 - 2 = ___.
Think about the addition toolbox we created in the last module. What would you put in your subtraction toolbox? Draw and/or write your ideas in the toolbox page below.

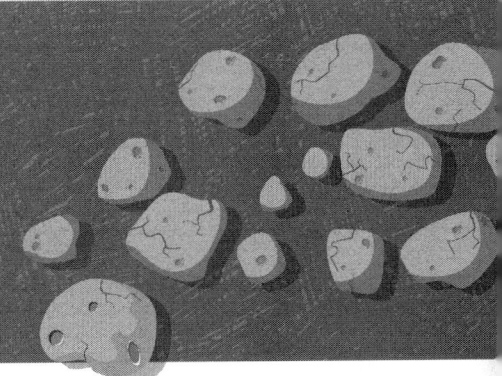

Example: I use counters and take them away. 6 - 4 = 2

Helpful Hints:
- What are some of the manipulatives you use to help you subtract?
- What are the steps you take when you find the difference of a subtraction sentence?
- Are there any addition toolbox strategies we can also use for subtraction?

47

4.1 Take From (Up to 20)

Name: _____ Date: _____

Add and Subtract Doubles

Use your counters to help you solve these addition sentences. First, move your counters into the part-part-whole chart to represent the addition sentence. Use the same number of counters to help you find the related subtraction sentence. **Remember, addition and subtraction doubles facts use the same parts and whole.** Then, record your answers by drawing dots with a crayon for each counter on your part-part-whole chart. **Don't forget to record the sum and the related doubles subtraction sentence!**

Example:

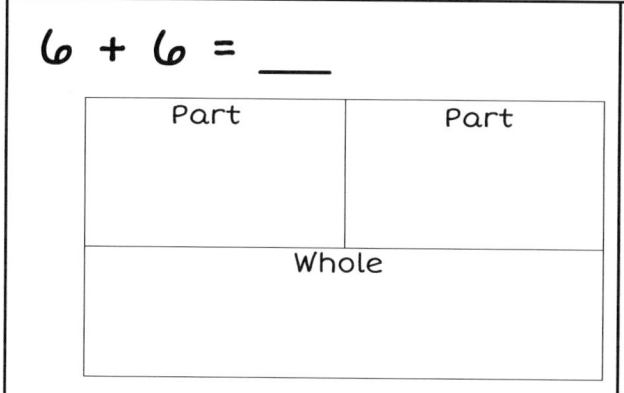

1 + 1 = 2

Part •	Part •
Whole • •	

2 - 1 = 1

Whole • •	
Part •	Part •

6 + 6 = ___

Part	Part
Whole	

___ - ___ = ___

Whole	
Part	Part

4.2 Subtract Doubles

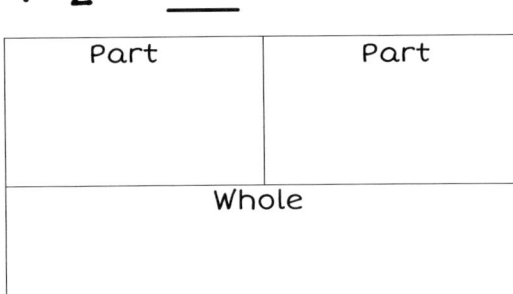

2 + 2 = ___

Part	Part
Whole	

___ - ___ = ___

Whole	
Part	Part

7 + 7 = ___

Part	Part
Whole	

___ - ___ = ___

Whole	
Part	Part

3 + 3 = ___

Part	Part
Whole	

___ - ___ = ___

Whole	
Part	Part

9 + 9 = ___

Part	Part
Whole	

___ - ___ = ___

Whole	
Part	Part

4.2 Subtract Doubles

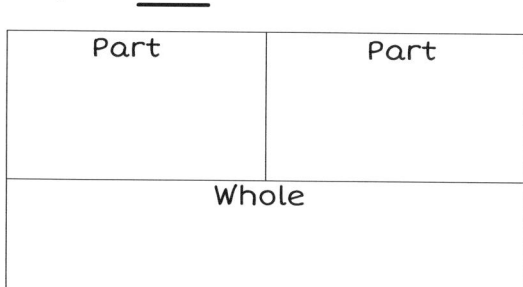

1 + 1 = ___

Part	Part
Whole	

___ - ___ = ___

Whole	
Part	Part

5 + 5 = ___

Part	Part
Whole	

___ - ___ = ___

Whole	
Part	Part

8 + 8 = ___

Part	Part
Whole	

___ - ___ = ___

Whole	
Part	Part

4 + 4 = ___

Part	Part
Whole	

___ - ___ = ___

Whole	
Part	Part

4.2 Subtract Doubles

Next page

10 + 10 = ___

Part	Part
Whole	

___ - ___ = ___

Whole	
Part	Part

4.2 Subtract Doubles

Name: _____ Date: _____

Subtracting Doubles Instructions

To play this game you will need:
1. Pencil
2. Paper clip
3. 25 counters

Spin the spinner by placing your paper clip in the middle of the circle. Then place your pencil tip in the center of the circle, through a space in your paper clip. Hold the pencil tightly against the paper, and flick the paper clip with a finger on your other hand. The paper clip should spin around the circle like a spinner. This takes some practice, so don't get frustrated!

After you spin the spinner, write the subtraction sentence and the difference on your worksheet. Look back at your game board, and cover the difference on the game board square with a counter. You can cover only 1 number for each spin. When your game board has 5 counters in a row, your game is done! Please note that your worksheet may have empty spaces for subtraction sentences even when you are done with the game. That is okay!

Bonus challenge: To challenge yourself even more, try to cover each number on the game board with a counter!

4.2 Subtract Doubles

Next page

Find the Doubles!

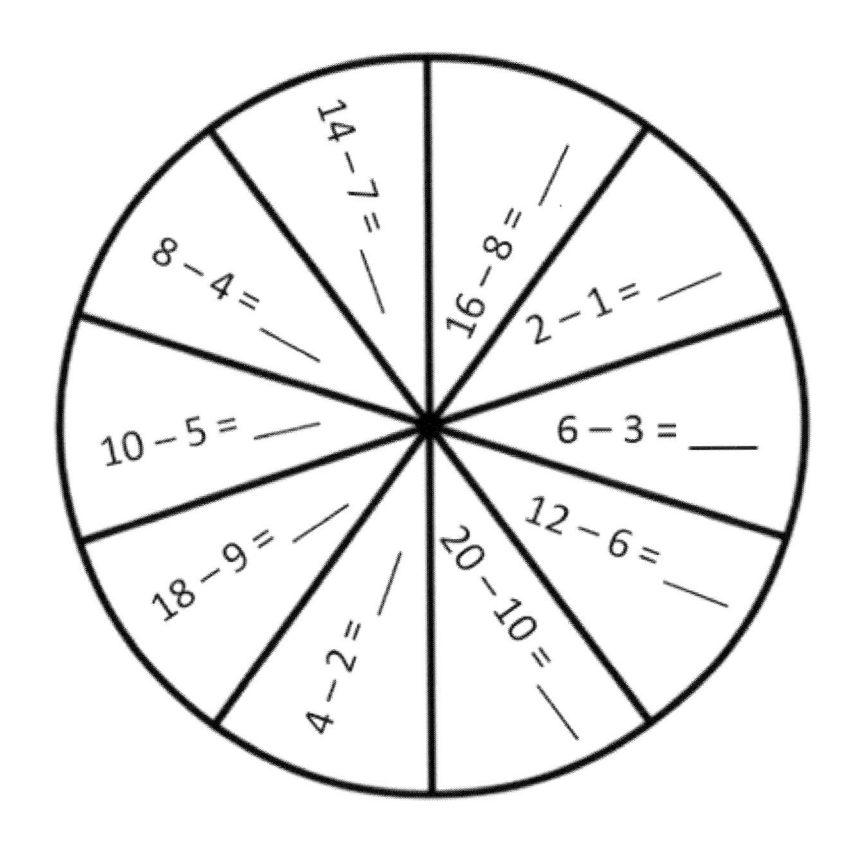

14 − 7 = ___
16 − 8 = ___
8 − 4 = ___
2 − 1 = ___
10 − 5 = ___
6 − 3 = ___
18 − 9 = ___
12 − 6 = ___
4 − 2 = ___
20 − 10 = ___

5	8	6	9	2
7	3	2	1	6
3	6	4	5	10
1	5	7	9	3
4	9	10	8	2

4.2 Subtract Doubles

Example:

Let's pretend you spun the paper clip and it landed on "8 - 4 = ___."
Record the subtraction sentence on a line below. Then use a counter to cover the difference on your game board.

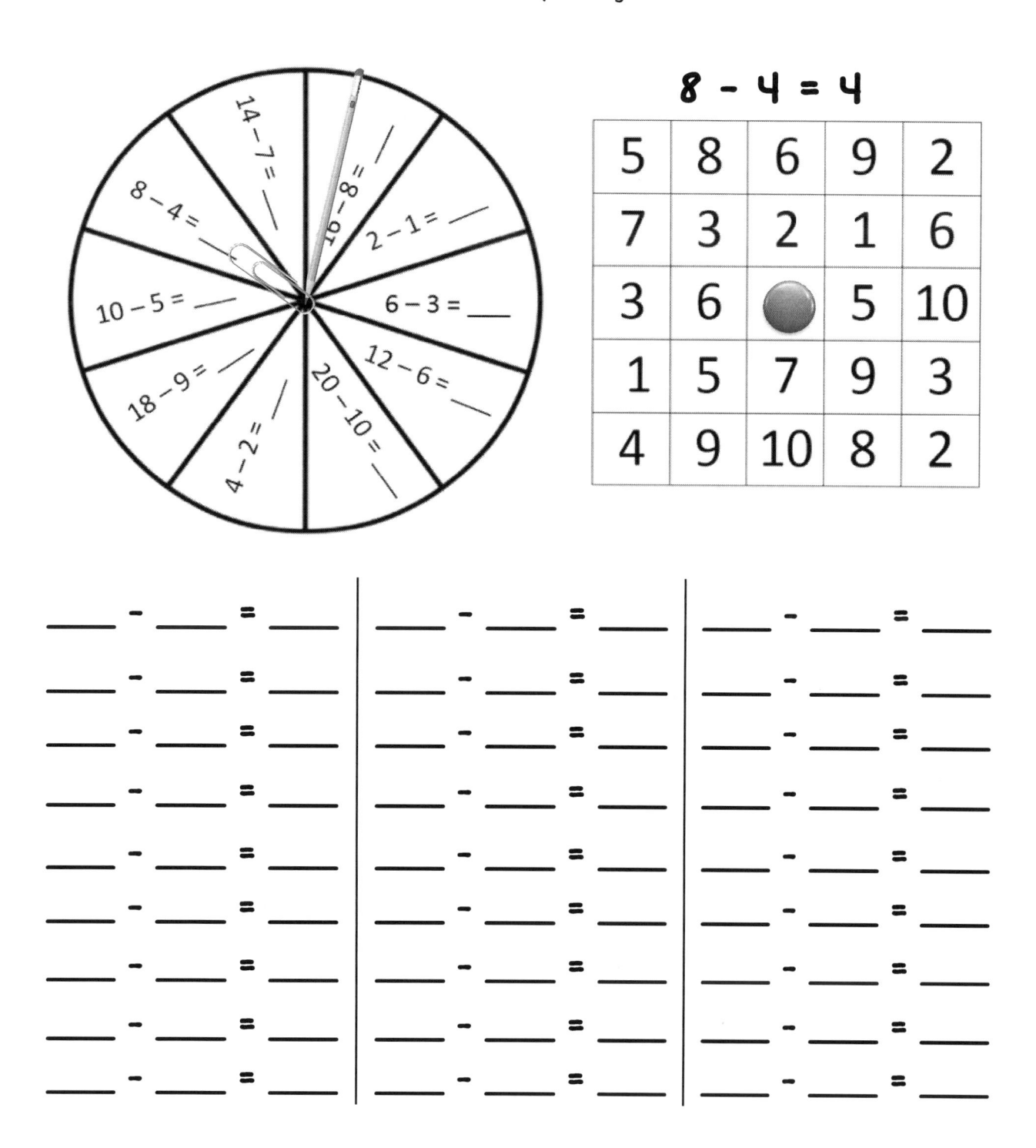

Spinner sections: 14 - 7 =, 16 - 8 =, 2 - 1 =, 6 - 3 =, 12 - 6 =, 20 - 10 =, 4 - 2 =, 18 - 9 =, 10 - 5 =, 8 - 4 =

8 - 4 = 4

5	8	6	9	2
7	3	2	1	6
3	6	●	5	10
1	5	7	9	3
4	9	10	8	2

___ - ___ = ___   ___ - ___ = ___   ___ - ___ = ___

___ - ___ = ___   ___ - ___ = ___   ___ - ___ = ___

___ - ___ = ___   ___ - ___ = ___   ___ - ___ = ___

___ - ___ = ___   ___ - ___ = ___   ___ - ___ = ___

___ - ___ = ___   ___ - ___ = ___   ___ - ___ = ___

___ - ___ = ___   ___ - ___ = ___   ___ - ___ = ___

___ - ___ = ___   ___ - ___ = ___   ___ - ___ = ___

___ - ___ = ___   ___ - ___ = ___   ___ - ___ = ___

___ - ___ = ___   ___ - ___ = ___   ___ - ___ = ___

4.2 Subtract Doubles

Name: _____ Date: _____

Rewrite to Subtract

Let's use what we've learned to help Jenny move more boxes. Follow the directions below using the part-part-whole chart to help you find the parts and the whole and write the subtraction sentence for each problem.

1. Fill out the part-part-whole chart with the whole and the part we know.
2. Rewrite the subtraction sentence to take away the part we know.
3. Put x's over the number of cubes you need to take away.
4. Find the difference by counting the boxes that are left over!

Example: 13 - _?_ = 6
         13 - _6_ = _7_

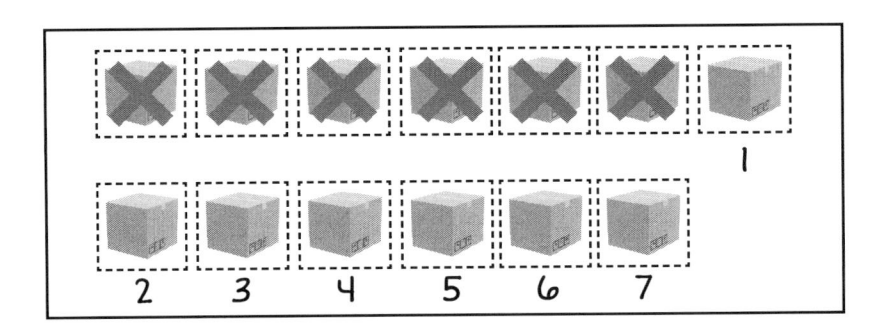

1. 12 - _?_ = 4
   12 - ___ = ___

55

4.3 Missing Numbers

Next page

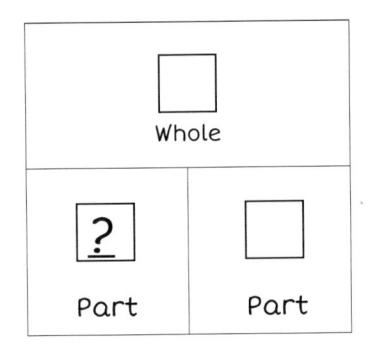

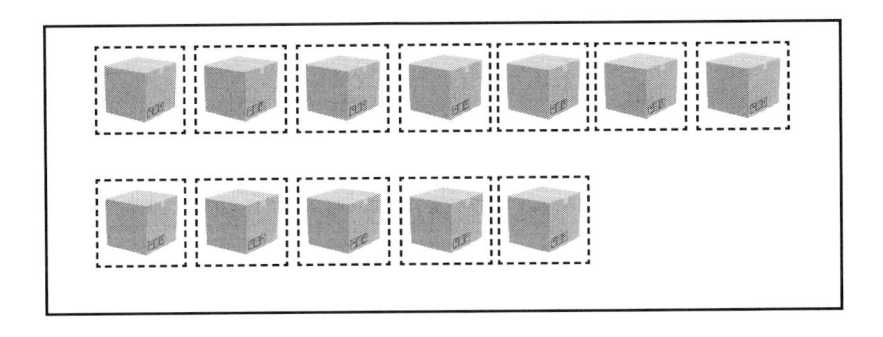

2. 14 − ? = 9
   14 − ___ = ___

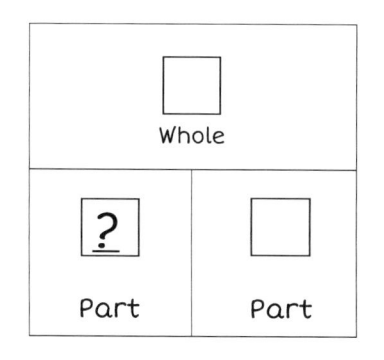

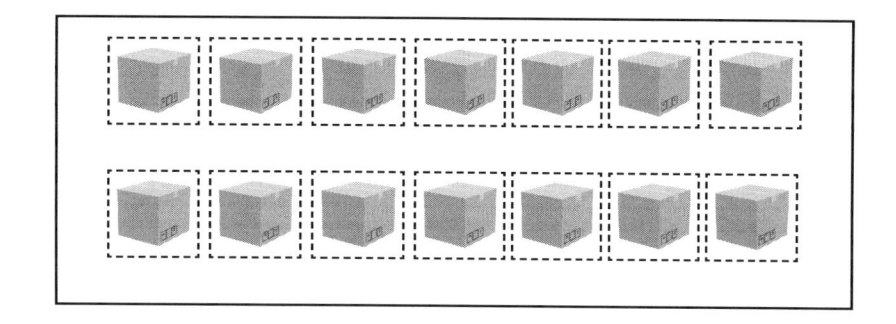

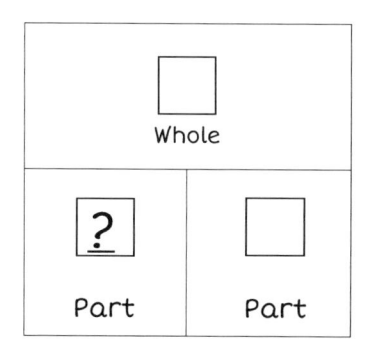

3. 15 − ? = 5
   15 − ___ = ___

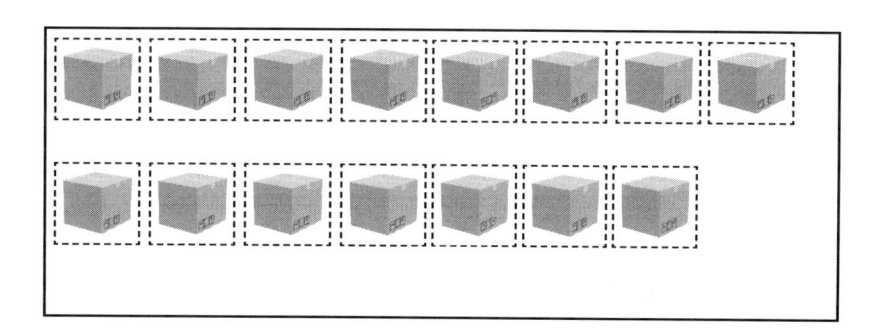

4. 11 − ? = 6
   11 − ___ = ___

4.3 Missing Numbers

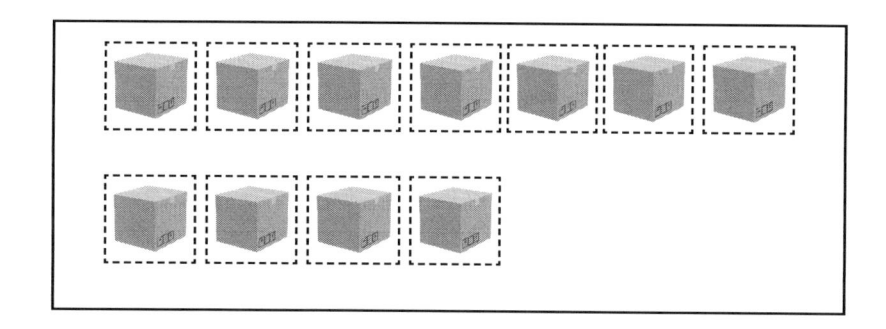

5. 16 - ? = 7
16 - ___ = ___

Whole

? Part   Part

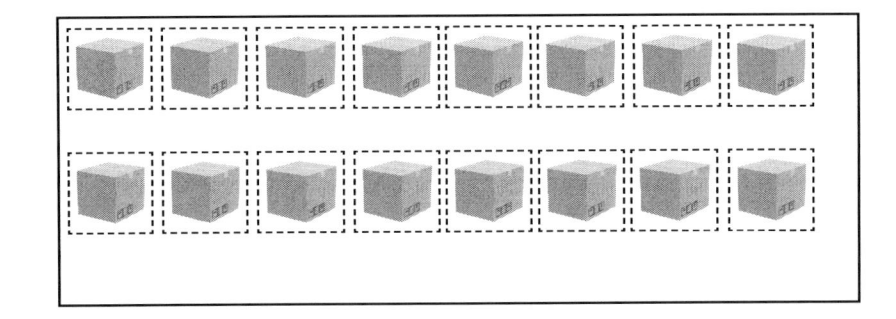

Extra Practice: Can you think of an addition sentence that uses the same parts as each of the subtraction sentences? Write the addition sentence above each of the pictures!

Name: _____ Date: _____

Subtract on a Number Line

Can you help the astronaut jump?
1. Draw a dot above the whole on the number line.
2. Draw jumps from the whole to the left. You will jump the same number as the part!
3. Write the difference on the empty line.

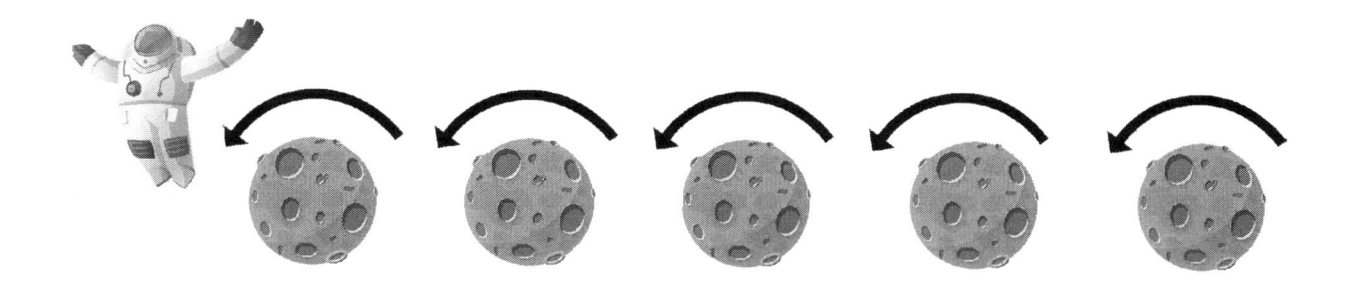

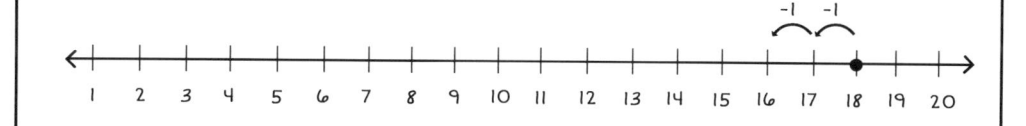

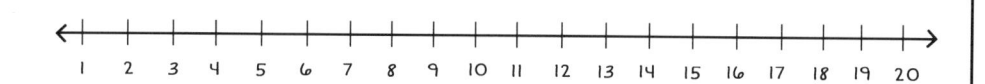

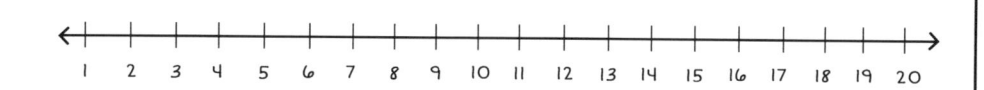

Example:	
18 − 2 = 16	number line 1–20 with -1, -1 jumps from 18 to 16
9 − 4 = ___	number line 1–20
20 − 11 = ___	number line 1–20

4.4 Subtract on a Number Line

58

Next page

18 - 5 = ____	←—1—2—3—4—5—6—7—8—9—10—11—12—13—14—15—16—17—18—19—20—→
11 - 2 = ____	←—1—2—3—4—5—6—7—8—9—10—11—12—13—14—15—16—17—18—19—20—→
14 - 7 = ____	←—1—2—3—4—5—6—7—8—9—10—11—12—13—14—15—16—17—18—19—20—→
17 - 3 = ____	←—1—2—3—4—5—6—7—8—9—10—11—12—13—14—15—16—17—18—19—20—→
12 - 8 = ____	←—1—2—3—4—5—6—7—8—9—10—11—12—13—14—15—16—17—18—19—20—→
19 - 5 = ____	←—1—2—3—4—5—6—7—8—9—10—11—12—13—14—15—16—17—18—19—20—→
8 - 6 = ____	←—1—2—3—4—5—6—7—8—9—10—11—12—13—14—15—16—17—18—19—20—→

4.4 Subtract on a Number Line

Bonus Question:

This number line represents 13 - 5. How do you know that the answer is 8? Please record your answer using a complete sentence.

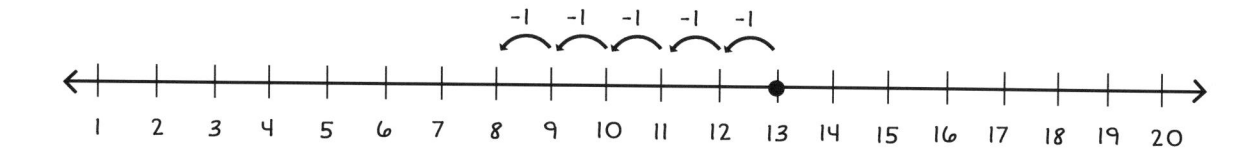

_____

_____

_____

4.4 Subtract on a Number Line

Name: _____ Date: _____

Counting by 5s to 100

Can you skip count by 5s to 100? Take your stacking cubes and make stacks of 5 cubes. Write the number sequence in the blank under each stack. Take a picture of your paper when you are done!

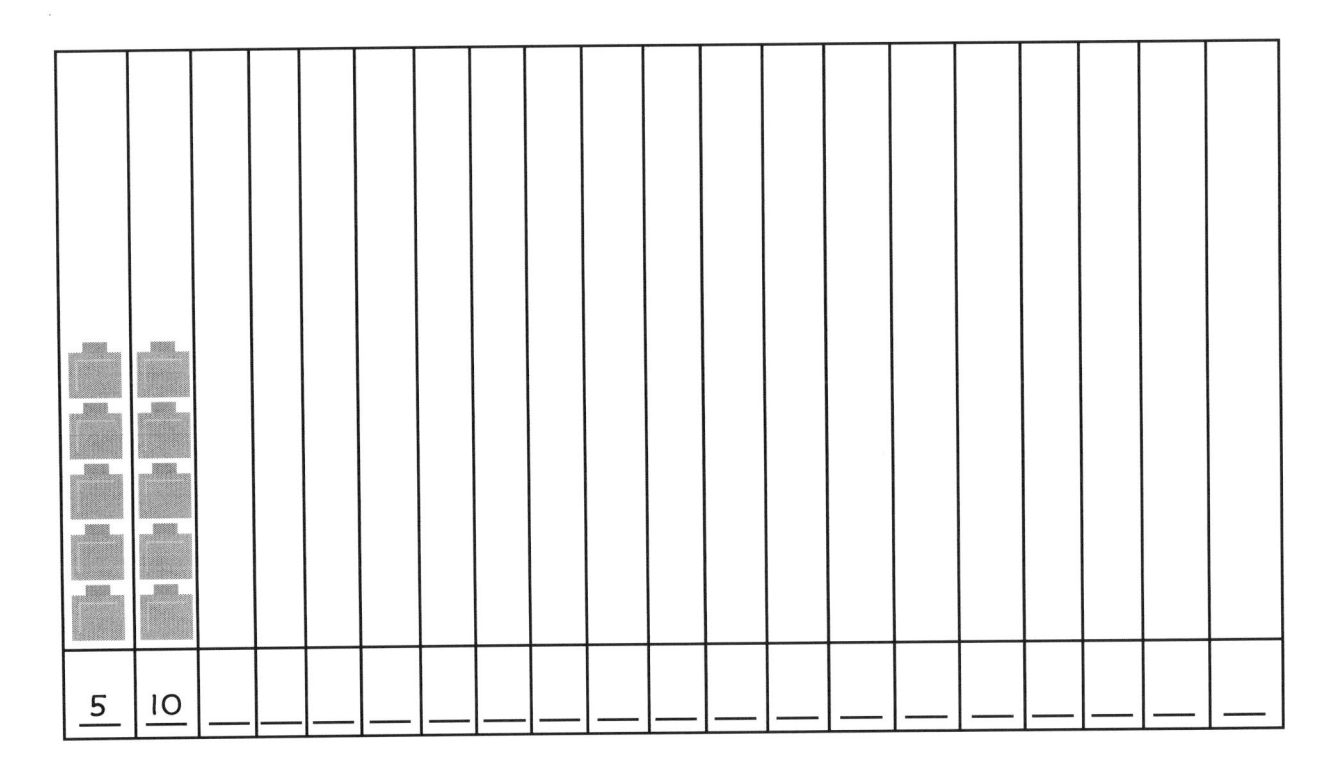

| 5 | 10 | __ | __ | __ | __ | __ | __ | __ | __ | __ | __ | __ | __ | __ | __ | __ | __ | __ | __ |

61   5.1 Counting by 5s to 100

Name: _____ Date: _____

Counting by 10s to 100

Janie works with a wildlife reserve. She is in charge of searching for lions and recording where they live in savannas and grasslands. Janie is using place-value blocks to help her add quickly. Each rod represents 10 lions. Help Janie record the correct number of lions by placing your place-value rods in the blank rectangles below. Then, record the number sequence that matches your rods on the blank lines.

Example:

10, 20, 30, 40, 50, 60, 70

5.2 Counting by 10s to 100

62

Next page

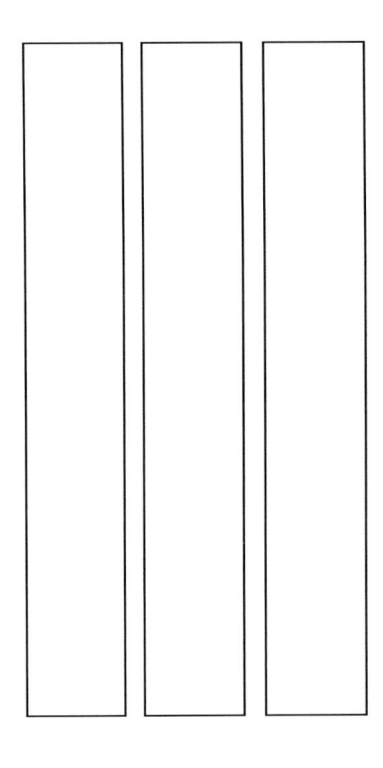

1.

_____, _____, _____

2.

_____, _____, _____, _____, _____, _____, _____, _____, _____

5.2 Counting by 10s to 100

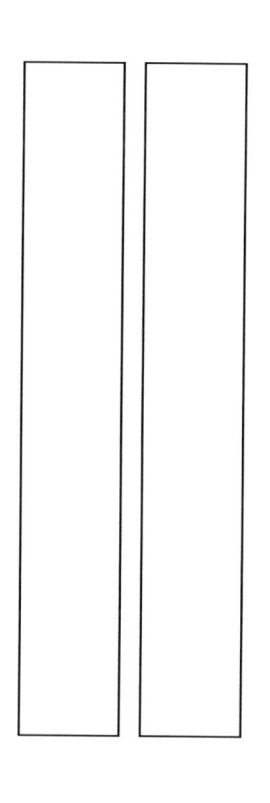

3.

___, ___, ___, ___, ___

4.

___, ___

5.2 Counting by 10s to 100

Next page

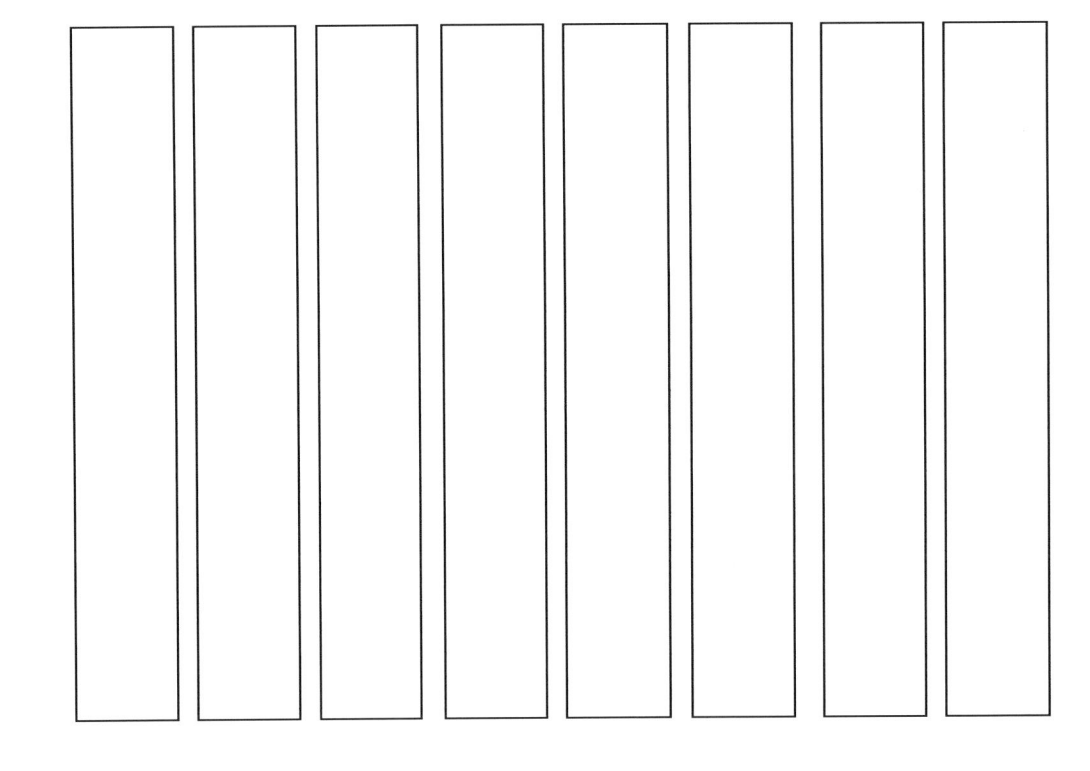

5.

___, ___, ___, ___, ___, ___

6.

___, ___, ___, ___, ___, ___, ___, ___

5.2 Counting by 10s to 100

7.

_____,

8.

_____, _____, _____, _____

9.

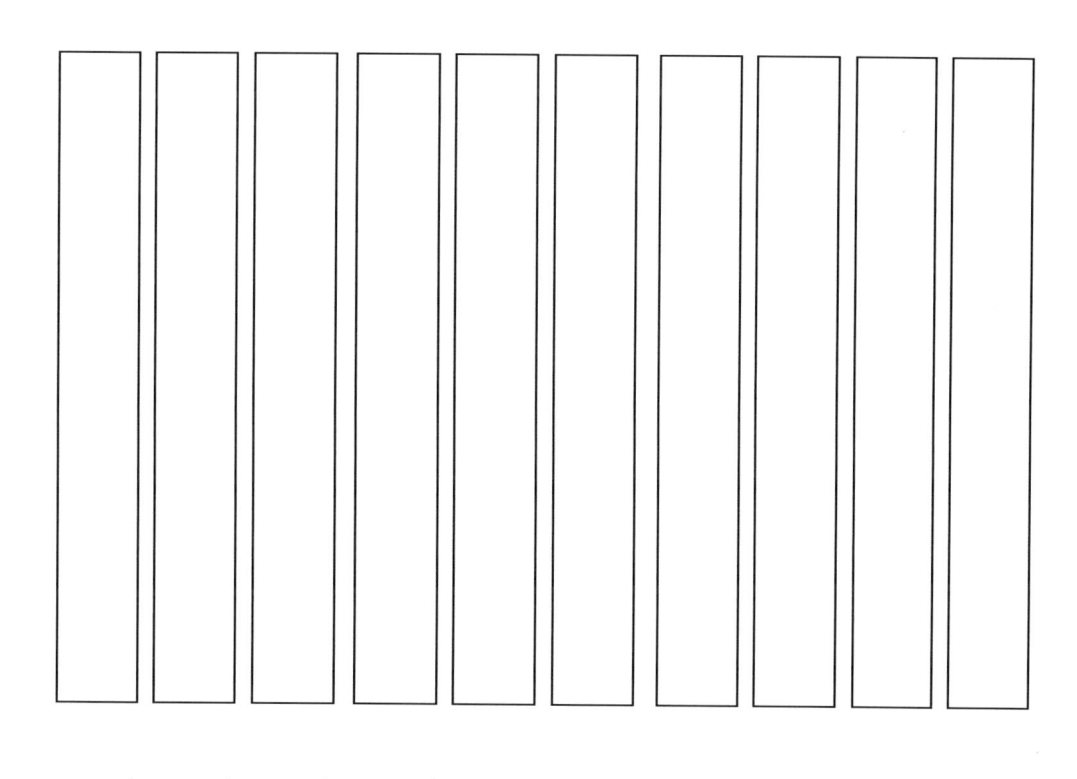

_____, _____, _____, _____, _____, _____, _____, _____, _____, _____

5.2 Counting by 10s to 100

Name: _____ Date: _____

Find the Missing Numbers

Janie is writing a list of numbers to track the lions. Help her by filling in the missing numbers below. Then, color in the missing number in its hundreds chart.

Example:

30, 40, <u>50</u>, 60, 70

1	2	3	4	5	6	7	8	9	10
11	12	13	14	15	16	17	18	19	20
21	22	23	24	25	26	27	28	29	30
31	32	33	34	35	36	37	38	39	40
41	42	43	44	45	46	47	48	49	**50**
51	52	53	54	55	56	57	58	59	60
61	62	63	64	65	66	67	68	69	70
71	72	73	74	75	76	77	78	79	80
81	82	83	84	85	86	87	88	89	90
91	92	93	94	95	96	97	98	99	100

___ , 20, 30, 40, 50

1	2	3	4	5	6	7	8	9	10
11	12	13	14	15	16	17	18	19	20
21	22	23	24	25	26	27	28	29	30
31	32	33	34	35	36	37	38	39	40
41	42	43	44	45	46	47	48	49	50
51	52	53	54	55	56	57	58	59	60
61	62	63	64	65	66	67	68	69	70
71	72	73	74	75	76	77	78	79	80
81	82	83	84	85	86	87	88	89	90
91	92	93	94	95	96	97	98	99	100

60, 70, ___ , 90, 100

1	2	3	4	5	6	7	8	9	10
11	12	13	14	15	16	17	18	19	20
21	22	23	24	25	26	27	28	29	30
31	32	33	34	35	36	37	38	39	40
41	42	43	44	45	46	47	48	49	50
51	52	53	54	55	56	57	58	59	60
61	62	63	64	65	66	67	68	69	70
71	72	73	74	75	76	77	78	79	80
81	82	83	84	85	86	87	88	89	90
91	92	93	94	95	96	97	98	99	100

5.2 Counting by 10s to 100

40, __ , 60, 70, __

10, __ , 30, __ , 50

60, 70, __ , __ , 100

5.2 Counting by 10s to 100

Name: _____ Date: _____

Find the Missing 100

Pablo found counting caterpillars, but each one has a missing number. Use the thousands chart at the top of the page to write the missing number in each caterpillar to help Pablo count!

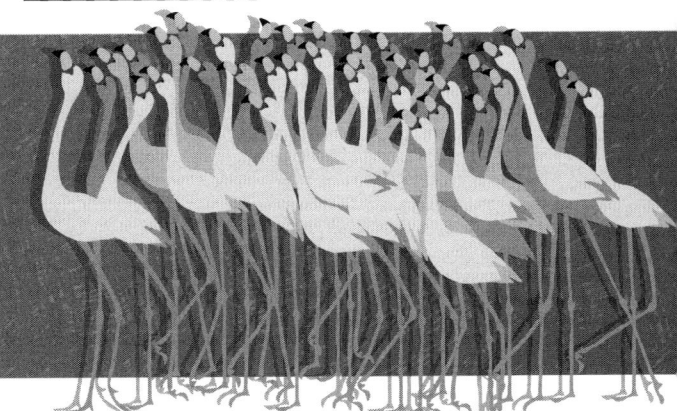

10	20	30	40	50	60	70	80	90	100
110	120	130	140	150	160	170	180	190	200
210	220	230	240	250	260	270	280	290	300
310	320	330	340	350	360	370	380	390	400
410	420	430	440	450	460	470	480	490	500
510	520	530	540	550	560	570	580	590	600
610	620	630	640	650	660	670	680	690	700
710	720	730	740	750	760	770	780	790	800
810	820	830	840	850	860	870	880	890	900
910	920	930	940	950	960	970	980	990	1000

Example:

100 | 200 | 300 | 400 | <u>500</u> | 600 | 700 | 800 | 900

---

100 | 200 | 300 | 400 | 500 | 600 | ___ | 800

69

5.3 Counting by 100s to 1000

10	20	30	40	50	60	70	80	90	100
110	120	130	140	150	160	170	180	190	200
210	220	230	240	250	260	270	280	290	300
310	320	330	340	350	360	370	380	390	400
410	420	430	440	450	460	470	480	490	500
510	520	530	540	550	560	570	580	590	600
610	620	630	640	650	660	670	680	690	700
710	720	730	740	750	760	770	780	790	800
810	820	830	840	850	860	870	880	890	900
910	920	930	940	950	960	970	980	990	1000

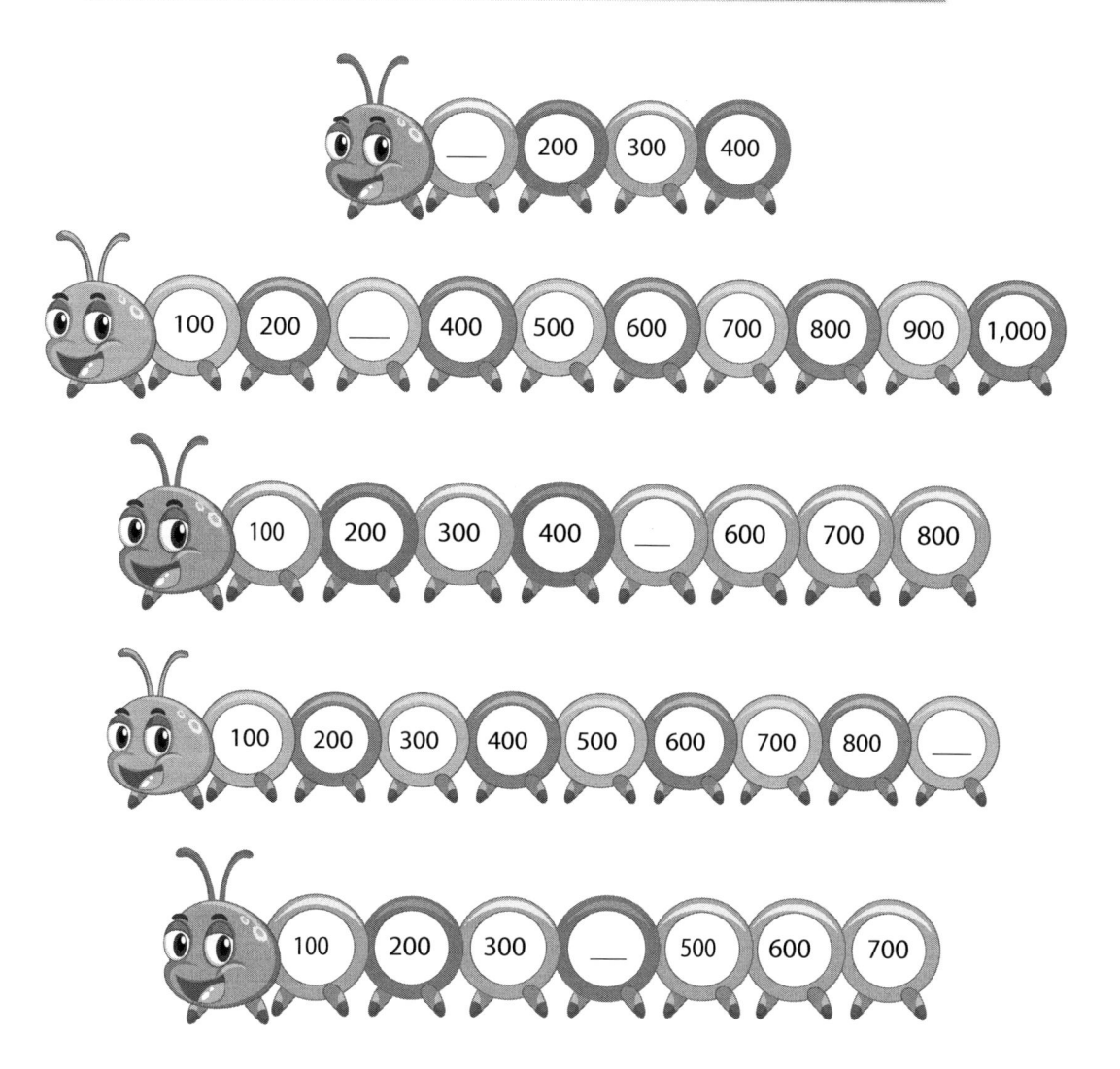

____ 200 300 400

100 200 ____ 400 500 600 700 800 900 1,000

100 200 300 400 ____ 600 700 800

100 200 300 400 500 600 700 800 ____

100 200 300 ____ 500 600 700

5.3 Counting by 100s to 1000

Name: _____ Date: _____

Counting to 1,000
Let's practice skip counting by 1s, 10s, and 100s!

Let's practice skip counting by 1s and 10s!

1. Fill in the missing numbers by skip counting by 1s.
2. Skip count by 10s and circle each number in your number sequence.

1	2	3	4	5	6	7	8	9	10
11	___	13	14	___	16	17	18	19	20
21	22	23	24	25	26	27	___	29	30
31	32	33	34	35	36	37	38	39	40
___	42	43	44		46	47	48	___	50
51	52	53	54	55	56	___	58	59	60
61	62	63	___	65	66	67	68	69	70
71	72	73	74	75	76	77	78	79	80
81	82	___	84	85	86	87	88	___	90
91	92	93	94	95	96	97	98	99	100

5.4 Counting by 100s, 10s and 1s

Next pa

Let's skip count by 100s!

3. Skip count by 100s and circle each number in your number sequence.

10	20	30	40	50	60	70	80	90	100
110	120	130	140	150	160	170	180	190	200
210	220	230	240	250	260	270	280	290	300
310	320	330	340	350	360	370	380	390	400
410	420	430	440	450	460	470	480	490	500
510	520	530	540	550	560	570	580	590	600
610	620	630	640	650	660	670	680	690	700
710	720	730	740	750	760	770	780	790	800
810	820	830	840	850	860	870	880	890	900
910	920	930	940	950	960	970	980	990	1000

5.4 Counting by 100s, 10s and 1s

Name: _____ Date: _____

Place-Value Chart

Use this place-value chart with your blocks to make numbers! Refer to the lesson for the numbers you need to make.

1 10

Tens	Ones

6.1 Number Structure (Tens and Ones)

Name: _____ Date: _____

Make a Number

Use your base-ten blocks to draw the rods and cubes on the place-value chart. Then write the number they make on the line. Match the color to the correct answer on the picture to color in the bunny!

Example:

What number is made from 2 rods and 3 cubes?

Tens	Ones

23   PURPLE

1. What number is made from 1 rod and 5 cubes?

Tens	Ones

___   BROWN

2. What number is made from 8 rods and 2 cubes?

Tens	Ones

___   BLUE

6.1 Number Structure (Tens and Ones)

74

Next page

3. What number is made from 6 rods and 0 cubes?

Tens	Ones

☐ YELLOW

4. What number is made from 3 rods and 3 cubes?

Tens	Ones

☐ ORANGE

5. What number is made from 4 rods and 7 cubes?

Tens	Ones

☐ PINK

6.1 Number Structure (Tens and Ones)

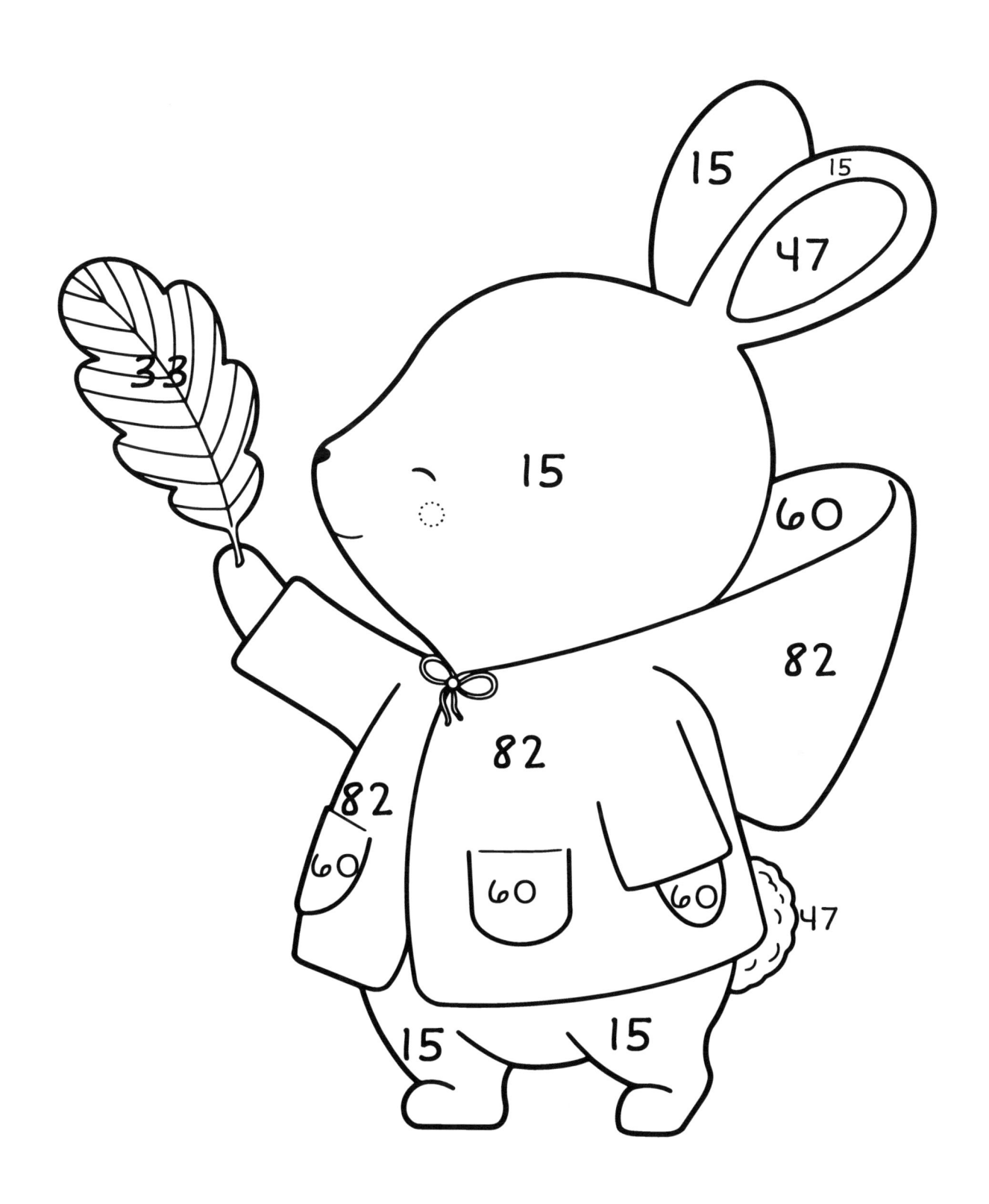

76

Name: _____ Date: _____

Place-Value Chart

Use this place-value chart with your blocks to make numbers! Refer to the lesson for the numbers you need to make.

Hundreds	Tens	Ones

6.2 Number Structure (Hundreds)

Name: _____ Date: _____

Compare with Blocks

Harper sees more pumpkins! Can you compare groups of pumpkins? Use your place-value chart and blocks. Then, circle the number that is greater than the other.

Example: Which is bigger: 23 or 26?

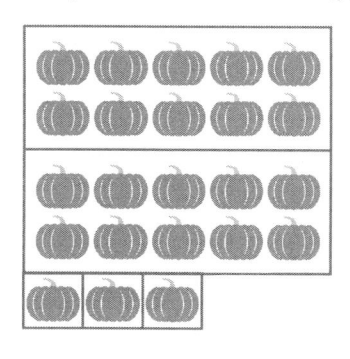

23

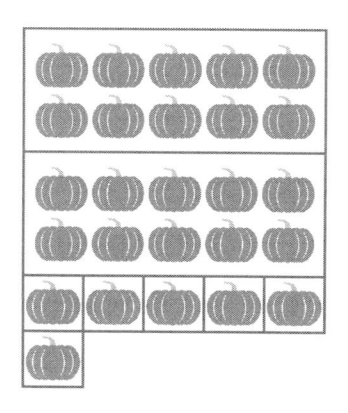

(26)

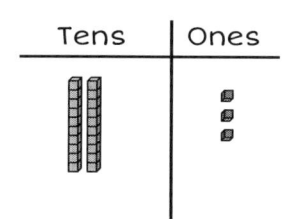

Tens	Ones

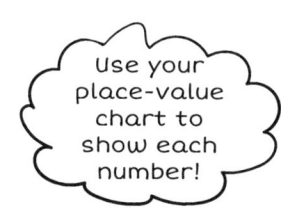

Use your place-value chart to show each number!

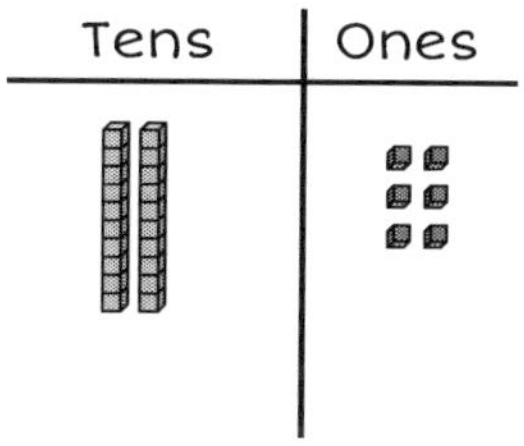

Tens	Ones

---

1. Which number is bigger: 33 or 39?

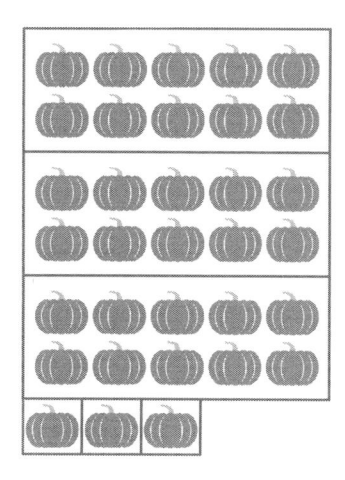

33

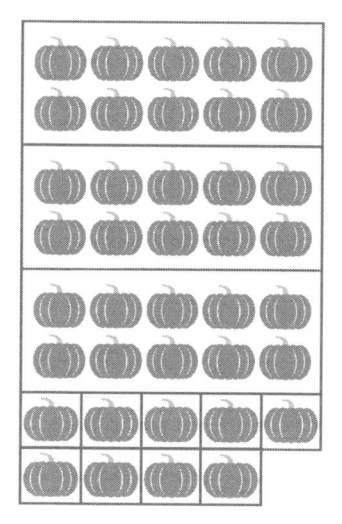

39

6.3 Make Groups of 10s and 1s to Compare

78

Next page

2. Which number is bigger: 31 or 21?

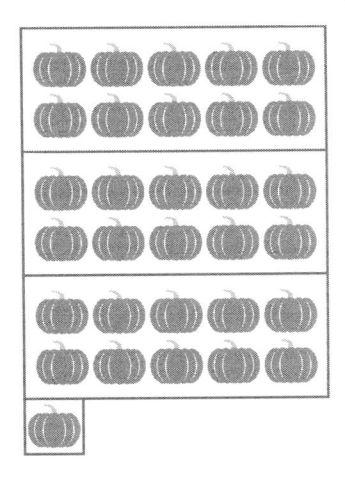

31

21

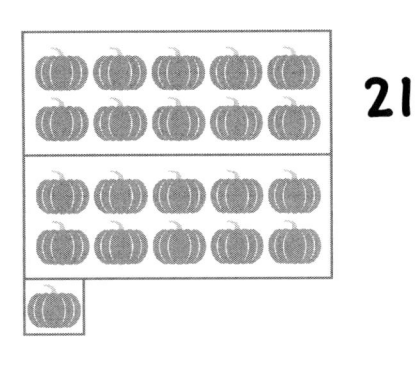

3. Which number is bigger: 45 or 52?

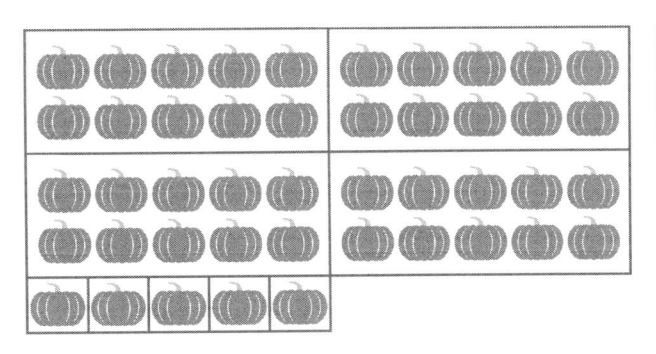

45

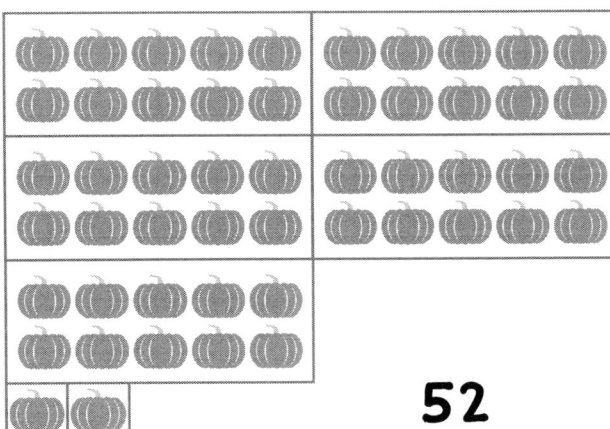

52

4. Which number is bigger: 70 or 64?

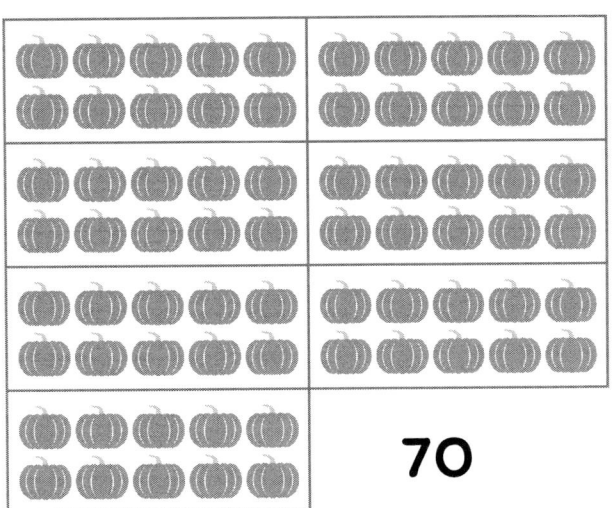

70

64

5. Which number is bigger: 88 or 87?

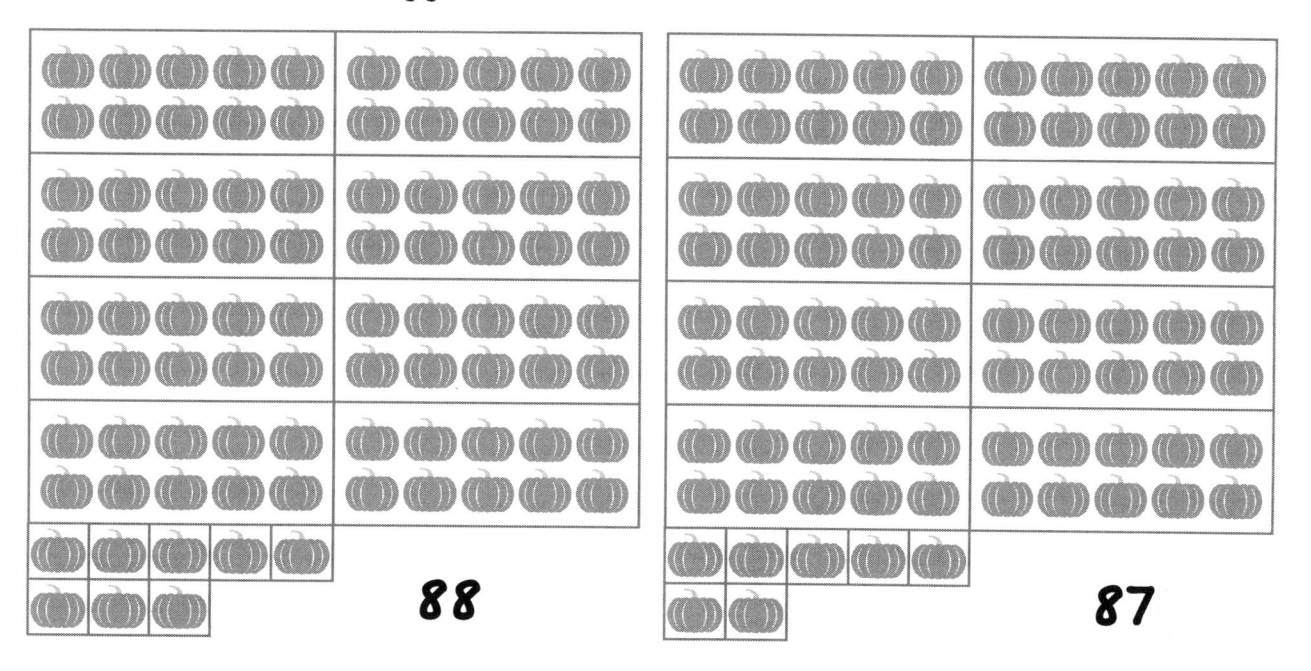

88   **87**

Challenge: What is the biggest number you can make with 9 rods and 9 cubes? Use your blocks and write the number on the line below.

Tens	Ones

The biggest number is ____.

6.3 Make Groups of 10s and 1s to Compare

Name: _____ Date: _____

Make Groups of 100s to Compare 3-Digit Numbers

Let's practice comparing numbers by looking at the 100s, 10s, and 1s. Use your place-value blocks to make each number. Draw the correct number of blocks on each of the charts. Then, write < or > to compare the numbers.

Example:

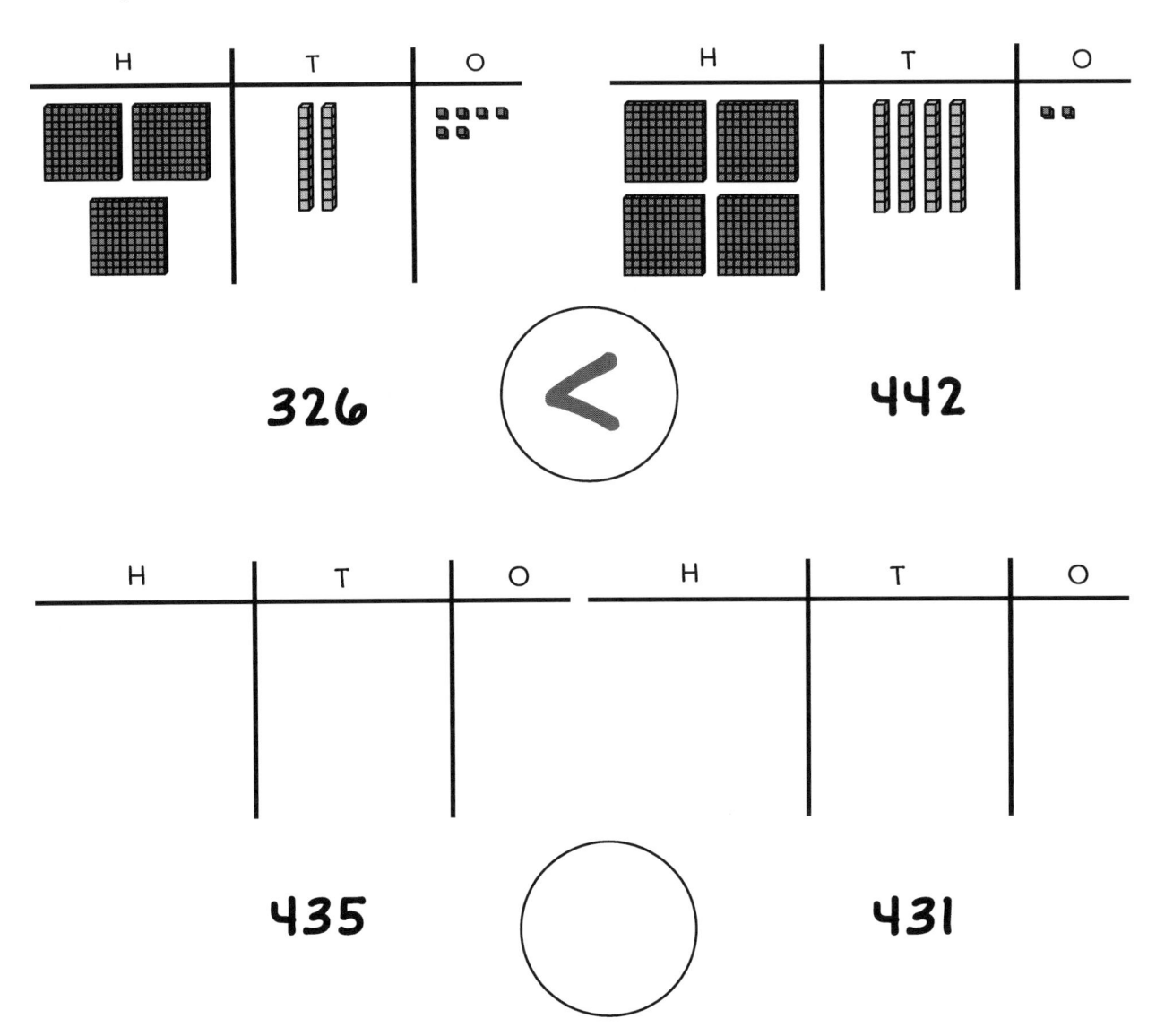

H	T	O

326 (<) 442

H	T	O

435 ( ) 431

81

6.4 Make Groups of 100s to Compare 3-Digit Numbers

H	T	O		H	T	O

185 ◯ 247

H	T	O		H	T	O

394 ◯ 633

H	T	O		H	T	O

529 ◯ 306

6.4 Make Groups of 100s to Compare 3-Digit Numbers

Next page

| H | T | O | | H | T | O |

701   ◯   650

6.4 Make Groups of 100s to Compare 3-Digit Numbers

Name: _____ Date: _____

Make and Compare Numbers

Use your number cards from the cutout section to make three-digit numbers. Write the numbers you used in the boxes. Circle the place that you used to find out which number is bigger. Then draw > or < in the middle.

Example:

Make the numbers 435 and 562. Show which is bigger and the place you used.

| 4 | 3 | 5 | (<) | (5) | 6 | 2 |

1. Make the numbers 145 and 173. Show which is bigger and which place you used.

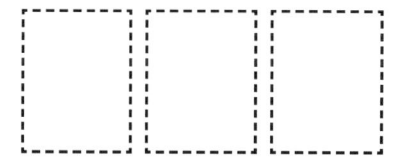

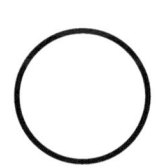

2. Make the numbers 289 and 286. Show which is bigger and which place you used.

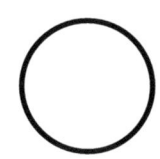

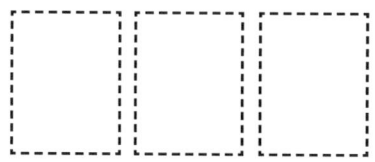

3. Make the numbers 625 and 791. Show which is bigger and which place you used.

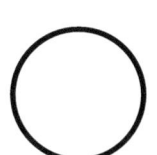

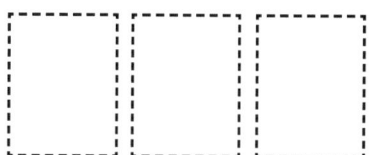

6.5 Problem Solving Strategy: Reasoning

Next page

4. Make the numbers 901 and 900. Show which is bigger and which place you used.

5. Make the numbers 814 and 824. Show which is bigger and which place you used.

Challenge: What is the biggest number you can make with your cards? What is the smallest number you can make with your cards? Write them in the boxes below. Then write < or > in the circle.

6.5 Problem Solving Strategy: Reasoning

Name: _____ Date: _____

Hundred Chart

Use this hundred chart with your counters to make number sequences! Refer to the lesson for the number sequences you need to make.

100

1	2	3	4	5	6	7	8	9	10
11	12	13	14	15	16	17	18	19	20
21	22	23	24	25	26	27	28	29	30
31	32	33	34	35	36	37	38	39	40
41	42	43	44	45	46	47	48	49	50
51	52	53	54	55	56	57	58	59	60
61	62	63	64	65	66	67	68	69	70
71	72	73	74	75	76	77	78	79	80
81	82	83	84	85	86	87	88	89	90
91	92	93	94	95	96	97	98	99	100

7.1 Tens and Ones

Name: _____ Date: _____

Create Number Sequences

Make the number sequences below by coloring in the numbers on each hundred chart and filling in the blanks.

Example: **Skip count by 10s, starting at 3.**

1	2	3	4	5	6	7	8	9	10
11	12	13	14	15	16	17	18	19	20
21	22	23	24	25	26	27	28	29	30
31	32	33	34	35	36	37	38	39	40
41	42	43	44	45	46	47	48	49	50
51	52	53	54	55	56	57	58	59	60
61	62	63	64	65	66	67	68	69	70
71	72	73	74	75	76	77	78	79	80
81	82	83	84	85	86	87	88	89	90
91	92	93	94	95	96	97	98	99	100

__3__ __13__ __23__ __33__ __43__

1. **Skip count by 10s, starting at 55.**

1	2	3	4	5	6	7	8	9	10
11	12	13	14	15	16	17	18	19	20
21	22	23	24	25	26	27	28	29	30
31	32	33	34	35	36	37	38	39	40
41	42	43	44	45	46	47	48	49	50
51	52	53	54	55	56	57	58	59	60
61	62	63	64	65	66	67	68	69	70
71	72	73	74	75	76	77	78	79	80
81	82	83	84	85	86	87	88	89	90
91	92	93	94	95	96	97	98	99	100

___ ___ ___ ___ ___

7.1 Tens and Ones

Next pa

2. Skip count by 5s, starting at 30.

1	2	3	4	5	6	7	8	9	10
11	12	13	14	15	16	17	18	19	20
21	22	23	24	25	26	27	28	29	30
31	32	33	34	35	36	37	38	39	40
41	42	43	44	45	46	47	48	49	50
51	52	53	54	55	56	57	58	59	60
61	62	63	64	65	66	67	68	69	70
71	72	73	74	75	76	77	78	79	80
81	82	83	84	85	86	87	88	89	90
91	92	93	94	95	96	97	98	99	100

5. Skip count by 10s, starting at 10.

1	2	3	4	5	6	7	8	9	10
11	12	13	14	15	16	17	18	19	20
21	22	23	24	25	26	27	28	29	30
31	32	33	34	35	36	37	38	39	40
41	42	43	44	45	46	47	48	49	50
51	52	53	54	55	56	57	58	59	60
61	62	63	64	65	66	67	68	69	70
71	72	73	74	75	76	77	78	79	80
81	82	83	84	85	86	87	88	89	90
91	92	93	94	95	96	97	98	99	100

3. Skip count by 10s, starting at 48.

1	2	3	4	5	6	7	8	9	10
11	12	13	14	15	16	17	18	19	20
21	22	23	24	25	26	27	28	29	30
31	32	33	34	35	36	37	38	39	40
41	42	43	44	45	46	47	48	49	50
51	52	53	54	55	56	57	58	59	60
61	62	63	64	65	66	67	68	69	70
71	72	73	74	75	76	77	78	79	80
81	82	83	84	85	86	87	88	89	90
91	92	93	94	95	96	97	98	99	100

6. Skip count by 5s, starting at 44.

1	2	3	4	5	6	7	8	9	10
11	12	13	14	15	16	17	18	19	20
21	22	23	24	25	26	27	28	29	30
31	32	33	34	35	36	37	38	39	40
41	42	43	44	45	46	47	48	49	50
51	52	53	54	55	56	57	58	59	60
61	62	63	64	65	66	67	68	69	70
71	72	73	74	75	76	77	78	79	80
81	82	83	84	85	86	87	88	89	90
91	92	93	94	95	96	97	98	99	100

4. Skip count by 5s, starting at 45.

1	2	3	4	5	6	7	8	9	10
11	12	13	14	15	16	17	18	19	20
21	22	23	24	25	26	27	28	29	30
31	32	33	34	35	36	37	38	39	40
41	42	43	44	45	46	47	48	49	50
51	52	53	54	55	56	57	58	59	60
61	62	63	64	65	66	67	68	69	70
71	72	73	74	75	76	77	78	79	80
81	82	83	84	85	86	87	88	89	90
91	92	93	94	95	96	97	98	99	100

7. Skip count by 10s, starting at 9.

1	2	3	4	5	6	7	8	9	10
11	12	13	14	15	16	17	18	19	20
21	22	23	24	25	26	27	28	29	30
31	32	33	34	35	36	37	38	39	40
41	42	43	44	45	46	47	48	49	50
51	52	53	54	55	56	57	58	59	60
61	62	63	64	65	66	67	68	69	70
71	72	73	74	75	76	77	78	79	80
81	82	83	84	85	86	87	88	89	90
91	92	93	94	95	96	97	98	99	100

7.1 Tens and Ones

Next page

8. Skip count by 5s, starting at 3.

1	2	3	4	5	6	7	8	9	10
11	12	13	14	15	16	17	18	19	20
21	22	23	24	25	26	27	28	29	30
31	32	33	34	35	36	37	38	39	40
41	42	43	44	45	46	47	48	49	50
51	52	53	54	55	56	57	58	59	60
61	62	63	64	65	66	67	68	69	70
71	72	73	74	75	76	77	78	79	80
81	82	83	84	85	86	87	88	89	90
91	92	93	94	95	96	97	98	99	100

___ ___ ___ ___ ___ ___

9. Skip count by 10s, starting at 15.

1	2	3	4	5	6	7	8	9	10
11	12	13	14	15	16	17	18	19	20
21	22	23	24	25	26	27	28	29	30
31	32	33	34	35	36	37	38	39	40
41	42	43	44	45	46	47	48	49	50
51	52	53	54	55	56	57	58	59	60
61	62	63	64	65	66	67	68	69	70
71	72	73	74	75	76	77	78	79	80
81	82	83	84	85	86	87	88	89	90
91	92	93	94	95	96	97	98	99	100

___ ___ ___ ___ ___

10. Skip count by 5s, starting at 65.

1	2	3	4	5	6	7	8	9	10
11	12	13	14	15	16	17	18	19	20
21	22	23	24	25	26	27	28	29	30
31	32	33	34	35	36	37	38	39	40
41	42	43	44	45	46	47	48	49	50
51	52	53	54	55	56	57	58	59	60
61	62	63	64	65	66	67	68	69	70
71	72	73	74	75	76	77	78	79	80
81	82	83	84	85	86	87	88	89	90
91	92	93	94	95	96	97	98	99	100

___ ___ ___ ___ ___

Name: _____ Date: _____

Thousand Chart Number Patterns

Color in each place as you count by 100s. Color the ones place blue. Color the tens place yellow. Color the hundreds place red. Then fill in the numbers on the lines in each color. Be sure to box the last number. That is your answer!

Example:

130 + 200

1 3 0, 2 _ _ 3 0 | 3 3 0 |

1. 150 + 300

1 5 0, _ _ _ , _ _ _ , _ _ _

2. 280 + 400

2 8 0, _ _ _ , _ _ _ , _ _ _ _ _ _

7.2 Hundreds

90

Next page

3. 330 + 500

3 3 0, _ _ _, _ _ _, _ _ _
_ _ _, _ _ _

4. 180 + 600

1 8 0, _ _ _, _ _ _, _ _ _
_ _ _, _ _ _

5. 60 + 700

6 0, _ _ _, _ _ _, _ _ _
_ _ _, _ _ _, _ _ _, _ _ _

7.2 Hundreds

Name: _____ Date: _____

Name the Number

Fill in the blanks using standard form, word form, or expanded form.

Standard Form	Word Form	Expanded Form
358	Three hundred fifty-eight	
	Nine hundred seventeen	
592		500 + 90 + 2
		200 + 70 + 3

7.4 Read and Write Numbers to 1,000

Name: _____ Date: _____

Find the Larger Number

Use your blocks to find the larger number. Make each number on your Hundreds Place-Value Chart. Then draw the blocks you used on the charts below. Write the expanded form of each number. Then find the larger number using < or >.

Example:

Which number is larger?

624 < 629

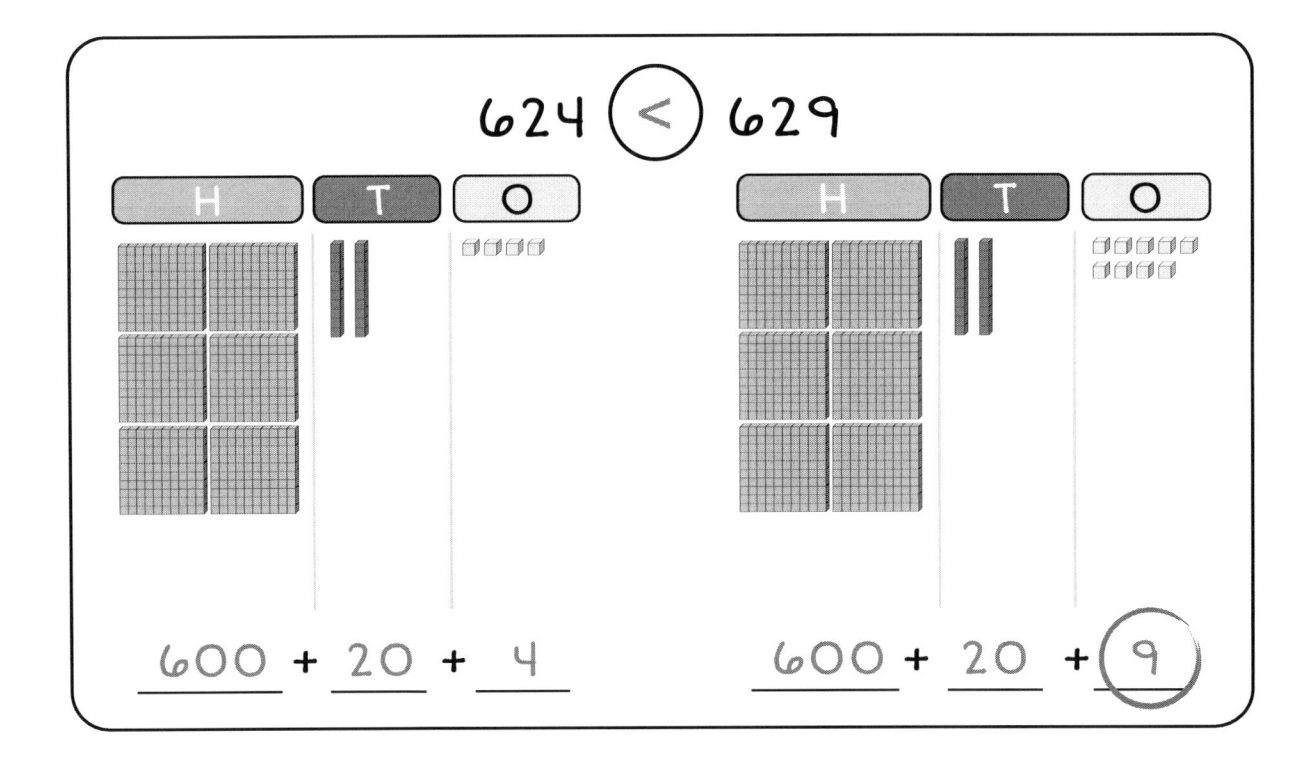

600 + 20 + 4   600 + 20 + (9)

7.5 Compare Numbers to 1,000

1. Which number is larger?

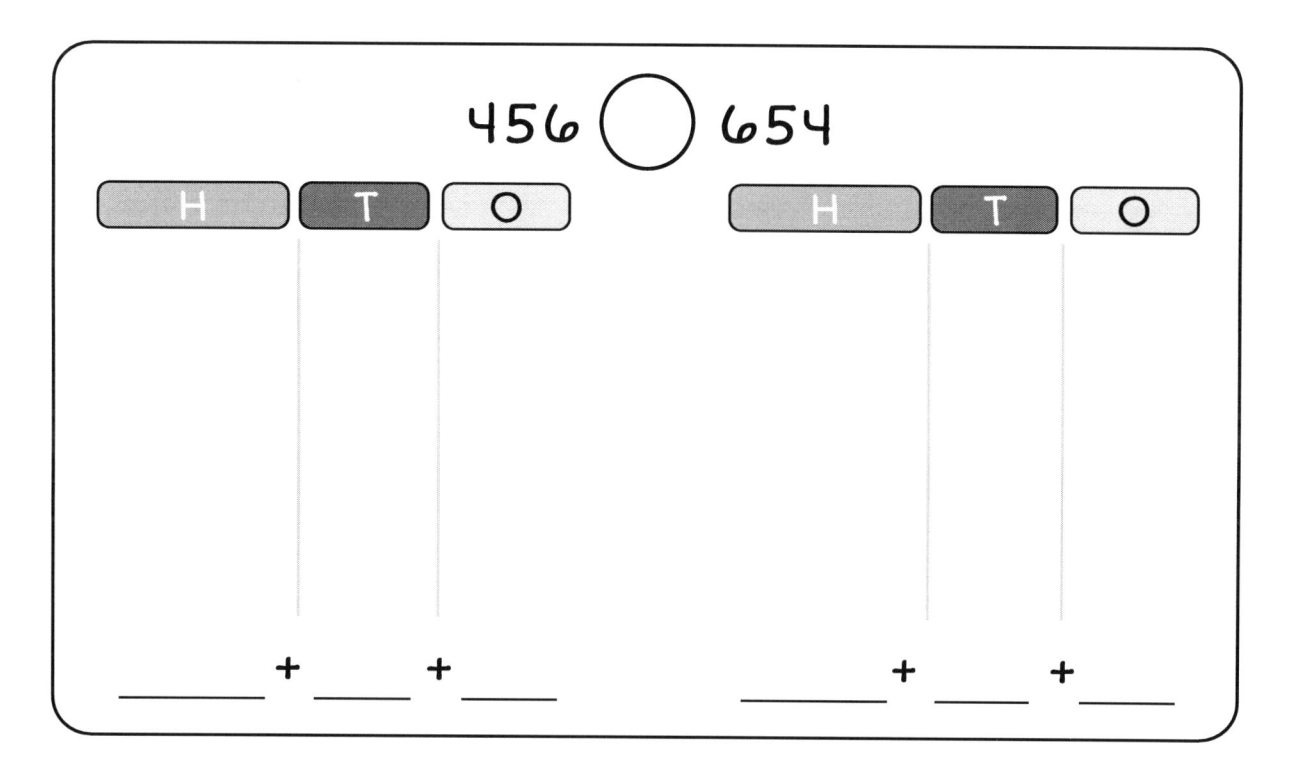

456 ◯ 654

H T O   H T O

___ + ___ + ___   ___ + ___ + ___

2. Which number is larger?

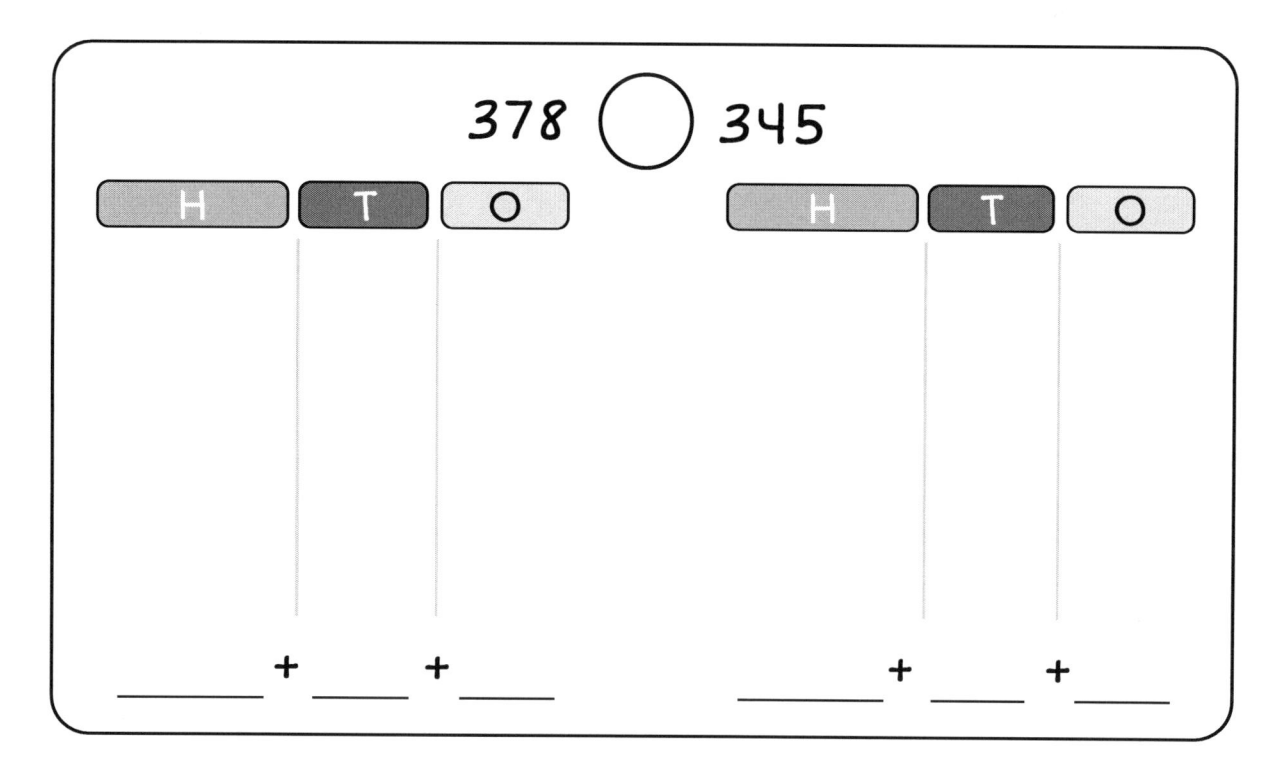

378 ◯ 345

H T O   H T O

___ + ___ + ___   ___ + ___ + ___

7.5 Compare Numbers to 1,000

3. Which number is larger?

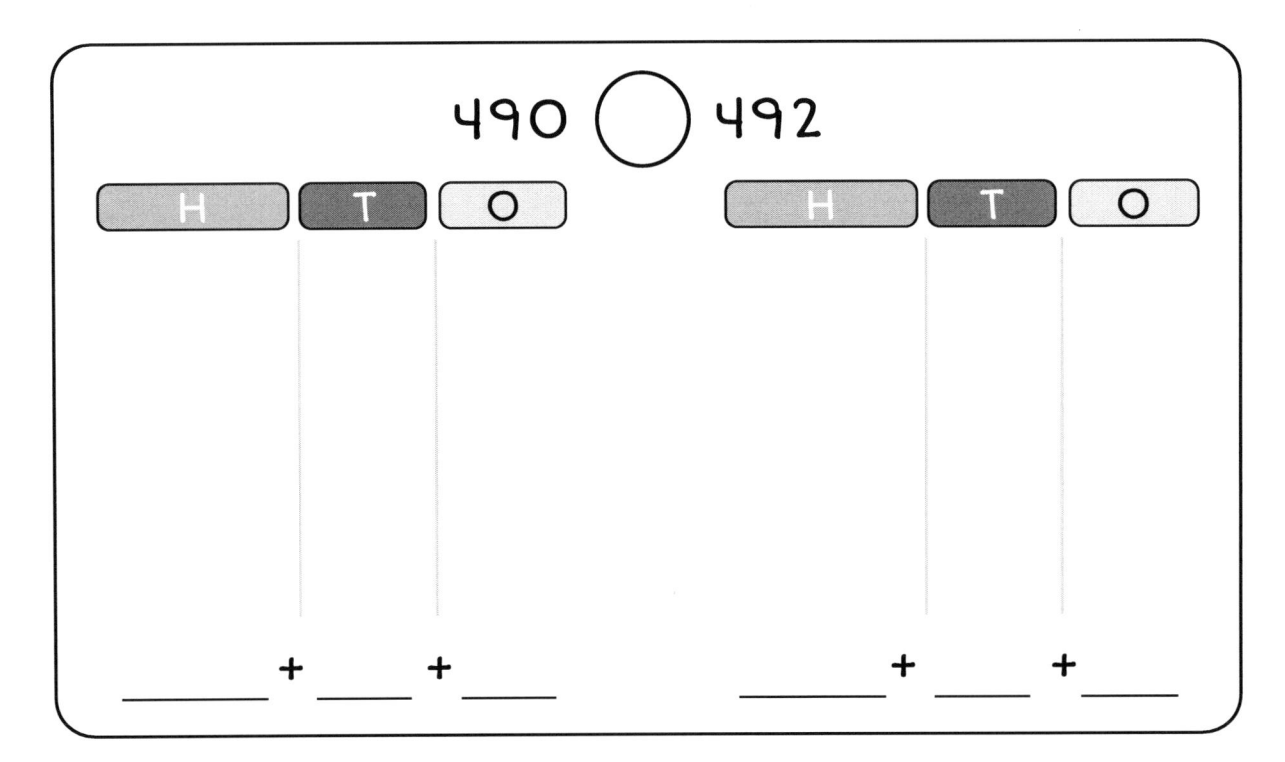

490 ◯ 492

| H | T | O | | H | T | O |

___ + ___ + ___   ___ + ___ + ___

4. Which number is larger?

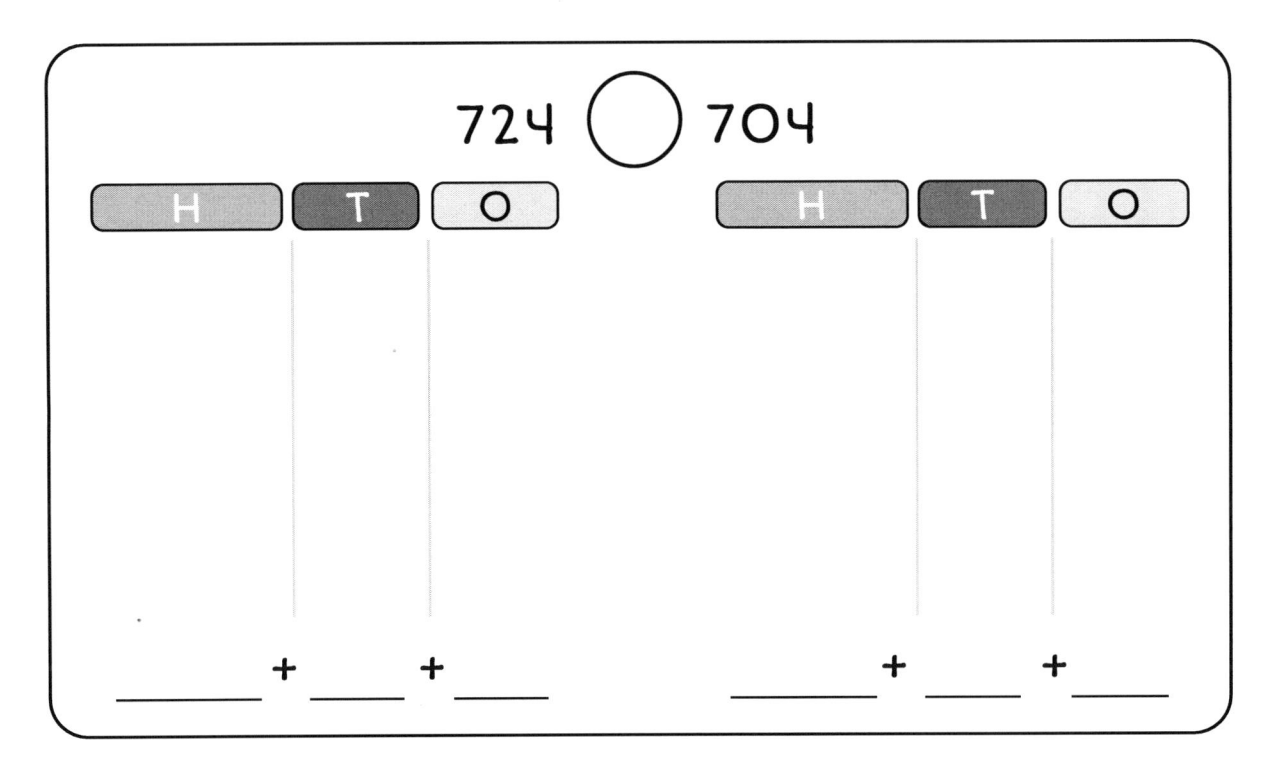

724 ◯ 704

| H | T | O | | H | T | O |

___ + ___ + ___   ___ + ___ + ___

5. Which number is larger?

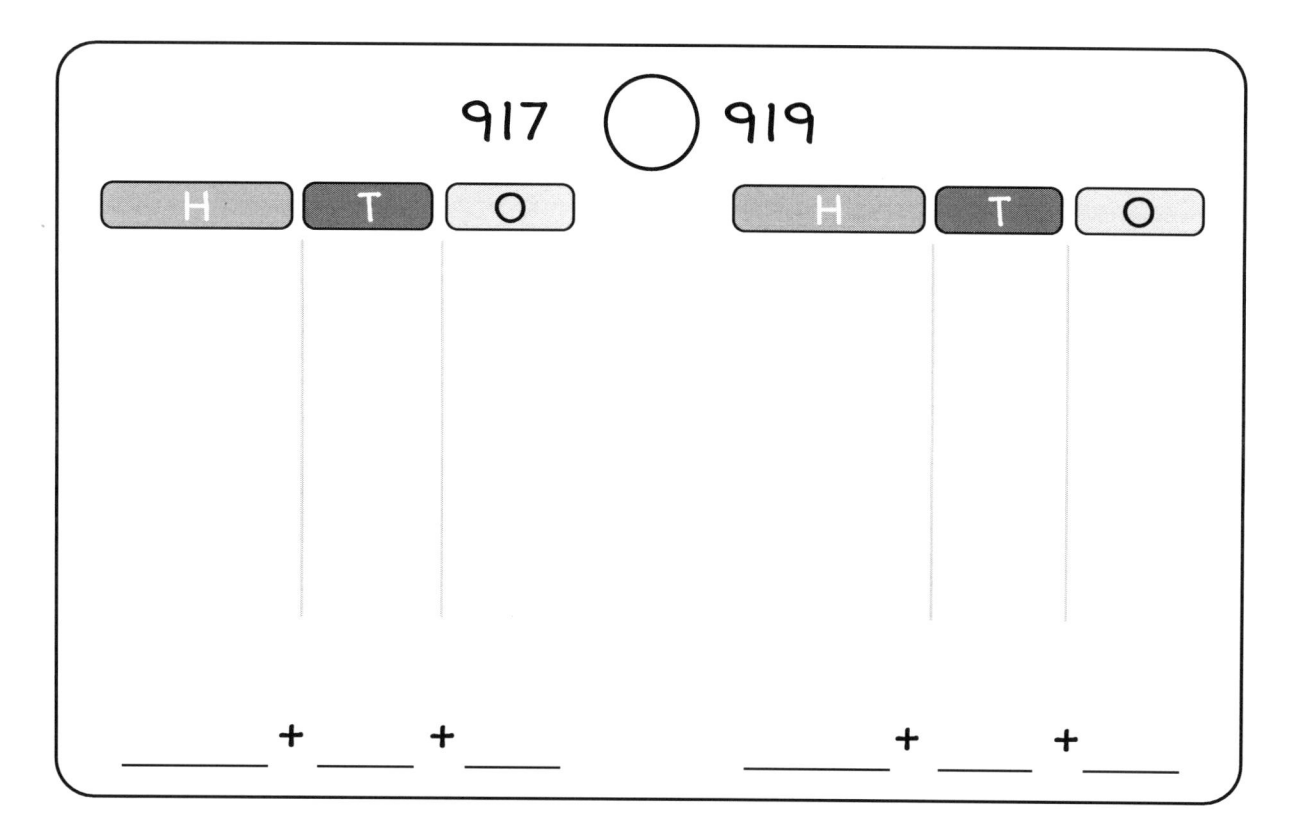

917 ◯ 919

| H | T | O | | H | T | O |

___ + ___ + ___   ___ + ___ + ___

Challenge

How did you know which number was bigger? Circle the number in the expanded forms you used to find this out. Do this for every question!
Ex. 900 + 10 + 3 and 900 + 10 + 5. Circle the 5.

7.5 Compare Numbers to 1,000

Name: _____ Date: _____

Number Line

Use this number line to round the numbers to the nearest 10. Refer to the lesson to check your work.

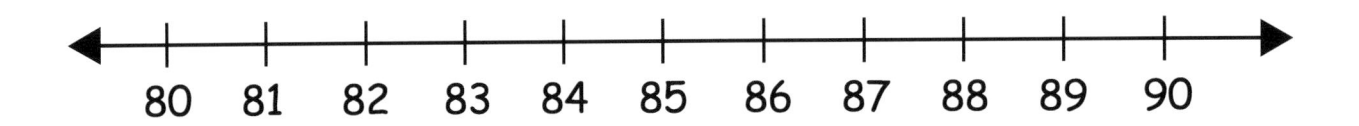

80 81 82 83 84 85 86 87 88 89 90

1. Round 81 to the nearest 10. _____

2. Round 87 to the nearest 10. _____

3. Round 84 to the nearest 10. _____

4. Round 85 to the nearest 10. _____

5. Round 89 to the nearest 10. _____

Name: _____ Date: _____

Round to the Nearest 10 from 0-100

Round each number to the nearest 10 using these number lines.

Example

Round 45 to the nearest 10.

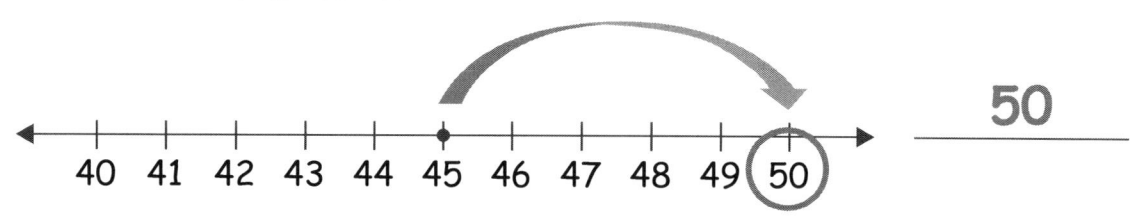

<------|----|----|----|----•----|----|----|----|----(50)------>   50
  40 41 42 43 44 45 46 47 48 49 50

Round 77 to the nearest 10.

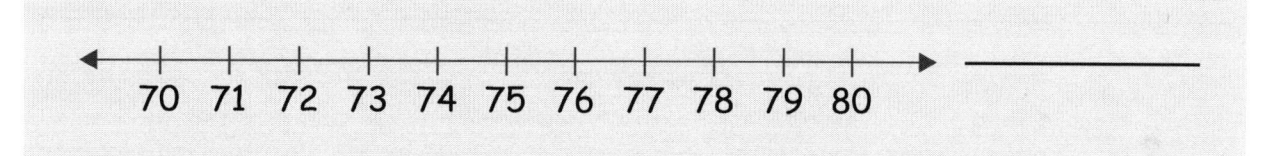

<------|----|----|----|----|----|----|----|----|----|------>   _____
  70 71 72 73 74 75 76 77 78 79 80

Round 18 to the nearest 10.

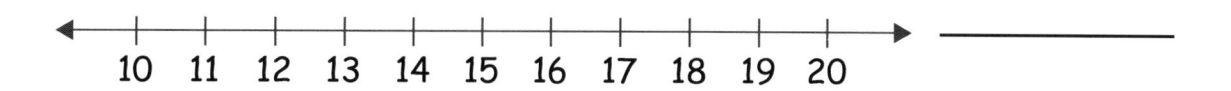

<------|----|----|----|----|----|----|----|----|----|------>   _____
  10 11 12 13 14 15 16 17 18 19 20

Round 96 to the nearest 10.

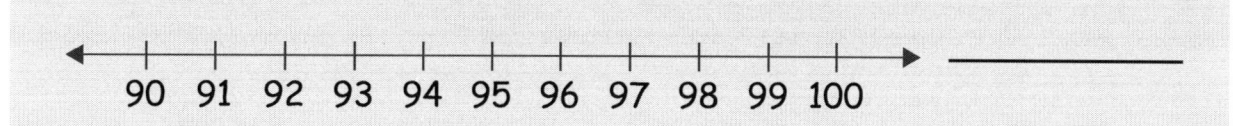

<------|----|----|----|----|----|----|----|----|----|------>   _____
  90 91 92 93 94 95 96 97 98 99 100

8.1 Round to the Nearest 10 from 0-100

Next page

Round 39 to the nearest 10.

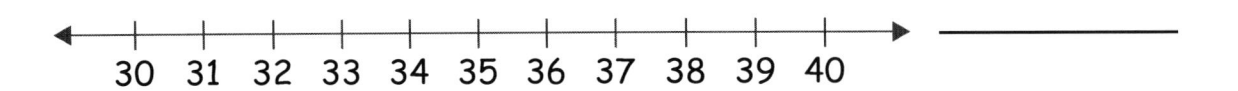

```
← — | — | — | — | — | — | — | — | — | — | — → _____
   30  31  32  33  34  35  36  37  38  39  40
```

Round 63 to the nearest 10.

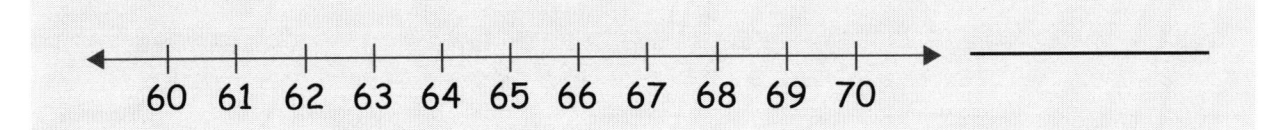

```
← — | — | — | — | — | — | — | — | — | — | — → _____
   60  61  62  63  64  65  66  67  68  69  70
```

Round 56 to the nearest 10.

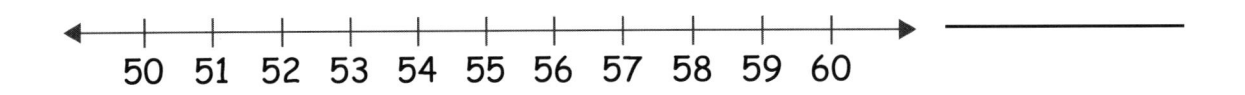

```
← — | — | — | — | — | — | — | — | — | — | — → _____
   50  51  52  53  54  55  56  57  58  59  60
```

Round 82 to the nearest 10

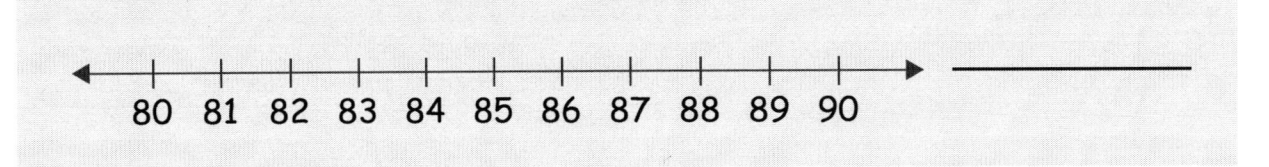

```
← — | — | — | — | — | — | — | — | — | — | — → _____
   80  81  82  83  84  85  86  87  88  89  90
```

Round 27 to the nearest 10.

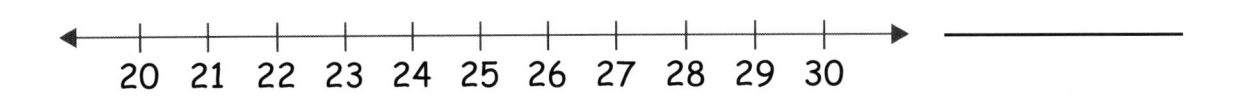

```
← — | — | — | — | — | — | — | — | — | — | — → _____
   20  21  22  23  24  25  26  27  28  29  30
```

8.1 Round to the Nearest 10 from 0-100

Round 84 to the nearest 10.

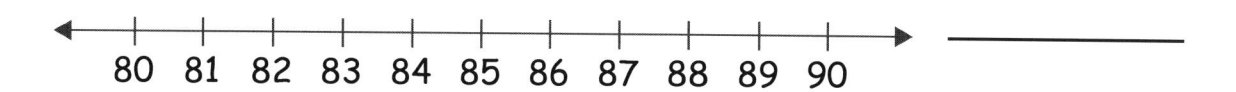

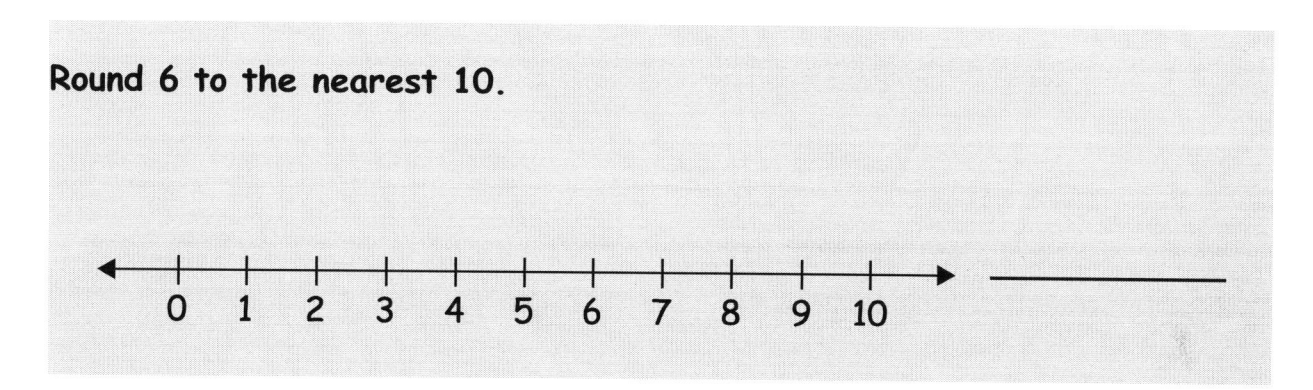

←—+—+—+—+—+—+—+—+—+—+—→ _____
 80 81 82 83 84 85 86 87 88 89 90

Round 6 to the nearest 10.

←—+—+—+—+—+—+—+—+—+—+—→ _____
 0 1 2 3 4 5 6 7 8 9 10

8.1 Round to the Nearest 10 from 0-100

Name: _____ Date: _____

Benchmark Number Lines

Use the number line and pieces of cereal to help you round 996 to the nearest whole ten. Use the lesson instructions to help you.

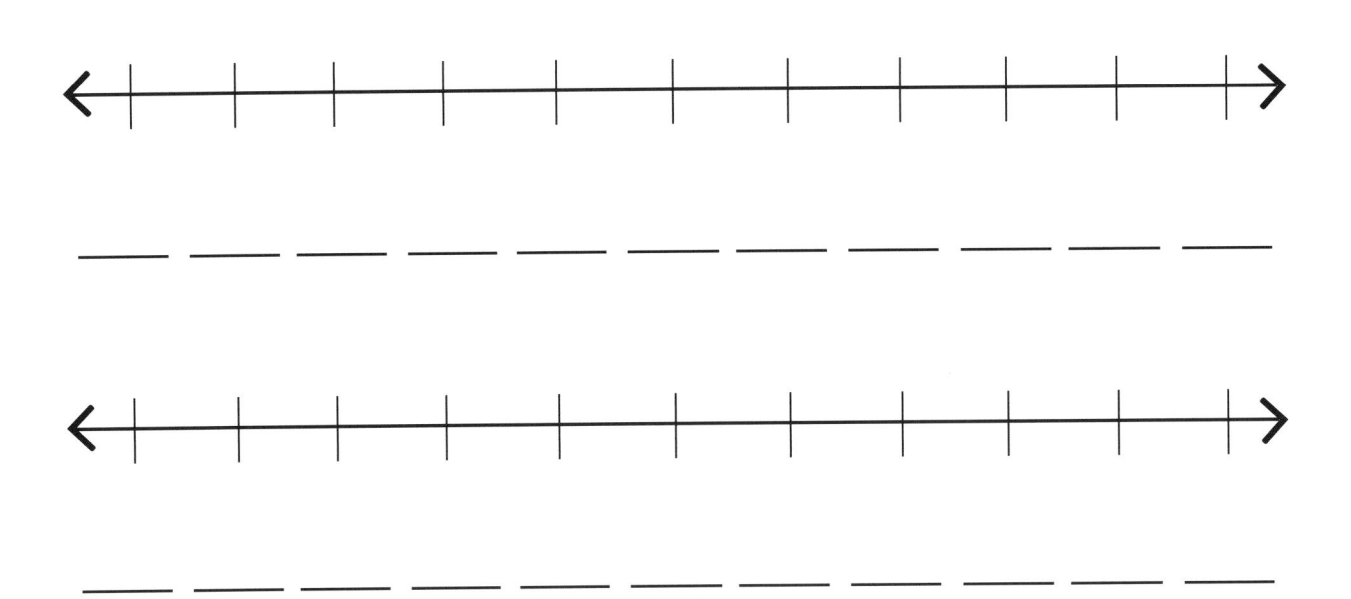

⟵|—|—|—|—|—|—|—|—|—|—|⟶

— — — — — — — — — — —

⟵|—|—|—|—|—|—|—|—|—|—|⟶

— — — — — — — — — — —

101

8.2 Round to the Nearest 10 from 0–1,000

Name: _____ Date: _____

Number Line Rounding

Can you round to the nearest whole ten? Put a dot to show the number you are rounding. Then, circle the number you are rounding to. Use the letter that goes with your answer to see a healthy treat!

Example:

Round 325 to the nearest 10 = **B**

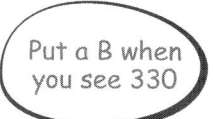

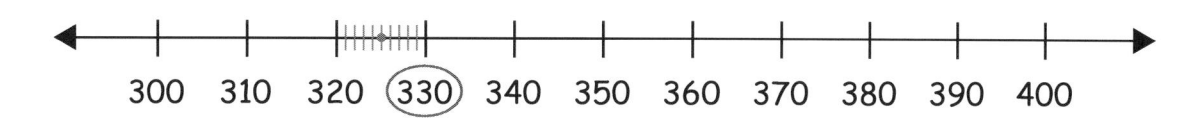

Put a B when you see 330

←―|―|―|―|―|―|―|―|―|―|―→
300 310 320 (330) 340 350 360 370 380 390 400

Round 152 to the nearest 10 = **E**

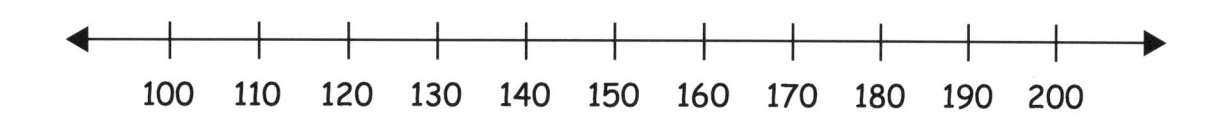

←―|―|―|―|―|―|―|―|―|―|―→
100 110 120 130 140 150 160 170 180 190 200

Round 548 to the nearest 10 = **R**

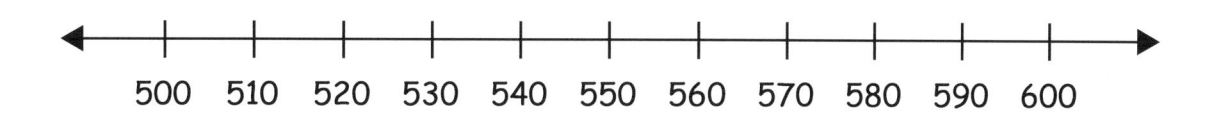

←―|―|―|―|―|―|―|―|―|―|―→
500 510 520 530 540 550 560 570 580 590 600

Round 865 to the nearest 10 = **S**

←―|―|―|―|―|―|―|―|―|―|―→
800 810 820 830 840 850 860 870 880 890 900

8.2 Round to the Nearest 10 from 0-1,000

Next page

Round 991 to the nearest 10 = **A**

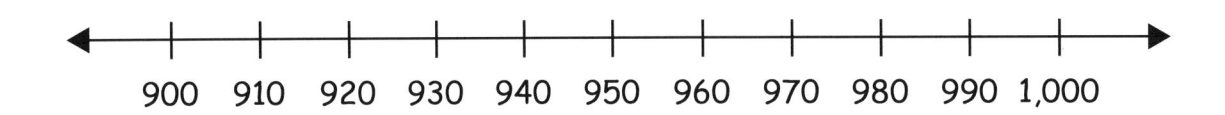

```
  900  910  920  930  940  950  960  970  980  990  1,000
```

Round 799 to the nearest 10 = **F**

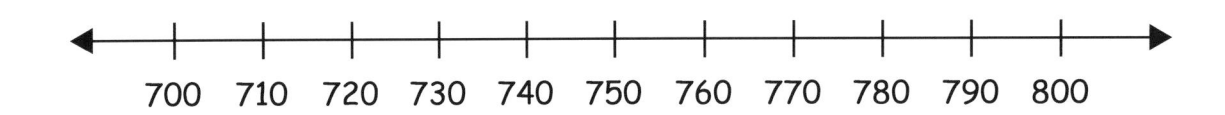

```
  700  710  720  730  740  750  760  770  780  790  800
```

_ _ _ _ H _ _ U I T _ N D V _ G _ T _ B L _ _
800 550 150 870 800 550   990   150 150 990   150 870

Challenge: Which number line rounds up? Which number line rounds down? Draw an arrow up to show rounding up. Draw an arrow down to show rounding down.

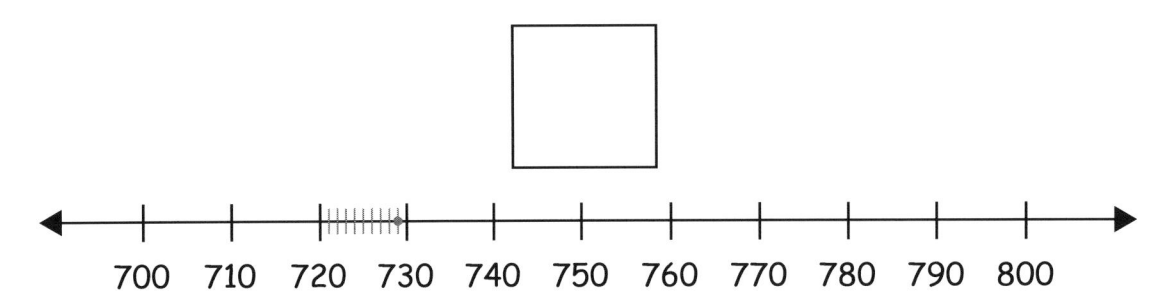

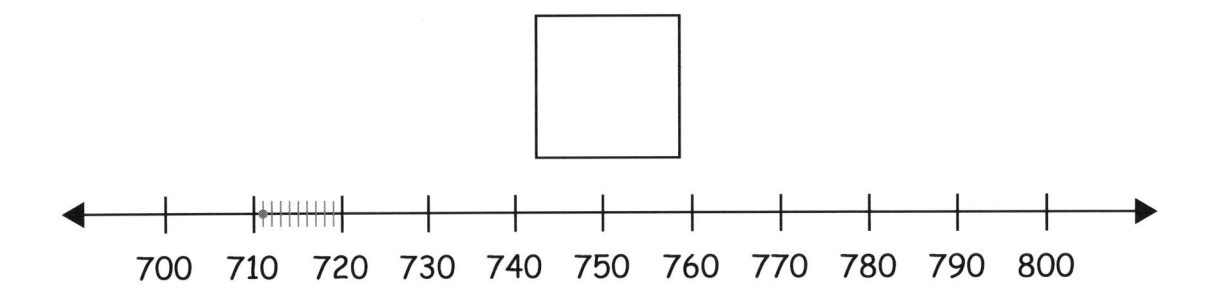

☐

```
  700  710  720  730  740  750  760  770  780  790  800
```

☐

```
  700  710  720  730  740  750  760  770  780  790  800
```

103   8.2 Round to the Nearest 10 from 0–1,000

Name: _____ Date: _____

Rounding on a Number Line and Thousand Chart

Round to the nearest 100. Circle your answer on the number line. Then circle whether you rounded up or down.

Example:

Round **783** to the nearest 100.

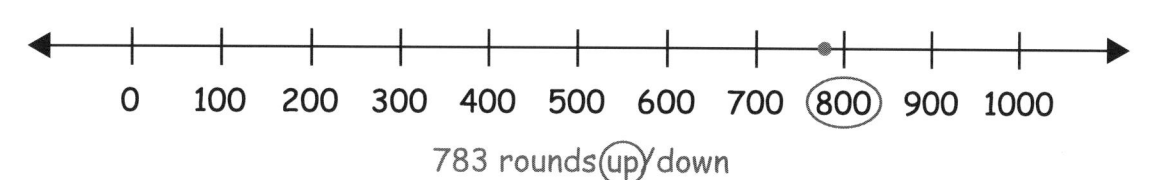

0 100 200 300 400 500 600 700 (800) 900 1000

783 rounds (up) / down

Use this chart to check your work

4 or less in the tens

5 or more in the tens

0	10	20	30	40	50	60	70	80	90	100
100	110	120	130	140	150	160	170	180	190	200
200	210	220	230	240	250	260	270	280	290	300
300	310	320	330	340	350	360	370	380	390	400
400	410	420	430	440	450	460	470	480	490	500
500	510	520	530	540	550	560	570	580	590	600
600	610	620	630	640	650	660	670	680	690	700
700	710	720	730	740	750	760	770	780	790	800
800	810	820	830	840	850	860	870	880	890	900
900	910	920	930	940	950	960	970	980	990	1000

8.3 Round to the Nearest 100 from 0-1,000

Next page

1. Round **469** to the nearest 100.

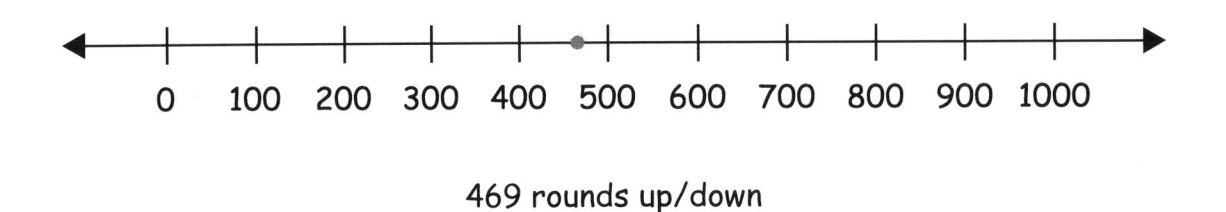

469 rounds up/down

2. Round **712** to the nearest 100.

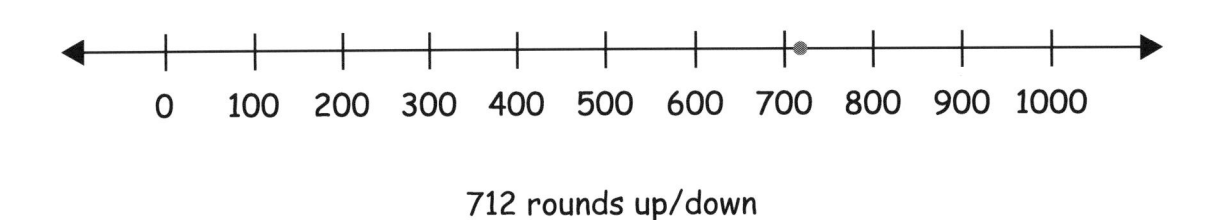

712 rounds up/down

3. Round **873** to the nearest 100.

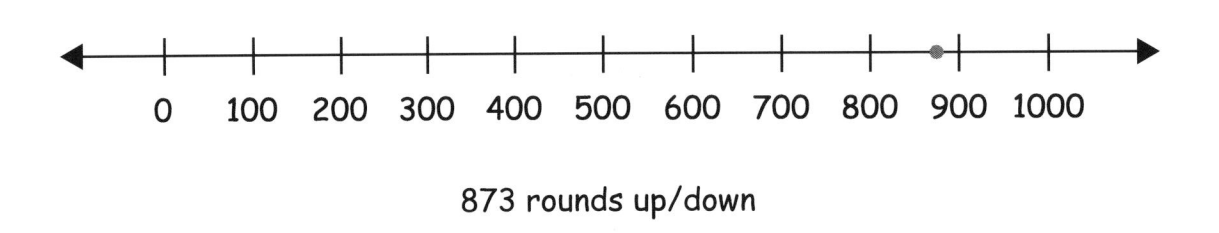

873 rounds up/down

4. Round **557** to the nearest 100.

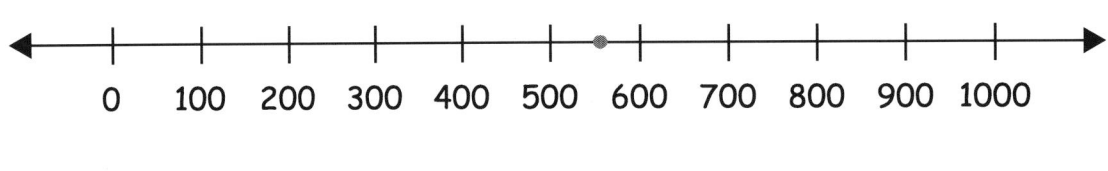

557 rounds up/down

8.3 Round to the Nearest 100 from 0-1,000

5. Round **990** to the nearest 100.

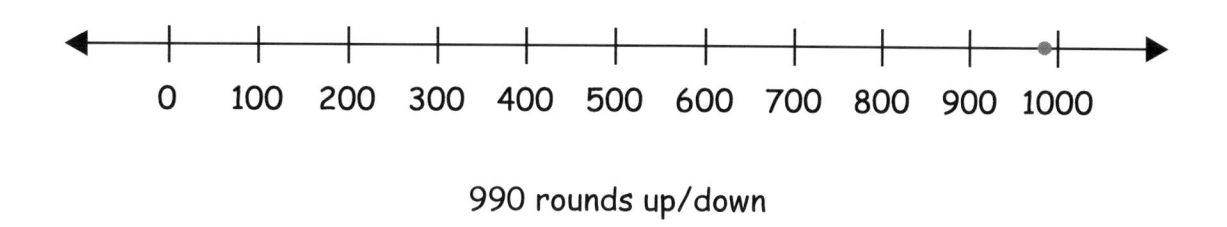

<-----|----|----|----|----|----|----|----|----|----•|----->
0   100 200 300 400 500 600 700 800 900 1000

990 rounds up/down

Challenge: Does 350 round up to 400 or down to 300. How do you know? Use words and pictures to show your answer.

8.3 Round to the Nearest 100 from 0-1,000

Name: _____ Date: _____

Number Line

Use the number line and two pieces of cereal to estimate the sums. Refer the lesson to check your work.

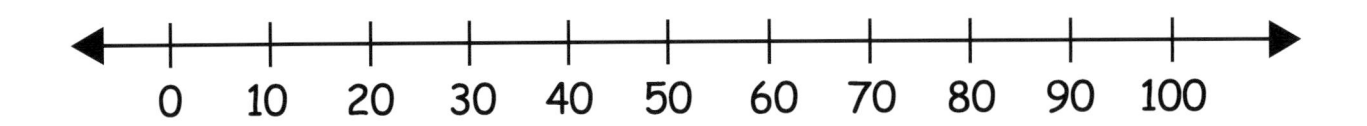

0 10 20 30 40 50 60 70 80 90 100

1. Estimate the sum: 12 + 48. _____

2. Estimate the sum: 77 + 31. _____

3. Estimate the sum: 35 + 45. _____

Name: _____ Date: _____

Estimate Sums

Estimate the sums below using a number line.

Addition Sentence	Number Line	Estimated Sum
32 + 84	0 10 20 (30) 40 50 60 70 (80) 90 100	30 + 80 = 110
77 + 8	0 10 20 30 40 50 60 70 80 90 100	__ + __ = __
45 + 61	0 10 20 30 40 50 60 70 80 90 100	__ + __ = __
56 + 64	0 10 20 30 40 50 60 70 80 90 100	__ + __ = __
25 + 24	0 10 20 30 40 50 60 70 80 90 100	__ + __ = __
4 + 82	0 10 20 30 40 50 60 70 80 90 100	__ + __ = __
41 + 99	0 10 20 30 40 50 60 70 80 90 100	__ + __ = __
68 + 27	0 10 20 30 40 50 60 70 80 90 100	__ + __ = __
59 + 25	0 10 20 30 40 50 60 70 80 90 100	__ + __ = __
86 + 18	0 10 20 30 40 50 60 70 80 90 100	__ + __ = __
72 + 11	0 10 20 30 40 50 60 70 80 90 100	__ + __ = __

8.5 Estimate Sums

Name: _____ Date: _____

Add Tens

Add the tens below and record your sum. Then match the sum to a color! Use place-value blocks if you need extra help adding.

10 + 60   80 + 10   0 + 70   20 + 60   30 + 40
___   ___   ___   ___   ___

50 + 20   40 + 40   60 + 30   50 + 30   40 + 50
___   ___   ___   ___   ___

70: [Yellow]   80: [Orange]   90: [Red]

109

9.1 Add Tens

Name: _____ Date: _____

Regroup Ones as Tens

These jars have different amounts of candy corn. How many tens and ones are in each jar? Circle groups of 10 candy corns. Then, write the number of tens and ones under each jar.

___ ten, ___ ones    ___ tens, ___ ones 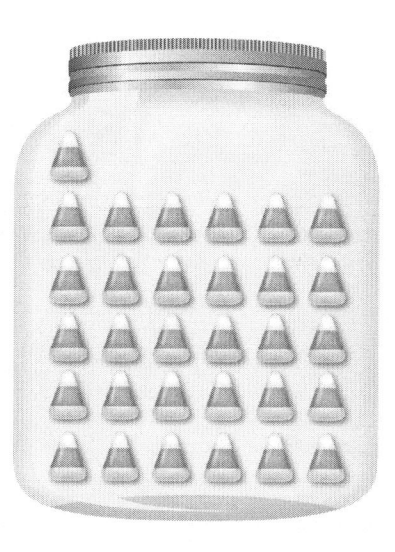   ___ tens, ___ one

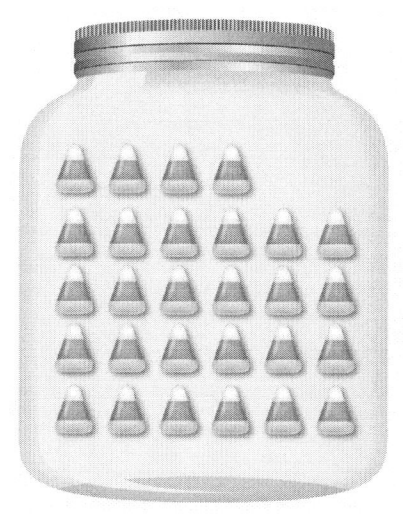

___ tens, ___ ones 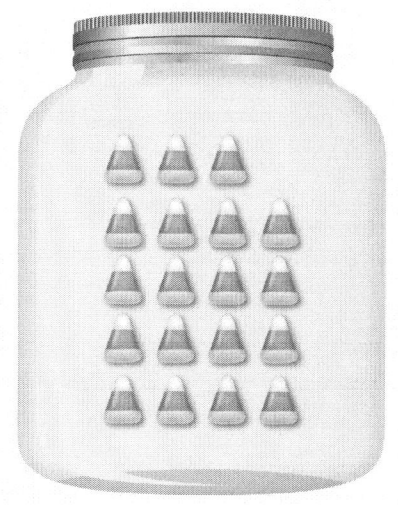   ___ ten, ___ ones 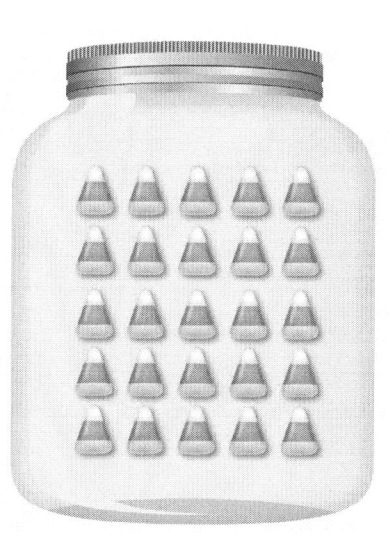   ___ tens, ___ ones

9.2 Regroup Ones as Tens

110

Next page

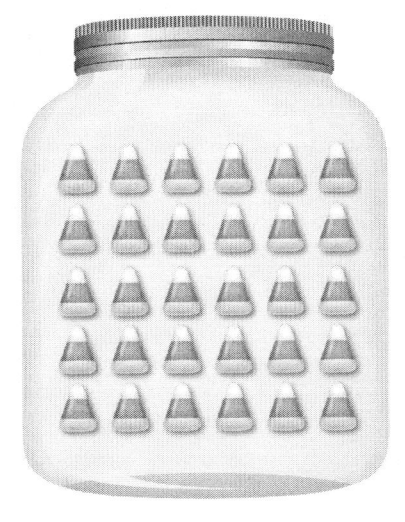

___ tens, ___ ones 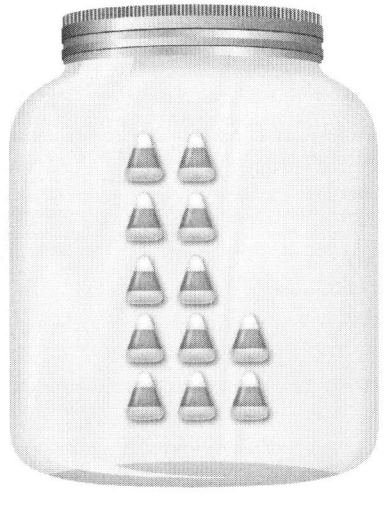   ___ ten, ___ ones 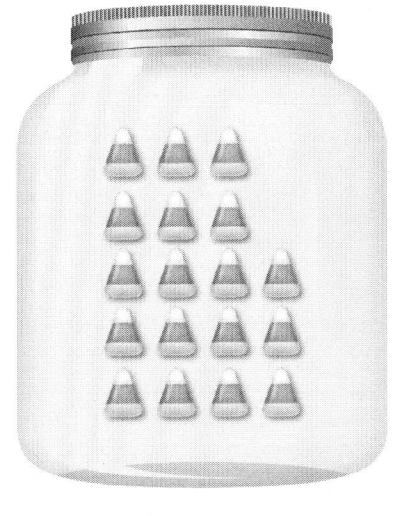   ___ ten, ___ ones

___ tens, ___ ones    ___ tens, ___ ones

9.2 Regroup Ones as Tens

Name: _____ Date: _____

Number Line

Use this number line to find the sum of 53 + 12 by following the directions in the lesson.

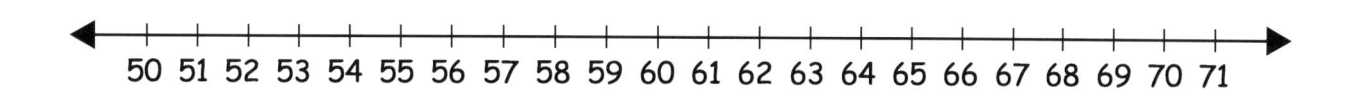

⟵ 50 51 52 53 54 55 56 57 58 59 60 61 62 63 64 65 66 67 68 69 70 71 ⟶

9.3 Add to a Two-Digit Number Using a Number Line

Name: _____ Date: _____

Add to a Two-Digit Number Using a Number Line

What is the sum? Use the number line to find out!

Addition Sentence	Number Line
57 + 3 = 60	50 51 52 53 54 55 56 57 58 59 60 61 62 63 64 65 66 67 68 69 70 71
34 + 4 = ___	30 31 32 33 34 35 36 37 38 39 40 41 42 43 44 45 46 47 48 49 50 51
21 + 11 = ___	20 21 22 23 24 25 26 27 28 29 30 31 32 33 34 35 36 37 38 39 40 41
4 + 43 = ___	30 31 32 33 34 35 36 37 38 39 40 41 42 43 44 45 46 47 48 49 50 51
60 + 18 = ___	60 61 62 63 64 65 66 67 68 69 70 71 72 73 74 75 76 77 78 79 80 81
82 + 2 = ___	70 71 72 73 74 75 76 77 78 79 80 81 82 83 84 85 86 87 88 89 90 91
16 + 25 = ___	25 26 27 28 29 30 31 32 33 34 35 36 37 38 39 40 41 42 43 44 45 46
30 + 6 = ___	30 31 32 33 34 35 36 37 38 39 40 41 42 43 44 45 46 47 48 49 50 51
5 + 65 = ___	55 56 57 58 59 60 61 62 63 64 65 66 67 68 69 70 71 72 73 74 75 76
44 + 8 = ___	35 36 37 38 39 40 41 42 43 44 45 46 47 48 49 50 51 52 53 54 55 56
12 + 10 = ___	10 11 12 13 14 15 16 17 18 19 20 21 22 23 24 25 26 27 28 29 30 31

9.3 Add to a Two-Digit Number Using a Number Line

Name: _____ Date: _____

Add a Two-Digit Number to a One-Digit Number

What is the sum? Use the place-value chart to find out! Draw an arrow if you need to move a ten frame to the ones section. Then, write the sum on the blank.

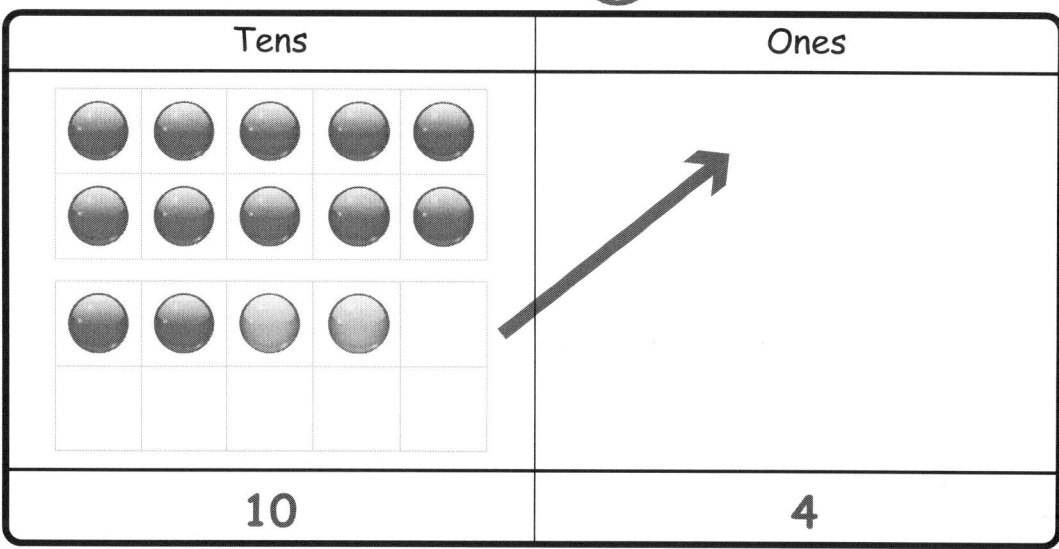

12 + 2 = (14)

Tens	Ones
10	4

17 + 3 = ____

Tens	Ones

9.4 Add a Two-Digit Number to a One-Digit Number

114

Next page

24 + 6 = ___

Tens	Ones

23 + 2 = ___

Tens	Ones

9.4 Add a Two-Digit Number to a One-Digit Number

18 + 4 = ___

Tens	Ones

35 + 6 = ___

Tens	Ones

9.4 Add a Two-Digit Number to a One-Digit Number

Name: _____ Date: _____

Addition Strategies

Answer questions 1-3 in your lesson using the given strategy. Check your answers in the lesson.

Base-Ten Blocks

Tens	Ones

9.5 Problem Solving Strategy: Write an Addition Sentence

Ten Frames

Tens	Ones

Number Line

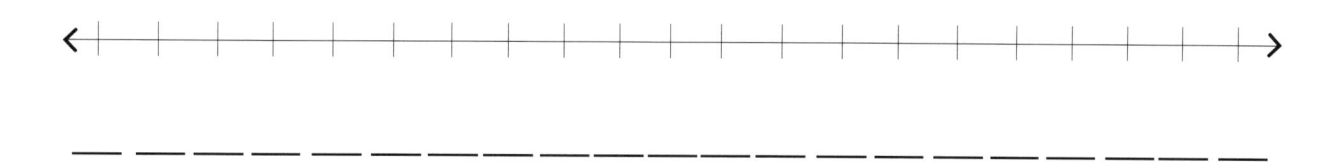

9.5 Problem Solving Strategy: Write an Addition Sentence

Name: _____ Date: _____

Write Addition Sentences

Can you find the addends and sum? Use the pictures below to find the addends and sums. Then, write them on the lines to create addition sentences!

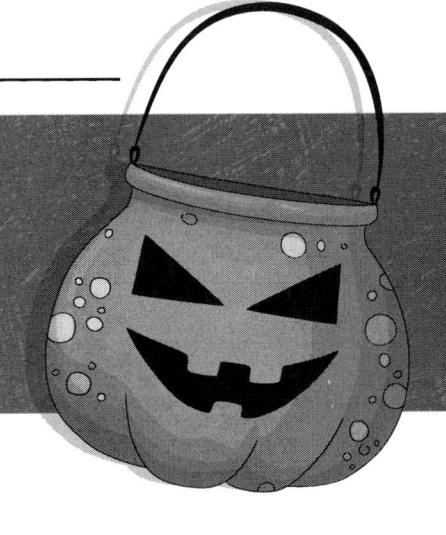

Example:

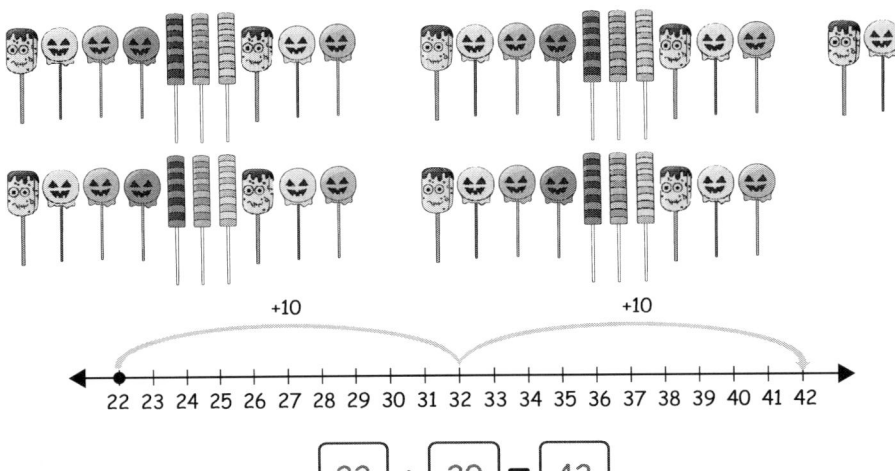

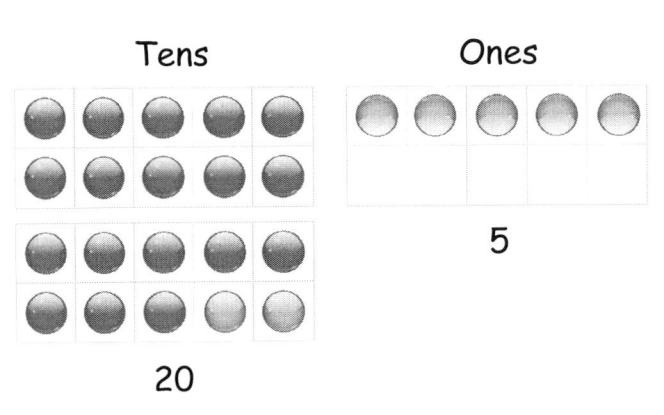

$$\boxed{22} + \boxed{20} = \boxed{42}$$

1.

Tens

Ones

20

5

$$\boxed{} + \boxed{} = \boxed{}$$

119   9.5 Problem Solving Strategy: Write an Addition Sentence

2.

☐ + ☐ = ☐

3.

☐ + ☐ = ☐

9.5 Problem Solving Strategy: Write an Addition Sentence

120

Next page

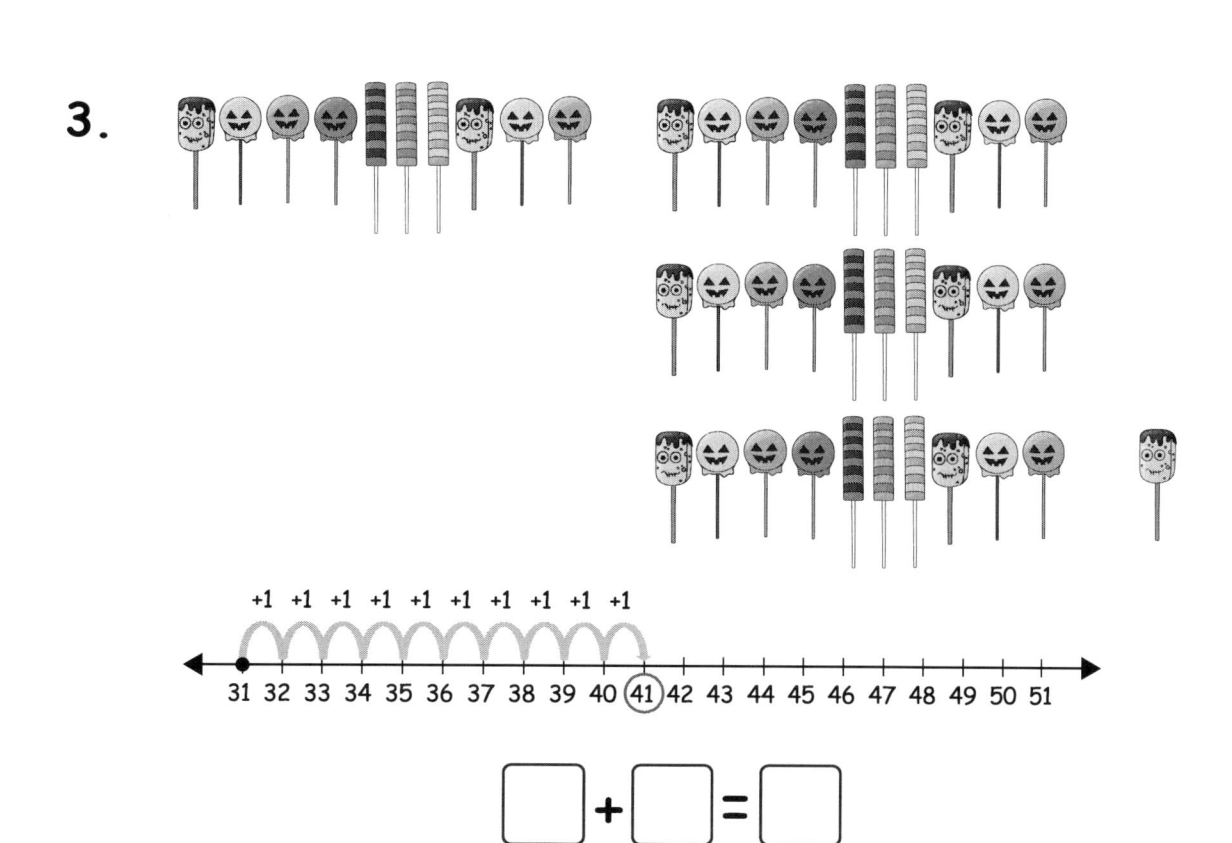

4.

Tens	Ones
	1

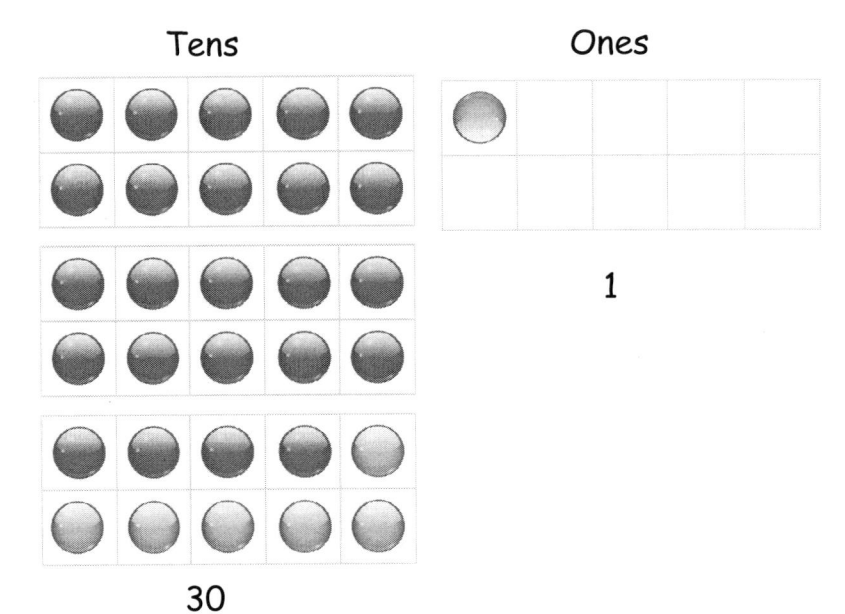

30

☐ + ☐ = ☐

121   9.5 Problem Solving Strategy: Write an Addition Sentence

5.

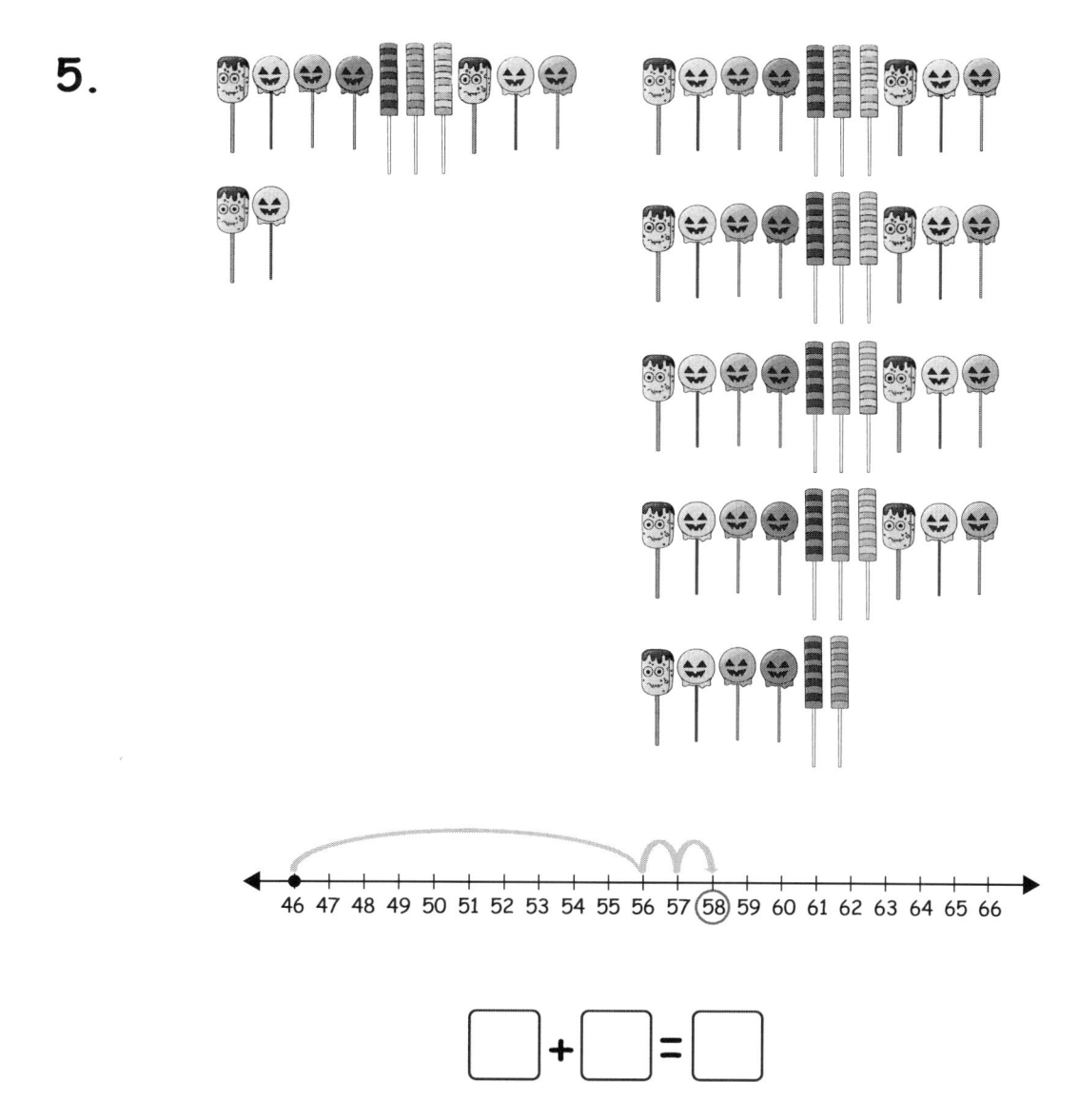

□ + □ = □

Example:
Write About It!

Which strategy did you like the most? Draw and write to show the one you like. Write at least one sentence to say why you like the strategy.

9.5 Problem Solving Strategy: Write an Addition Sentence

Name: _____ Date: _____

Place-Value Chart

Use this place-value chart to help you add. The lesson will walk you through how to use the chart!

Tens	Ones
_____	_____

10.1 Add a Two-Digit Number to a One-Digit Number with Regrouping

Name: _____ Date: _____

Counter Addition

Use your counters on the Tens Place-Value Chart. Write the sum on the line. Then, draw a line to match the place-value chart on the right to the correct addition sentence on the left.

Example:

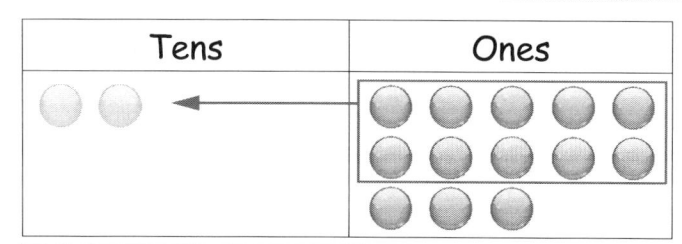

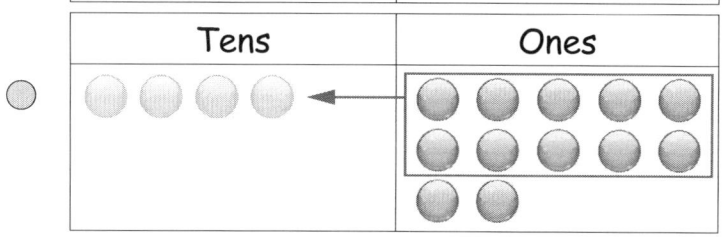

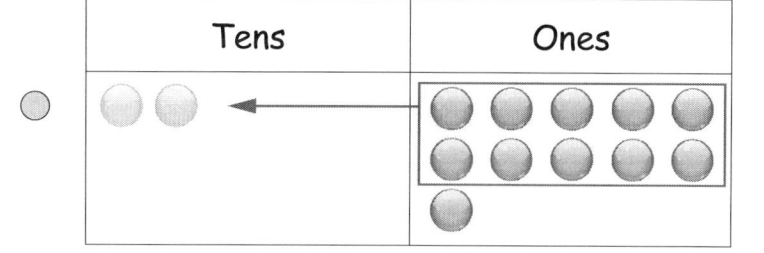

24 + 9 = 33

1. 15 + 7 = ___

2. 22 + 9 = ___

3. 37 + 6 = ___

4. 65 + 5 = ___

5. 44 + 8 = ___

10.1 Add a Two-Digit Number to a One-Digit Number with Regrouping

124

Next page

Challenge: What do you notice about the ones of both addends in 65 + 5? What happened to the ones place when you regrouped? Draw and write to show your answer.

Name: _____ Date: _____

Number Card Addition

Oscar needs help adding the leaves he is feeding to the pandas! Use the Place-Value Chart and Place-Value Number Cards to add. Then, write each number on the place-value charts below.

Example:

57 + 12 = 69

Tens	Ones
5	7
1	2
6	9

1. 34 + 11 =

Tens	Ones
___	___

2. 26 + 53 =

Tens	Ones
___	___

3. 42 + 21 =

Tens	Ones
___	___

4. 63 + 32 =

Tens	Ones
___	___

5. 16 + 72 =

Tens	Ones
___	___

10.2 Rewrite Two-Digit Addition

Name: _____ Date: _____

Two-Digit Addition Without Regrouping

Find the missing addends and sums. Match your answers with the color key. Then, color the monkey!

13 - Dark Brown
77 - Light Brown
38 - Dark Green
43 - Light Green
25 - Purple
51 - Red
23 - Pink
84 - Blue
19 - Orange
61 - White

```
   35          __          21          __          24
+  __       + 14        +  __       + 50        +  __
  ----        ----        ----        ----        ----
   58          75          34          88          67


   __          22          __          12          __
+ 40        +  __       + 15        +  __       + 21
  ----        ----        ----        ----        ----
   59          73          99          89          46
```

127

10.3 Two-Digit Addition Without Regrouping

Name: _____ Date: _____

Two-Digit Addition with Regrouping

Find the sums by adding and regrouping.
Match each letter with its sum.
The message will answer this joke:

What do you call a lion with a fancy hat?

___ ___ ___ ___ ___ ___ ___ ___ ___ ___
62   40 53 83 91 42   31 76 34 96

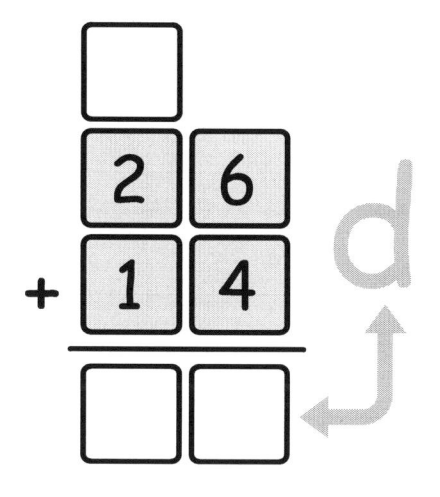

```
    2 6              3 7
+   1 4          +   5 9
  ─────            ─────
```

d

Match these letters with the sums in the blanks above

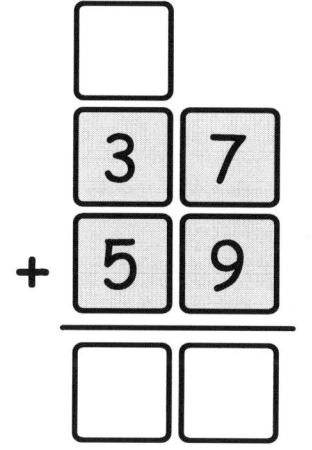

n

10.4 Two-Digit Addition With Regrouping

	4	8	i
+	2	8	

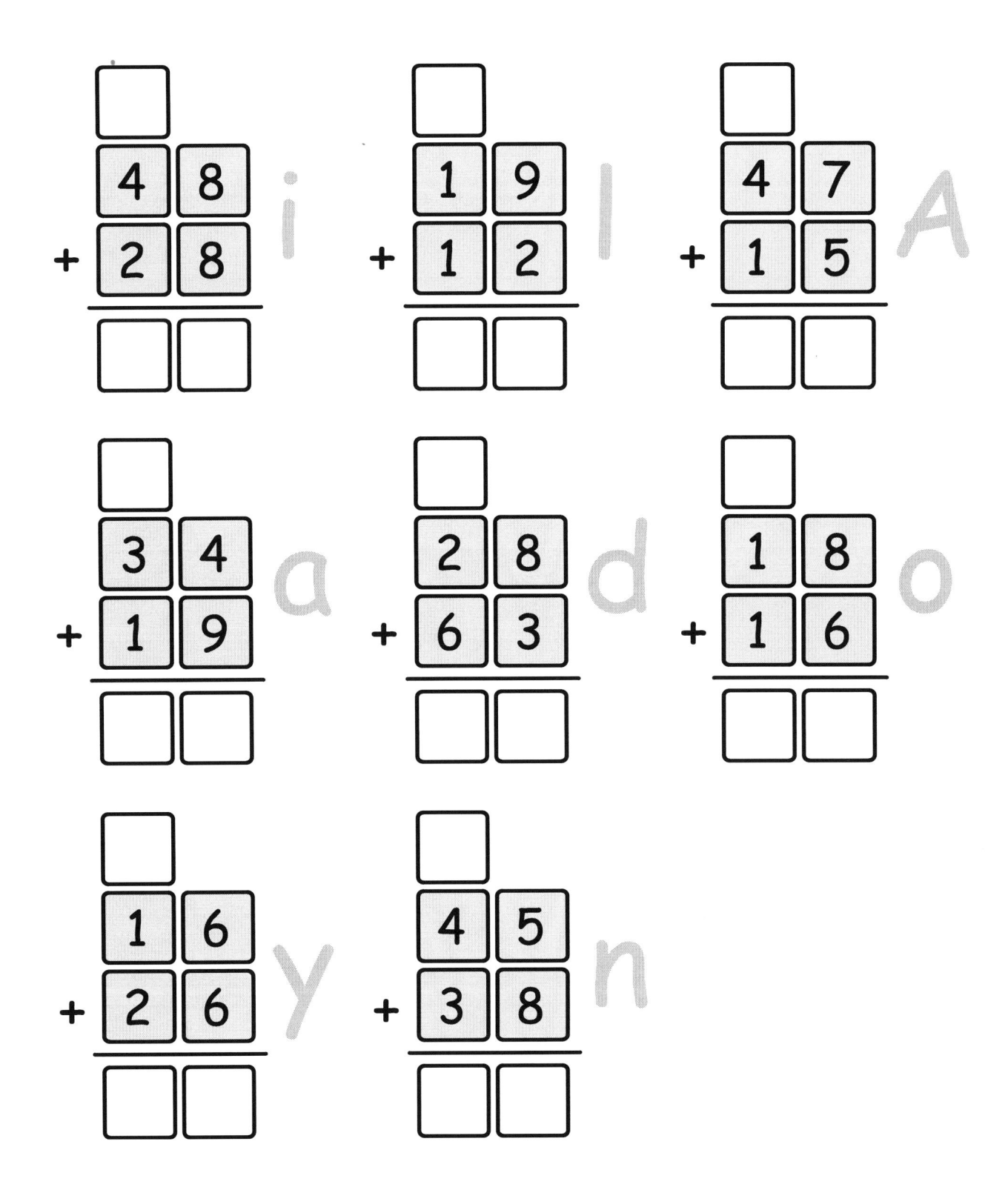

	1	9	l
+	1	2	

	4	7	A
+	1	5	

	3	4	a
+	1	9	

	2	8	d
+	6	3	

	1	8	o
+	1	6	

	1	6	y
+	2	6	

	4	5	n
+	3	8	

10.4 Two-Digit Addition With Regrouping

Name: _____ Date: _____

Input/Output Table

What are the missing numbers in the output column? Follow along in the lesson to check your work.

Input	Output
10	
20	
30	

Rule: +22

10.5 Input/Output Tables (Add)

Name: _____ Date: _____

Input/Output Tables (Add)

Can you find the numbers that belong in each output column? Use the spaces next to each input/output table to show your work.

Example:

Input	Output
5	37
10	42
15	47
20	52
Rule: +32	

5 + 32 37	10 + 32 42
15 + 32 47	20 + 32 52

Input	Output
10	
20	
30	
40	
Rule: +52	

Input	Output
44	
46	
48	
50	
Rule: +40	

131

10.5 Input/Output Tables (Add)

Input	Output
67	
68	
69	
70	
Rule: +19	

_____	_____
_____	_____

Input	Output
3	
6	
9	
12	
Rule: +15	

_____	_____
_____	_____

10.5 Input/Output Tables (Add)

Name: _____ Date: _____

Fact-Family Triangle

Follow along in the lesson to learn how to use this fact-family triangle to create related addition sentences.

___

____ + ____ = ____

____ + ____ = ____

___   ___

133   11.1 Two-Digit Fact Families

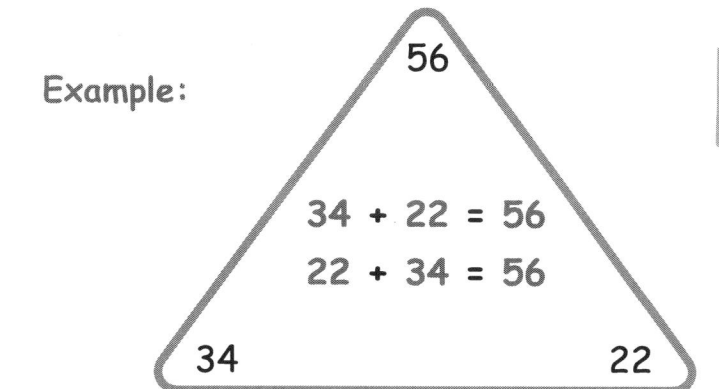

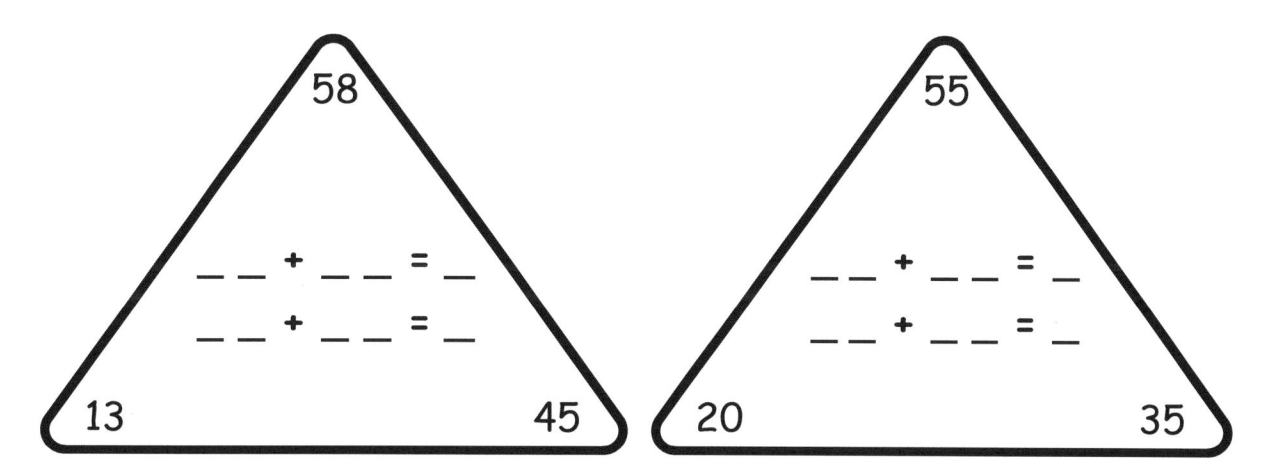

Name: ____________________________ Date: ____________

Two-Digit Fact Families

Can you create addition sentences from these fact-family triangles?

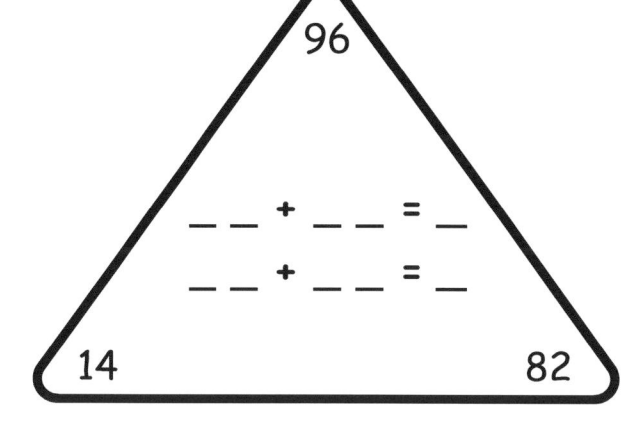

Example:

56

34 + 22 = 56

22 + 34 = 56

34 22

58

__ + __ = _

__ + __ = _

13 45

55

__ + __ = _

__ + __ = _

20 35

96

__ + __ = _

__ + __ = _

14 82

76

__ + __ = _

__ + __ = _

20 56

Triangle 1 (97, 46, 51)

46 + 51 = 97
51 + 46 = 97

Triangle 2 (94, 22, 72)

22 + 72 = 94
72 + 22 = 94

Triangle 3 (85, 21, 64)

21 + 64 = 85
64 + 21 = 85

Triangle 4 (67, 13, 54)

13 + 54 = 67
54 + 13 = 67

Triangle 5 (75, 30, 45)

30 + 45 = 75
45 + 30 = 75

Triangle 6 (89, 26, 63)

26 + 63 = 89
63 + 26 = 89

11.1 Two-Digit Fact Families

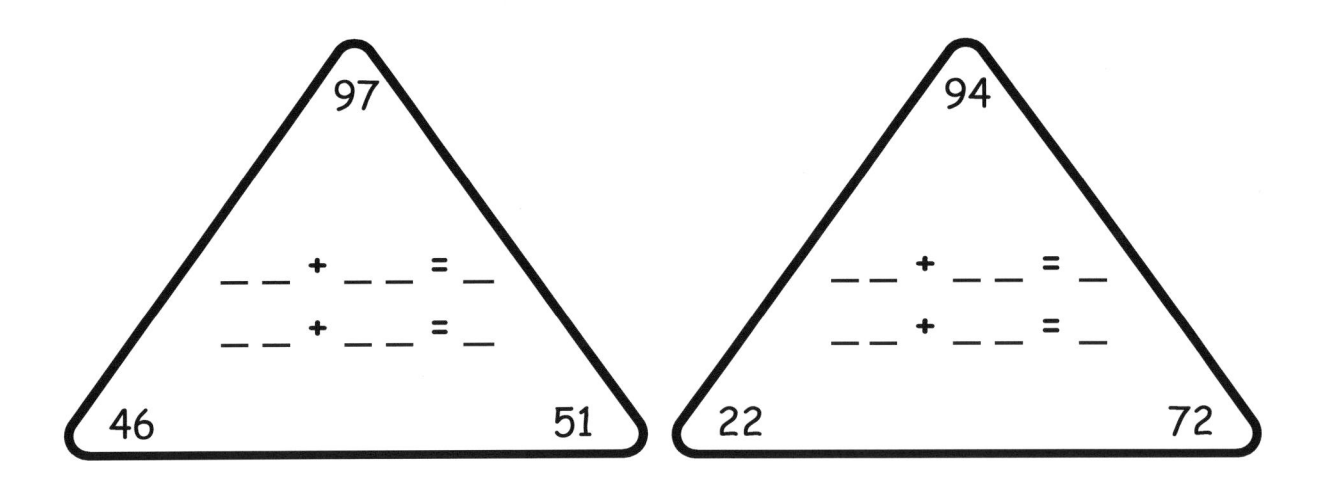

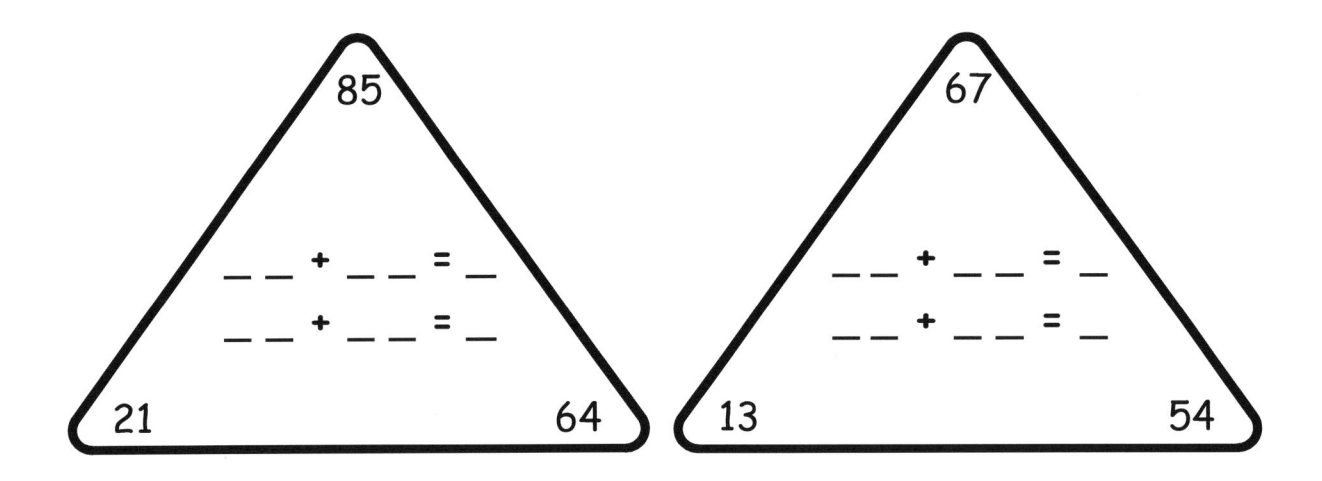

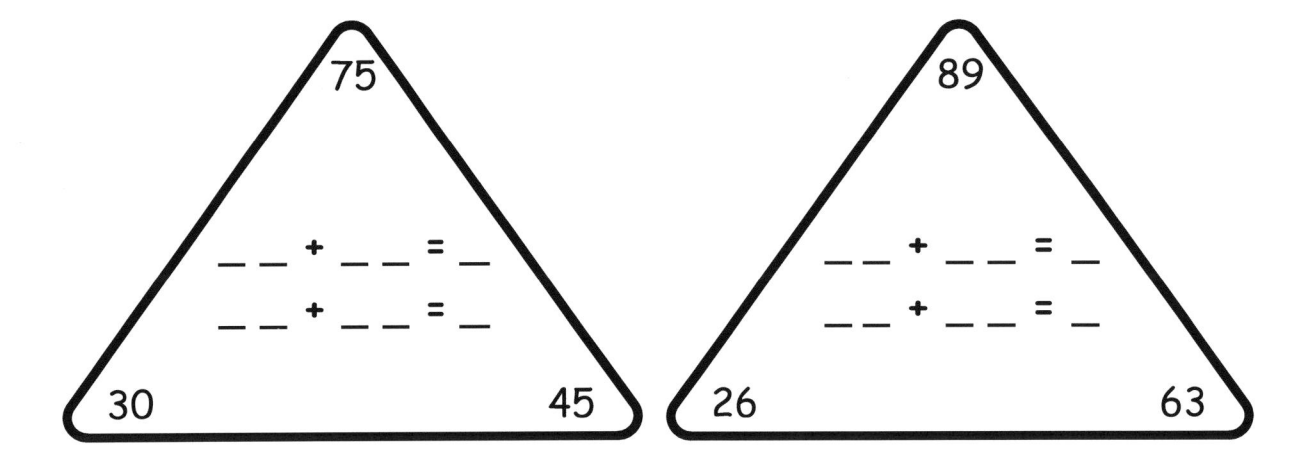

Mentally Add Two-Digit Numbers

Can you add these numbers in your head? Cross out the zeros to show which numbers you ignored! Then, match the sums with each letter. These letters will help you answer the question below.

Example: 1̸0 + 2̸0 = 30

6 + 50 = ___	a	20 + 2 = ___	h
70 + 5 = ___	d	7 + 30 = ___	A
90 + 4 = ___	o	80 + 3 = ___	c
10 + 60 = ___	w	10 + 30 = ___	-
40 + 20 = ___	g	40 + 50 = ___	t

What farm animal keeps the best time?

__   __ __ __ __ __ __ __ __ __
37   70 56 90 83 22 40 75 94 60

11.2 Mentally Add Two-Digit Numbers

Name: _____   Date: _____

Add In Parts

Can you add in parts? Fill in the missing numbers to get the correct sum. You can use your number cards and addition page to help you!

Example: 30 + 18 = 48

30 + 10 + 8

40 + 8

1. 20 + 15 = 35

   20 + 10 + 5

   ☐ + 5

2. 40 + 17 = 57

   40 + ☐ + 7

   50 + 7

3. 50 + 26 = 76

   50 + ☐ + 6

   ☐ + 6

4. 60 + 24 = 84

   60 + ☐ + 4

   ☐ + 4

5. 60 + 31 = 91

[ ] + [ ] + [1]

[ ] + [1]

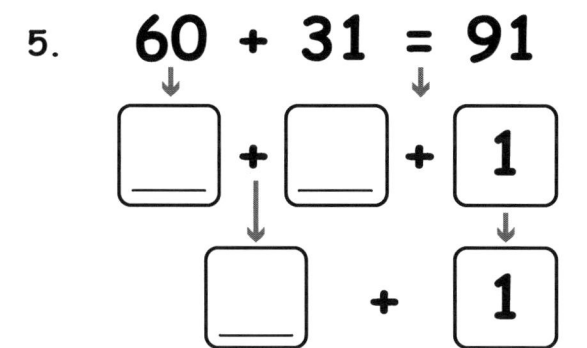

Challenge: Can you find the sum? Fill out all of the boxes and add in parts! Write the sum on the line.

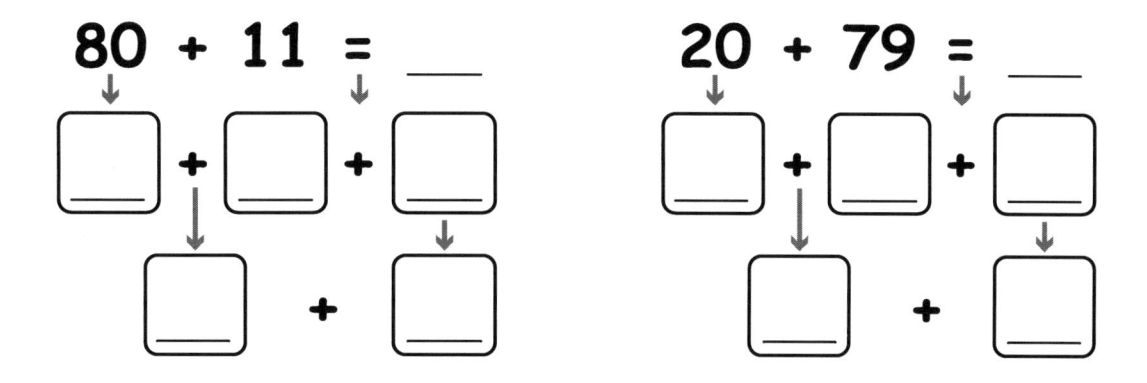

80 + 11 = ___

[ ] + [ ] + [ ]

[ ] + [ ]

20 + 79 = ___

[ ] + [ ] + [ ]

[ ] + [ ]

11.3 Add In Parts

Name: _____   Date: _____

Add In Parts

Can you add in parts? Use the numbers in the box to fill in the parts. Then write the sum on the line.

Example: **20 + 86 = 106**

[20] + [80] + [6]

[100] + [6]

| 6   6   20   80 |
| 100 |

1. **40 + 72 = ___**

[ ] + [ ] + [ ]

[ ] + [ ]

| 2   2   40   70 |
| 110 |

2. **58 + 60 = ___**

[ ] + [ ] + [ ]

[ ] + [ ]

| 8   8   50   60 |
| 110 |

139

11.4 Apply the Add in Parts Strategy

3. 60 + 85 = ___

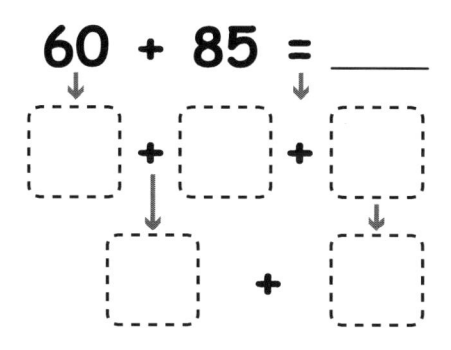

| 5 5 60 80 |
| 140 |

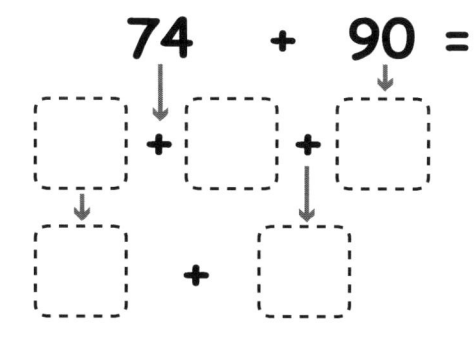

4. 74 + 90 = ___

| 4 4 70 90 |
| 160 |

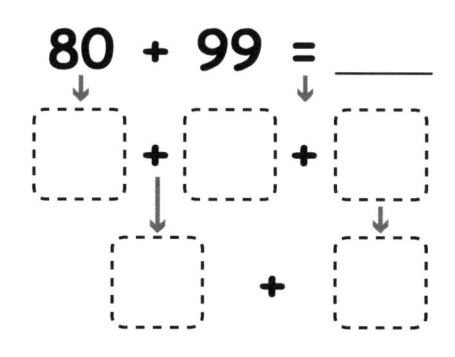

5. 80 + 99 = ___

| 9 9 80 90 |
| 170 |

11.4 Apply the Add in Parts Strategy

Name: _____ Date: _____

The Next Ten
Can you find the sum using the next-ten strategy?

Example:

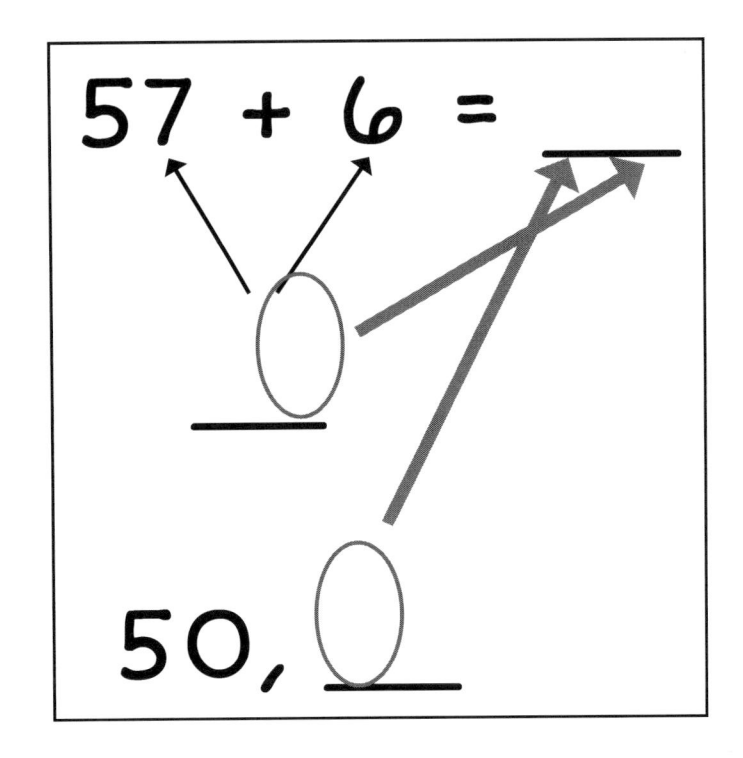

$35 + 9 = \underline{44}$

14

30, <u>40</u>

$57 + 6 = \underline{}$

50, ◯

141

11.5 The Next Ten

Name: _____ Date: _____

Add on a Hundred Chart

Use an addition strategy to find the sum. Then, check your work using a hundred chart. Color down and to the right with a green crayon. Circle the sum and see if it matches your first answer!

Example:

```
  54
+ 31
-----
  85
```

1.

```
  61
+ 35
-----
```

12.1 Add on a Hundred Chart

142

Next page

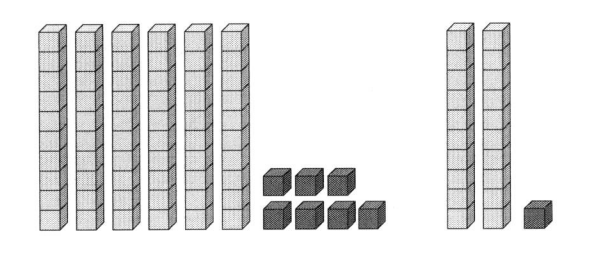

2.

11 + 54 =

Tens	Ones
●●●●● ●	●●●●●

1	2	3	4	5	6	7	8	9	10
11	12	13	14	15	16	17	18	19	20
21	22	23	24	25	26	27	28	29	30
31	32	33	34	35	36	37	38	39	40
41	42	43	44	45	46	47	48	49	50
51	52	53	54	55	56	57	58	59	60
61	62	63	64	65	66	67	68	69	70
71	72	73	74	75	76	77	78	79	80
81	82	83	84	85	86	87	88	89	90
91	92	93	94	95	96	97	98	99	100

3.

67 + 21 =

1	2	3	4	5	6	7	8	9	10
11	12	13	14	15	16	17	18	19	20
21	22	23	24	25	26	27	28	29	30
31	32	33	34	35	36	37	38	39	40
41	42	43	44	45	46	47	48	49	50
51	52	53	54	55	56	57	58	59	60
61	62	63	64	65	66	67	68	69	70
71	72	73	74	75	76	77	78	79	80
81	82	83	84	85	86	87	88	89	90
91	92	93	94	95	96	97	98	99	100

12.1 Add on a Hundred Chart

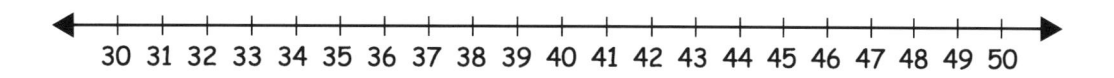

4.

$34 + 13 =$

```
← 30 31 32 33 34 35 36 37 38 39 40 41 42 43 44 45 46 47 48 49 50 →
```

1	2	3	4	5	6	7	8	9	10
11	12	13	14	15	16	17	18	19	20
21	22	23	24	25	26	27	28	29	30
31	32	33	34	35	36	37	38	39	40
41	42	43	44	45	46	47	48	49	50
51	52	53	54	55	56	57	58	59	60
61	62	63	64	65	66	67	68	69	70
71	72	73	74	75	76	77	78	79	80
81	82	83	84	85	86	87	88	89	90
91	92	93	94	95	96	97	98	99	100

5.

```
   55
+  32
 ----
```

1	2	3	4	5	6	7	8	9	10
11	12	13	14	15	16	17	18	19	20
21	22	23	24	25	26	27	28	29	30
31	32	33	34	35	36	37	38	39	40
41	42	43	44	45	46	47	48	49	50
51	52	53	54	55	56	57	58	59	60
61	62	63	64	65	66	67	68	69	70
71	72	73	74	75	76	77	78	79	80
81	82	83	84	85	86	87	88	89	90
91	92	93	94	95	96	97	98	99	100

12.1 Add on a Hundred Chart

Name: _____ Date: _____

Adding Page

Follow the directions in the lesson to help you add three numbers using the diagram below.

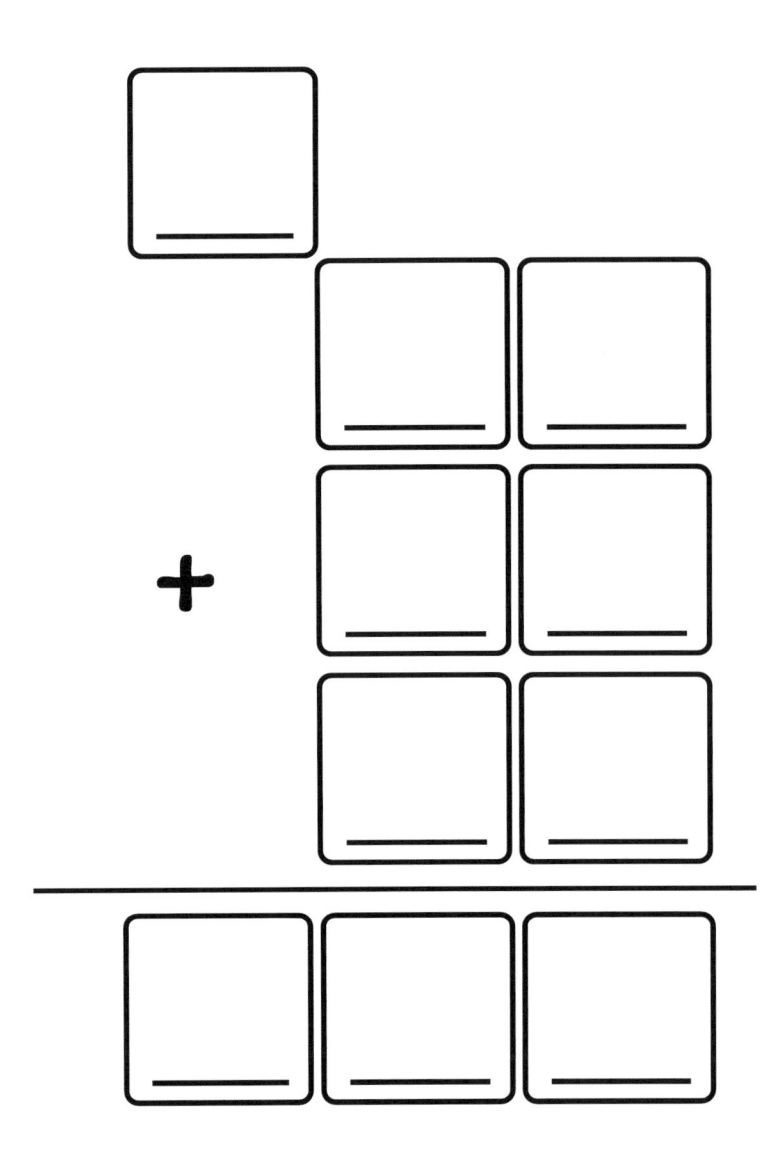

145

12.2 Add Three Numbers

Name: _____ Date: _____

Add Three Numbers

Can you solve these addition problems? Remember to add the digits in the ones place first. Then, add the digits in the tens place.

Example: What is the sum of 37 + 12 + 28?

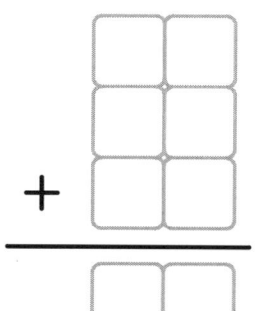

```
    1
    3 7
    1 2
  + 2 8
  -----
    7 7
```

1. What is the sum of 15 + 10 + 3?

2. There are 2 apples, 14 peaches, and 41 oranges. How many fruits are there in total?

3. There are 40 basketballs, 28 golf balls, and 11 footballs at the gym. How many balls are there altogether?

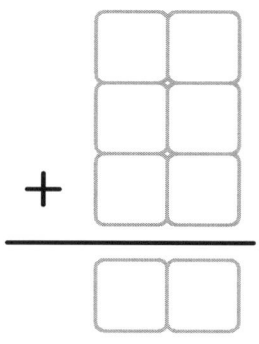

4. What is the sum of 12 + 22 + 15?

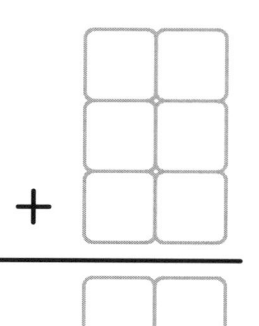

12.2 Add Three Numbers

146

Next page

5. What is the sum of 84 + 60 + 3?

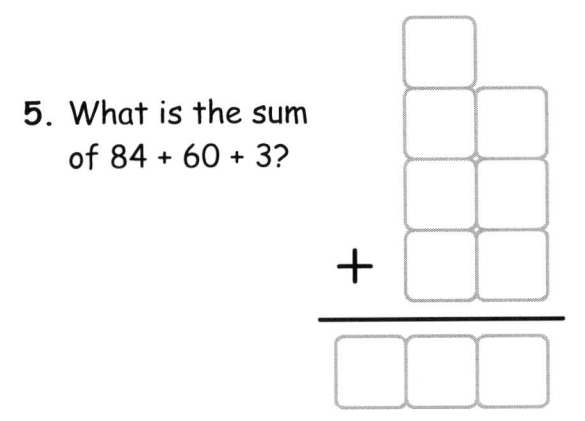

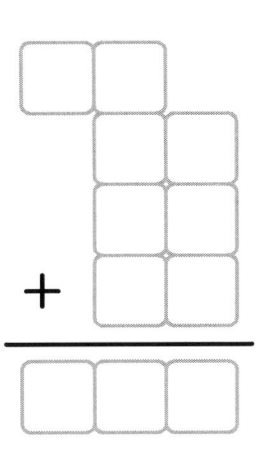

6. What is the sum of 55 + 17 + 29?

7. Anna counted 40 sheep, 11 pigs, and 4 cows on a farm. How many animals are there in total?

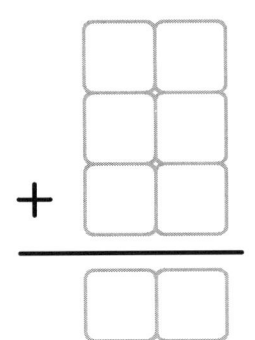

8. What is the sum of 33 + 24 + 9?

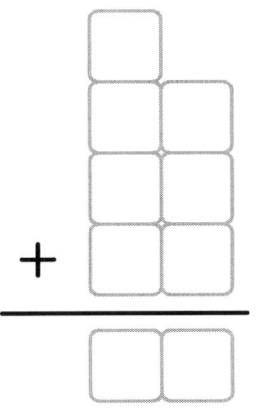

5. What is the sum of 80 + 9 + 9?

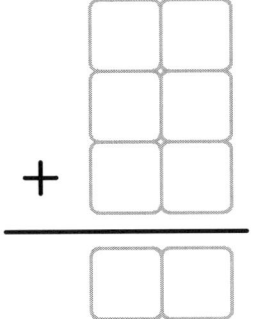

10. Tom saw 2 deer, 40 rabbits, and 85 birds in the woods. How many animals did he see altogether?

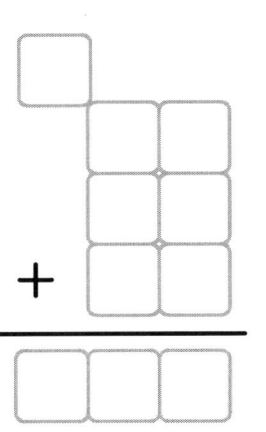

147

12.2 Add Three Numbers

Name: _____ Date: _____

Color the Sum

Can you help count the turkeys? Fill in the addends and find the sum. You can use your Adding Page and Number Cards to help you. Color in the turkey with the colors that go with each sum.

129
129
132
129
132
129
132
97
84
132
177
129
132

84

129

97   97

12.3 Add Four Numbers

148

Next page

Example:

There are 21 red turkeys, 52 brown turkeys, 67 yellow turkeys, and 38 orange turkeys. How many turkeys are there in all?

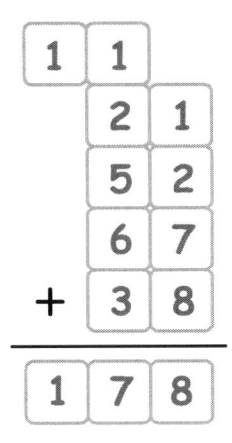

```
  1 1
    2 1
    5 2
    6 7
+   3 8
-------
  1 7 8
```

Color the picture purple where you see 178.

PURPLE

1. There are 26 red turkeys, 28 brown turkeys, 40 yellow turkeys, and 3 orange turkeys. How many turkeys are there in all?

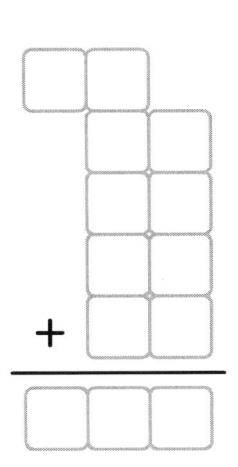

ORANGE

2. There are 13 red turkeys, 25 brown turkeys, 37 yellow turkeys, and 9 orange turkeys. How many turkeys are there in all?

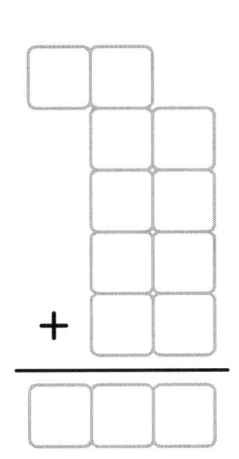

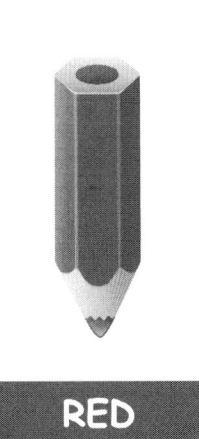

RED

12.3 Add Four Numbers

3. There are 28 red turkeys, 36 brown turkeys, 62 yellow turkeys, and 3 orange turkeys. How many turkeys are there in all?

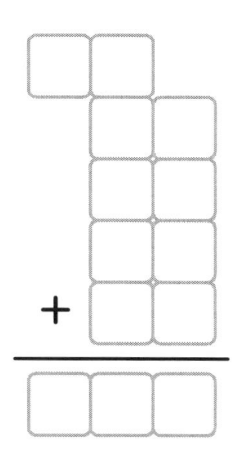

   BROWN

4. There are 16 red turkeys, 34 brown turkeys, 47 yellow turkeys, and 35 orange turkeys. How many turkeys are there in all?

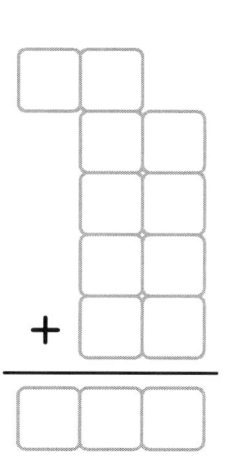

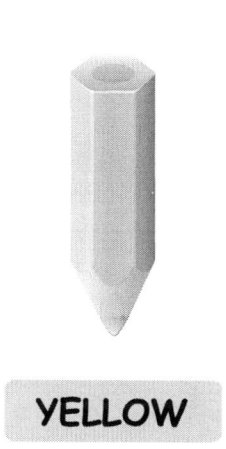

   YELLOW

5. There are 67 red turkeys, 43 brown turkeys, 29 yellow turkeys, and 38 orange turkeys. How many turkeys are there in all?

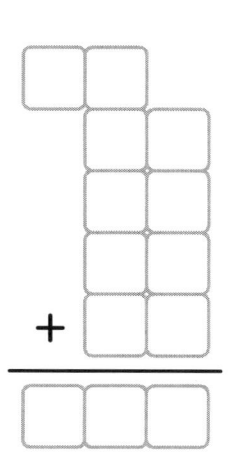

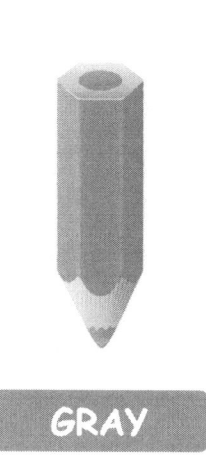

   GRAY

12.3 Add Four Numbers

Name: _____ Date: _____

Ways to Make a Number

Can you make 87 five different ways? Group your unit blocks and rods to make 87, then draw a square for each unit block and a line for each rod you used. Don't forget to record your addition sentences!

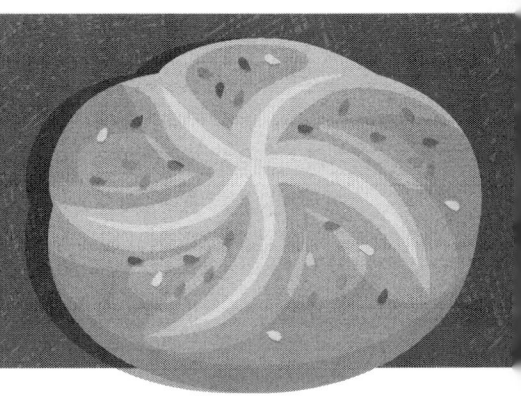

Addition sentence: __50 + 30 + 7__ = 87

Addition sentence: _____ = 87

151

12.4 Ways to Make a Number

Addition sentence: _____ = 87

Addition sentence: _____ = 87

Addition sentence: _____ = 87

12.4 Ways to Make a Number

Addition sentence: _____ = 87

Name: _____   Date: _____

Find the Missing Addend

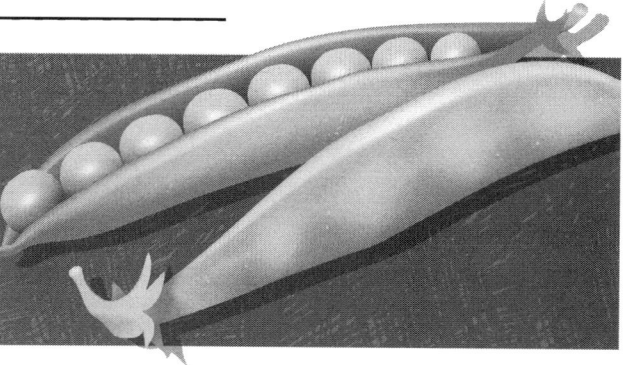

Use the number line to find the missing addend. You can use 10 and 1 jumps! Then write the missing addend on the line in the box.

Example:

42 + 7 = 38 + 11

49

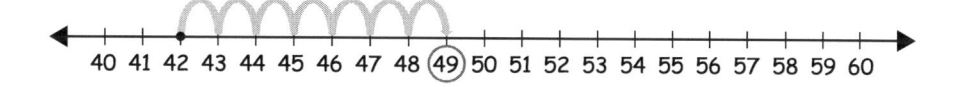

← 40 41 42 43 44 45 46 47 48 (49) 50 51 52 53 54 55 56 57 58 59 60 →

1.

21 + ☐ = 27 + 2

29

← 20 21 22 23 24 25 26 27 28 (29) 30 31 32 33 34 35 36 37 38 39 40 →

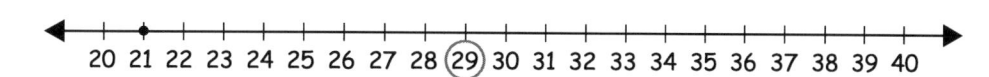

2.

25 + 6 = 22 + ☐

31

← 20 21 22 23 24 25 26 27 28 29 30 (31) 32 33 34 35 36 37 38 39 40 →

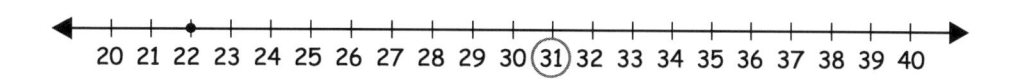

3.

26 + ☐ = 37 + 5

42

← 25 26 27 28 29 30 31 32 33 34 35 36 37 38 39 40 41 (42) 43 44 45 →

12.5 Find the Number

154

Next page

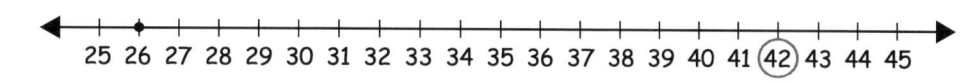

4. 35 + 8 = 29 + ☐

35 + 8 → 43

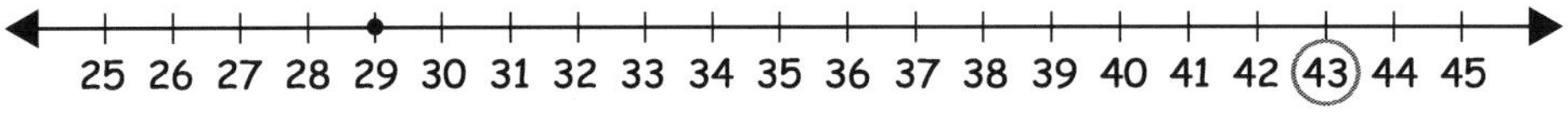
25 26 27 28 29 30 31 32 33 34 35 36 37 38 39 40 41 42 43 44 45

5. 72 + 17 = 76 + ☐

72 + 17 → 89

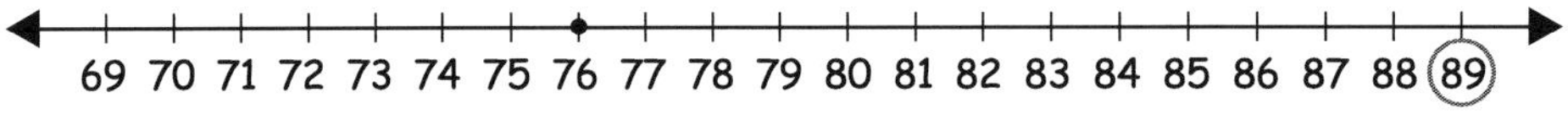
69 70 71 72 73 74 75 76 77 78 79 80 81 82 83 84 85 86 87 88 89

6. 42 + ☐ = 36 + 21

36 + 21 → 57

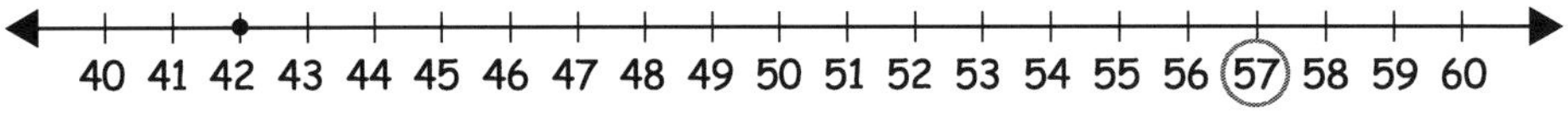
40 41 42 43 44 45 46 47 48 49 50 51 52 53 54 55 56 57 58 59 60

7. 37 + 23 = 41 + ☐

37 + 23 → 60

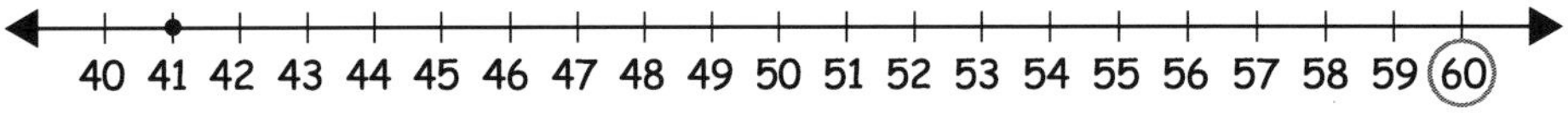
40 41 42 43 44 45 46 47 48 49 50 51 52 53 54 55 56 57 58 59 60

8.

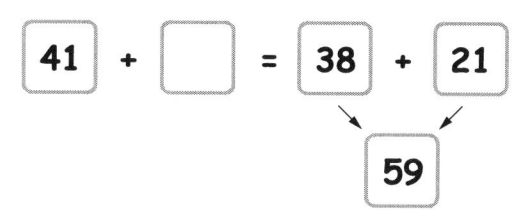

$\boxed{41} + \boxed{} = \boxed{38} + \boxed{21}$

$\boxed{59}$

```
←—+—•—+—+—+—+—+—+—+—+—+—+—+—+—+—+—+—+—+—⊕—+—→
   40 41 42 43 44 45 46 47 48 49 50 51 52 53 54 55 56 57 58 (59) 60
```

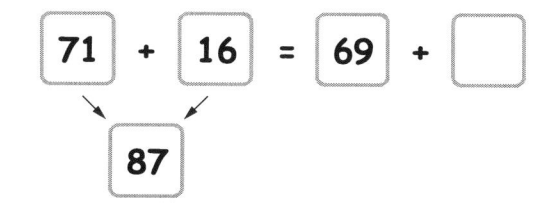

9.

$\boxed{71} + \boxed{16} = \boxed{69} + \boxed{}$

$\boxed{87}$

```
←—•—+—+—+—+—+—+—+—+—+—+—+—+—+—+—+—+—+—⊕—+—+—→
   69 70 71 72 73 74 75 76 77 78 79 80 81 82 83 84 85 86 (87) 88 89
```

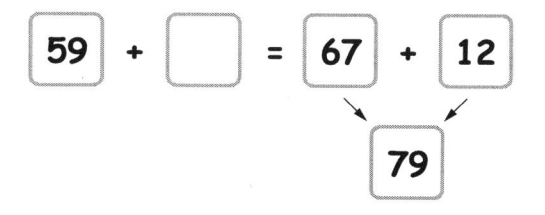

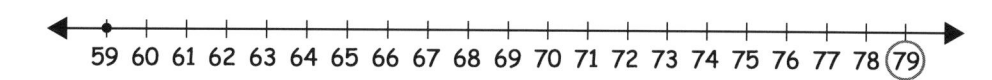

10.

$\boxed{59} + \boxed{} = \boxed{67} + \boxed{12}$

$\boxed{79}$

```
←—•—+—+—+—+—+—+—+—+—+—+—+—+—+—+—+—+—+—+—⊕—→
   59 60 61 62 63 64 65 66 67 68 69 70 71 72 73 74 75 76 77 78 (79)
```

Challenge: This is not the correct missing addend. Can you find the correct addend? Write it on the line below.

$$45 + ? = 30 + 26$$
$$45 + 12 = 56$$
$$57 \; ✗ \; 56$$

_____

12.5 Find the Number

156

Name: _____ Date: _____

Game Worksheet

Use this worksheet to help you play the Associative Property game found in the lesson.

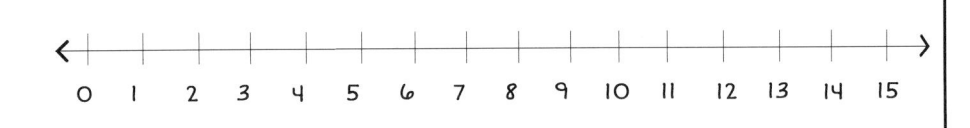

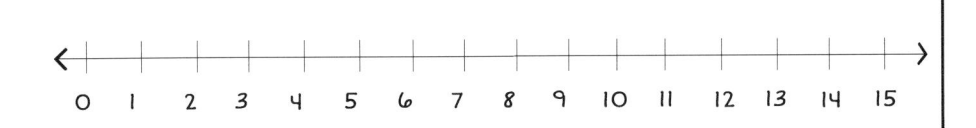

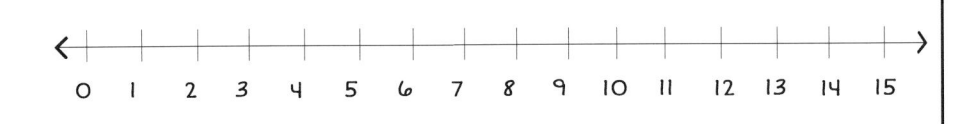

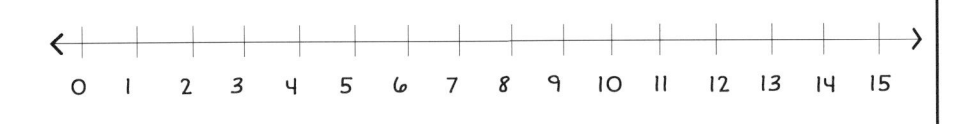

---

2 + 6 = ? + 5

___ = ? + 5

← 0 1 2 3 4 5 6 7 8 9 10 11 12 13 14 15 →

---

5 + ? = 18 + 1

5 + ? = ___

← 0 1 2 3 4 5 6 7 8 9 10 11 12 13 14 15 →

---

4 + 14 = 16 + ?

___ = 16 + ?

← 0 1 2 3 4 5 6 7 8 9 10 11 12 13 14 15 →

? + 4 = 2 + 10

? + 4 = ___

← 0 1 2 3 4 5 6 7 8 9 10 11 12 13 14 15 →

---

6 + 8 = ? + 2

___ = ? + 2

← 0 1 2 3 4 5 6 7 8 9 10 11 12 13 14 15 →

12.5 Find the Number

Name: _____ Date: _____

Subtract Tens
Find the difference and write your answer on each blank.

60 - 20 = ____

50 - 20 = ____

30 - 10 = ____

80 - 40 = ____

30 - 0 = ____

90 - 30 = ____

20 - 10 = ____

40 - 10 = ____

60 - 10 = ____

13.1 Subtract Tens

Name: _____ Date: _____

Place-Value Charts

Use this place-value chart with your blocks to help you subtract. The lesson will show you how to use the chart!

Tens	Ones

13.2 Subtract Tens and Ones

Name: _____ Date: _____

Subtract Tens and Ones

Draw base-ten blocks in each place-value chart to find the difference. Then, solve the riddle by matching the letters with your answers.

How does a scientist get fresh breath?

With an...

$$\overline{}\ \overline{}\ \overline{}\ \overline{}\ \overline{}\ \overline{}\ \ \overline{}\ \overline{}\ \overline{}\ \overline{}$$
13 32 33 10 31 11   15 51 16 21

Example: **33 - 1 = 32**

Tens	Ones
(3 tens blocks)	(3 ones blocks)

First, start with your place value blocks.

Tens	Ones
(3 tens drawn)	(3 ones drawn)

Then, draw your place value blocks.

Tens	Ones
(3 tens drawn)	(2 ones, 1 X'd)

Finally, draw your X's to find the answer.

13.2 Subtract Tens and Ones

160

Next page

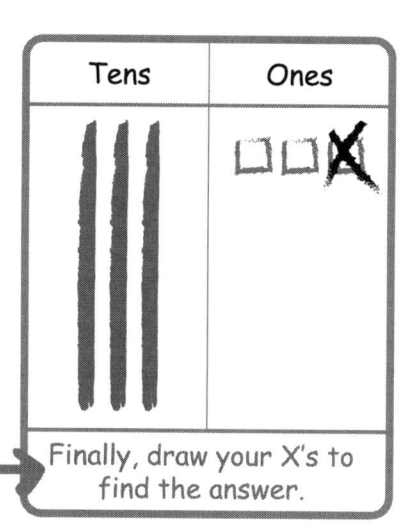

1. 41 - 31 = ___

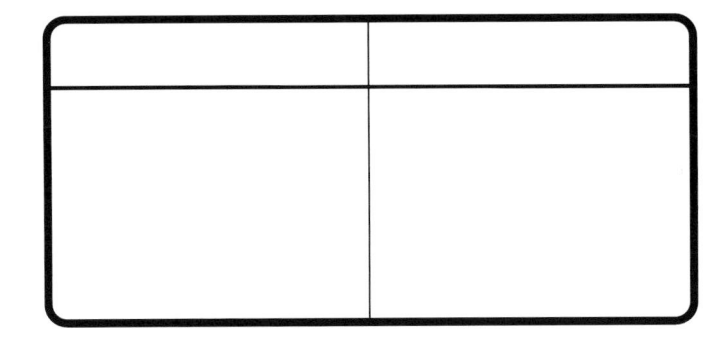

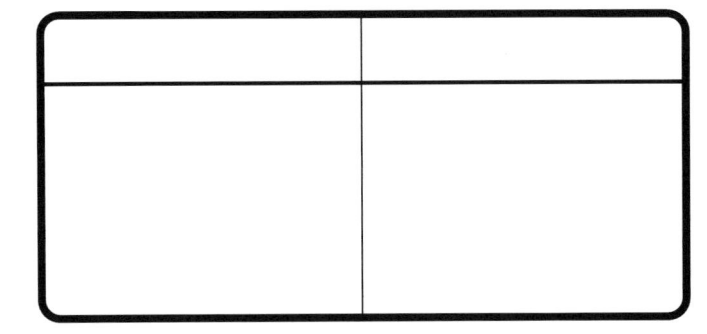

e

2. 64 - 53 = ___

i

3. 15 - 2 = ___

e

4. 59 - 28 = ___

r

5. 36 - 15 = ___

t

13.2 Subtract Tens and Ones

6. 47 - 32 = ___

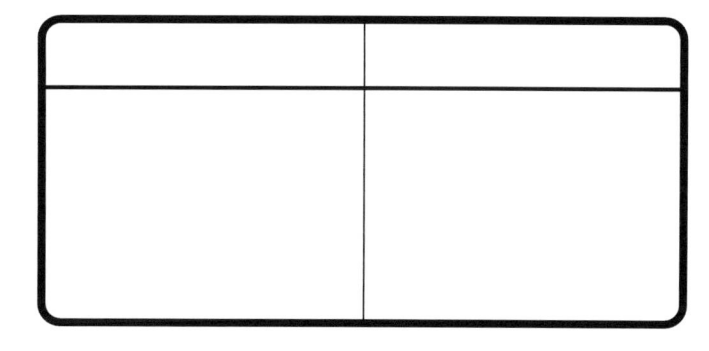

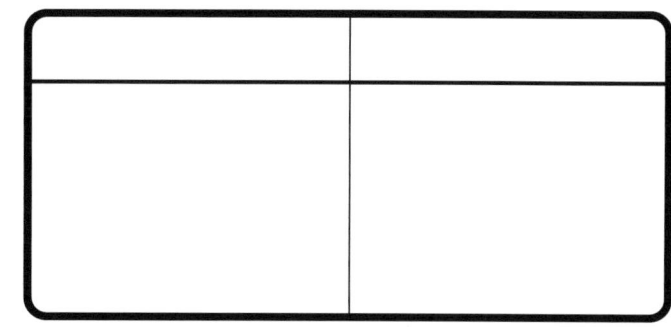

m

7. 76 - 44 = ___

x

8. 83 - 32 = ___

i

9. 28 - 12 = ___

n

10. 97 - 64 = ___

p

Name: _____ Date: _____

Number Line Subtraction

Can you count back to subtract?
Draw jumps on your number line to find the difference.
You can jump by tens and/or ones!
Write the difference in the box.

Example:

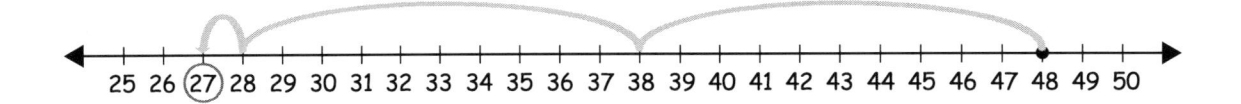

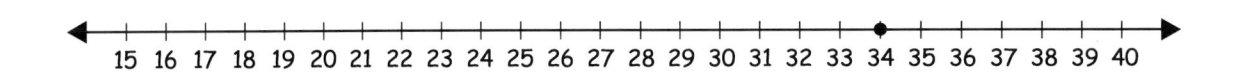

2 ten jumps and 1 one jump count back 21!

48 - 21 = 27

25 26 (27) 28 29 30 31 32 33 34 35 36 37 38 39 40 41 42 43 44 45 46 47 48 49 50

1. 36 - 5 = ☐

15 16 17 18 19 20 21 22 23 24 25 26 27 28 29 30 31 32 33 34 35 36 37 38 39 40

2. 34 - 7 = ☐

15 16 17 18 19 20 21 22 23 24 25 26 27 28 29 30 31 32 33 34 35 36 37 38 39 40

13.3 Subtract From a Two-Digit Number Using a Number Line

3. 48 - 13 = ☐

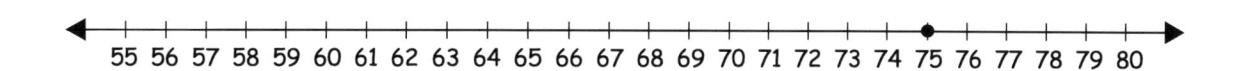

```
◄—+—+—+—+—+—+—+—+—+—+—+—+—+—+—+—+—+—+—+—+—+—+—+—►
  25 26 27 28 29 30 31 32 33 34 35 36 37 38 39 40 41 42 43 44 45 46 47 48 49 50
```

4. 50 - 22 = ☐

```
◄—+—+—+—+—+—+—+—+—+—+—+—+—+—+—+—+—+—+—+—+—+—+—+—►
  25 26 27 28 29 30 31 32 33 34 35 36 37 38 39 40 41 42 43 44 45 46 47 48 49 50
```

5. 75 - 19 = ☐

```
◄—+—+—+—+—+—+—+—+—+—+—+—+—+—+—+—+—+—+—+—+—+—+—+—►
  55 56 57 58 59 60 61 62 63 64 65 66 67 68 69 70 71 72 73 74 75 76 77 78 79 80
```

Write It Out!

Why didn't we use 21 one jumps to count back 21? Write and/or draw picture to explain!

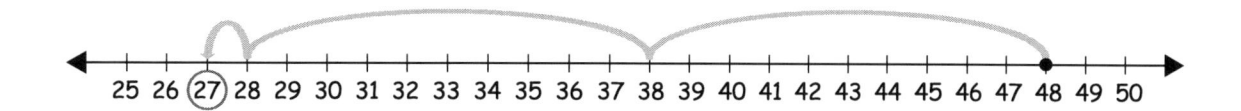

48 - 21 = 27

```
◄—+—+—+—+—+—+—+—+—+—+—+—+—+—+—+—+—+—+—+—+—+—+—+—►
  25 26 (27) 28 29 30 31 32 33 34 35 36 37 38 39 40 41 42 43 44 45 46 47 48 49 50
```

13.3 Subtract From a Two-Digit Number Using a Number Line

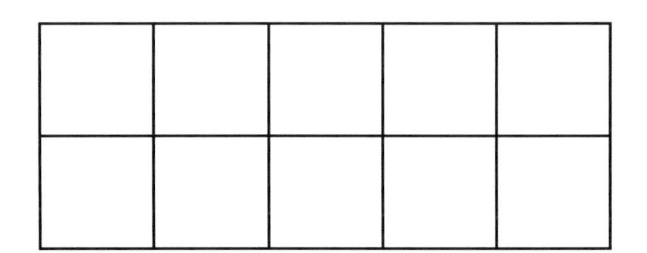

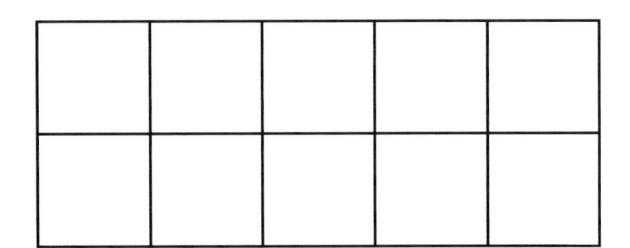

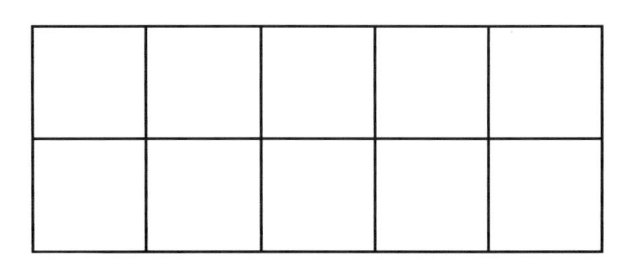

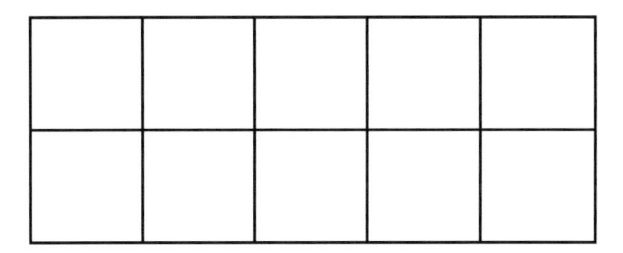

Name: _____ Date: _____

Ten Frames

Fill in the ten frames with the whole. Then cross out the part to subtract! Refer to the lesson to check your work!

45 - 9 = ☐

165   13.4 Subtract a One-Digit Number from a Two-Digit Number

Name: _____ Date: _____

Ten Frame Subtraction Match

Can you match the ten frames to the subtraction sentence?
Then fill in each difference.

Example:

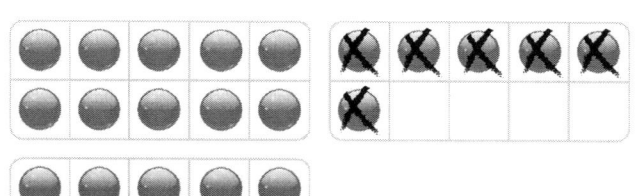

26 - 7 = 19

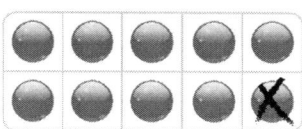

1.

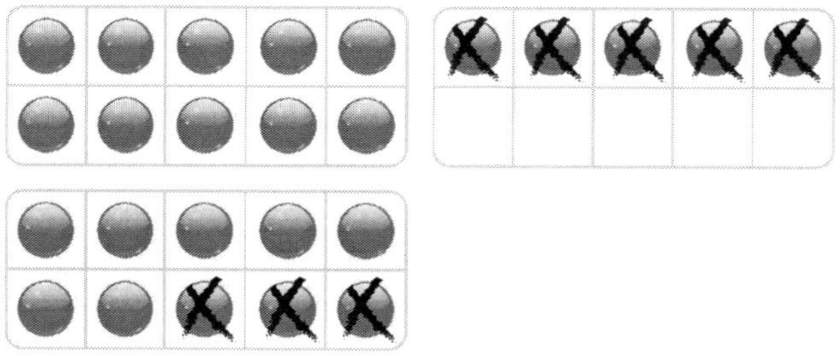

33 - 7 =

2.

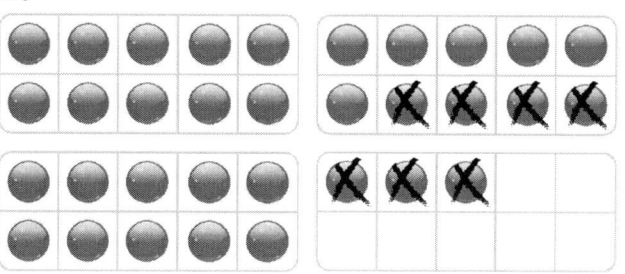

25 - 8 =

13.4 Subtract a One-Digit Number from a Two-Digit Number

Next page

3.

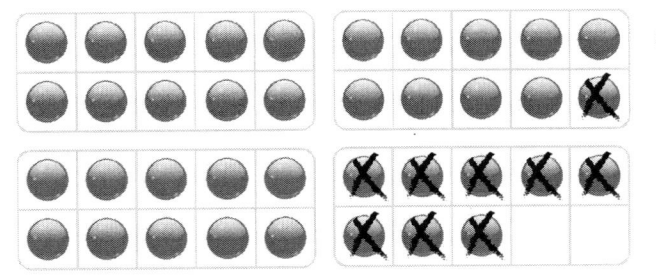

○   ○ 38 - 9 = ___

4.

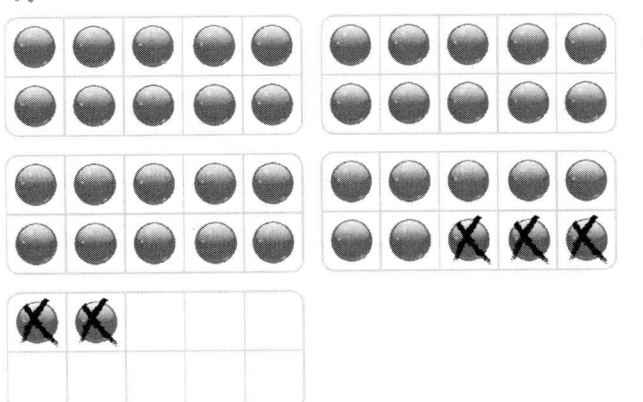

○   ○ 41 - 6 = ___

5.

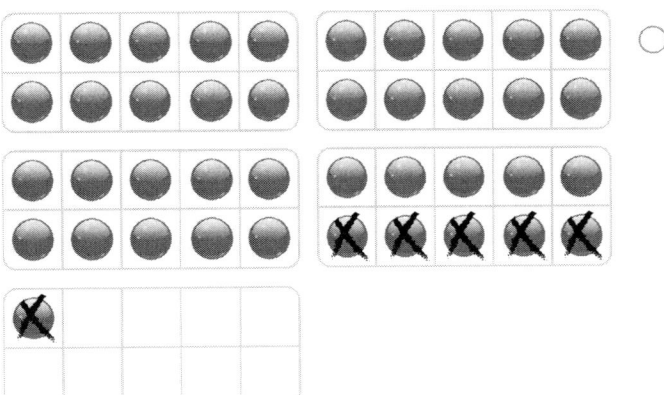

○   ○ 42 - 5 = ___

167   13.4 Subtract a One-Digit Number from a Two-Digit Number

Name: _____ Date: _____

Subtraction Sentences

Use this paper to record the subtraction sentences that are shown in the lesson. Make sure to check your work in the lesson!

_____ - _____ = _____

_____ - _____ = _____

_____ - _____ = _____

_____ - _____ = _____

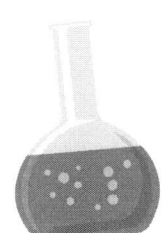

_____ - _____ = _____

13.5 Problem Solving Strategy: Write a Subtraction Sentence

Name: _____ Date: _____

Write Subtraction Sentences

What subtraction sentences do you see? Use the pictures below to find the parts and whole. Then, write them on the lines to create subtraction sentences!

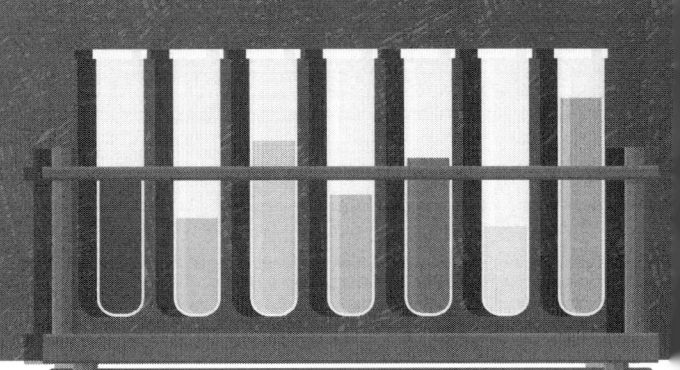

Example:

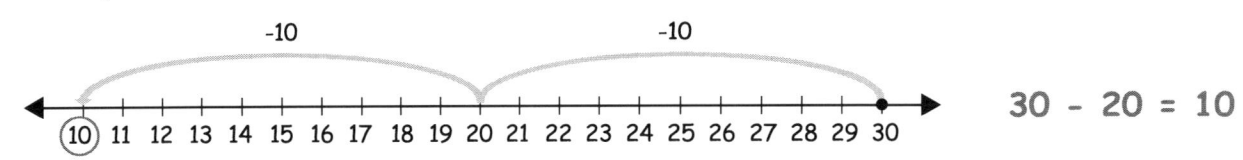

30 - 20 = 10

1.

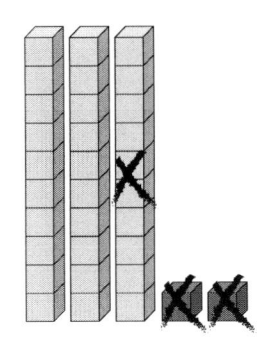

___ - ___ = ___

2.

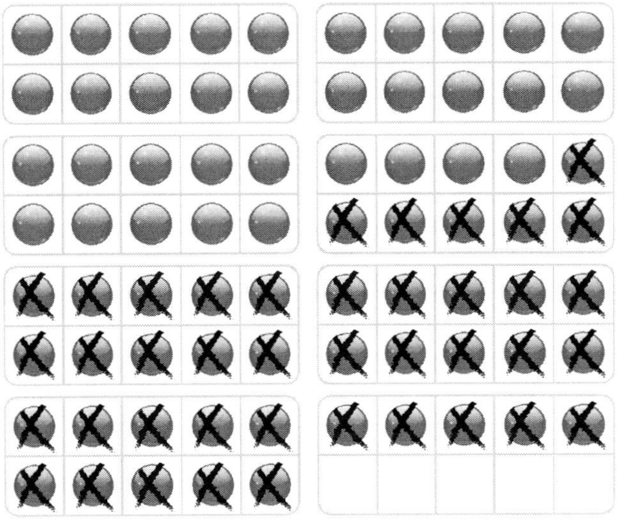

___ - ___ = ___

169   13.5 Problem Solving Strategy: Write a Subtraction Sentence

3. 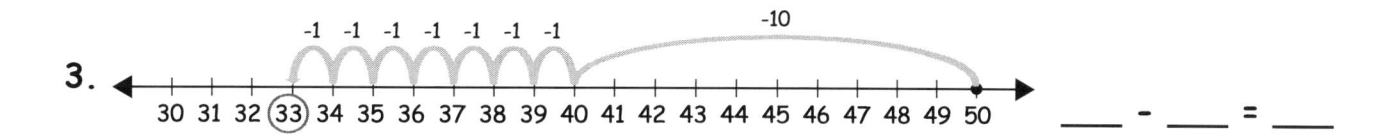 ___ - ___ = ___

4. 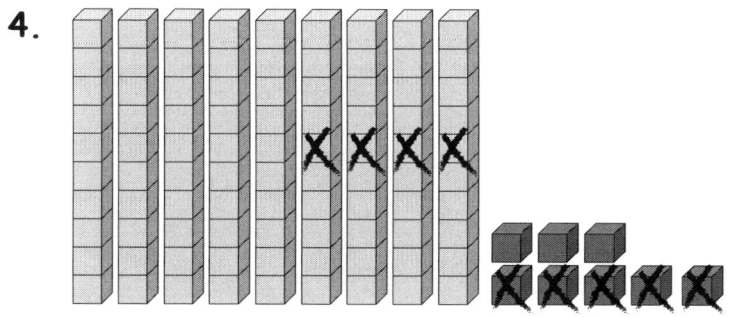 ___ - ___ = ___

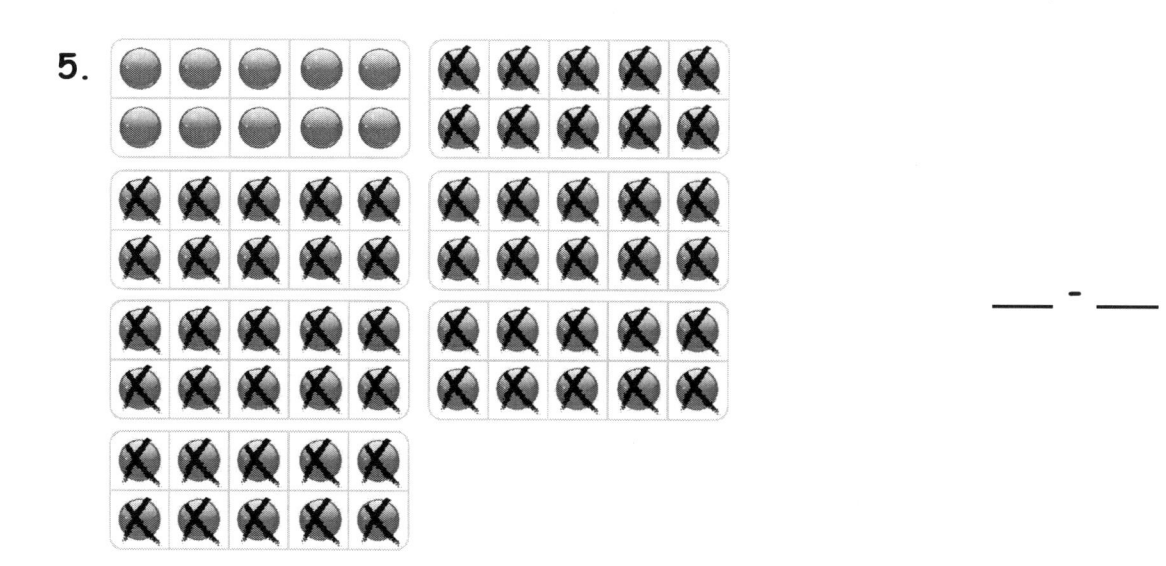

5. ___ - ___ = ___

6. 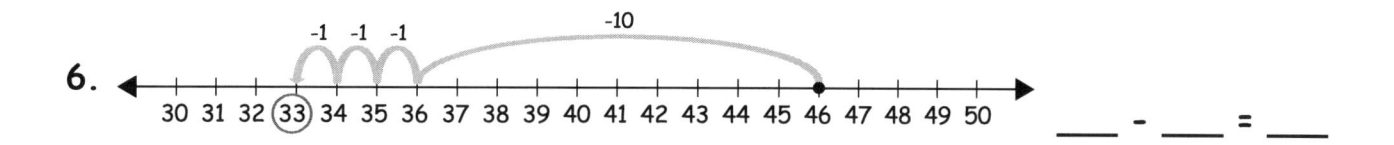 ___ - ___ = ___

13.5 Problem Solving Strategy: Write a Subtraction Sentence

170

7. ___ - ___ = ___

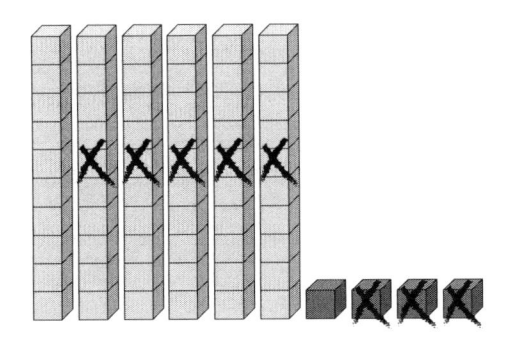

8. ___ - ___ = ___

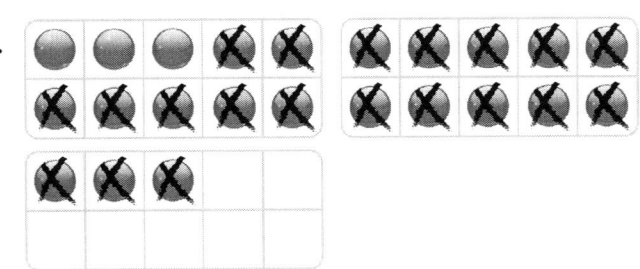

9. ___ - ___ = ___

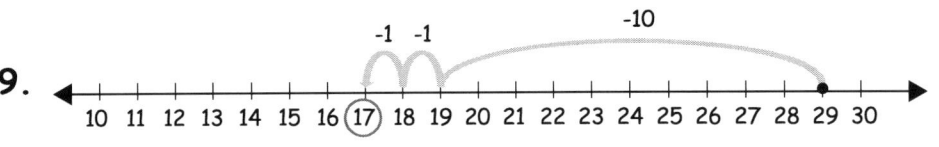

10. ___ - ___ = ___

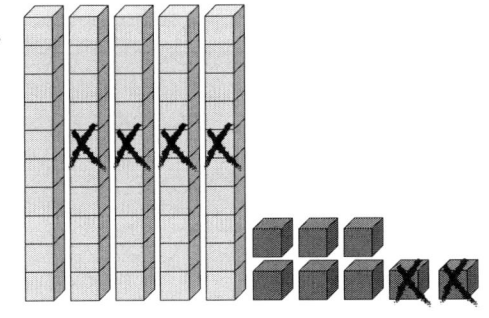

13.5 Problem Solving Strategy: Write a Subtraction Sentence

Name: _____ Date: _____

Regroup!

- Use rods and unit blocks to show the whole.
- Draw a line for each rod and a square for each unit block.
- Find the difference by regrouping! Regroup a ten by crossing it out with a red crayon. Draw ten unit blocks in the ones section.
- Then draw an X with a purple crayon over each square to represent the unit block you took away.
- Record your answer on the blank.

Example: 65 - 9 = 56

Tens	Ones

1. 52 - 5 = ___

Tens	Ones

2. 33 - 7 = ___

Tens	Ones

3. 20 - 8 = ___

Tens	Ones

4. 84 - 5 = ___

Tens	Ones

5. 11 - 4 = ___

Tens	Ones

14.1 Subtract a One-Digit Number from a Two-Digit Number with Regrouping

Name: _____ Date: _____

Rewriting Two-Digit Subtraction

Can you rewrite these subtraction sentences?
Use the place-value charts to help you find the difference.

Example: 37 - 21 = 16

Tens	Ones
3	7
2	1
1	6

1. 99 - 26 = ____

Tens	Ones
9	9
2	6

2. 42 - 11 = ____

Tens	Ones
4	2
1	1

3. 25 - 15 = ____

Tens	Ones
2	5
1	5

4. 86 - 34 = ____

Tens	Ones
8	6
3	4

14.2 Rewrite Two-Digit Subtraction

5. 66 - 45 = ____

Tens	Ones
6	6
4	5

6. 30 - 20 = ____

Tens	Ones
3	0
2	0

7. 73 - 42 = ____

Tens	Ones
7	3
4	2

8. 58 - 34 = ____

Tens	Ones
5	8
3	4

9. 91 - 81 = ____

Tens	Ones
9	1
8	1

10. 74 - 53 = ____

Tens	Ones
7	4
5	3

14.2 Rewrite Two-Digit Subtraction

Name: _____   Date: _____

Find the Missing Parts

Read the word problems and find the missing parts.

1. Jill has 35 cherries. She ate 13. How many cherries are left?

   35 − 13 = ☐ cherries

2. Tom wants to find a total of 79 acorns in the woods. He found some acorns, and he only needs to find 19 more. How many acorns does Tom already have?

   79 − ☐ = 19 acorns

3. A rabbit ate 88 flowers. 27 of the flowers were red. How many were blue?

   88 − 27 = ☐ flowers

4. Alex is playing baseball with his friends. He wants to hit the ball 43 times. He's already hit 11 balls! How many more balls does he need to hit?

   43 − 11 = ☐ balls

175   14.3 Two-Digit Subtraction Without Regrouping

5. Conner wants to ride his bike for 75 minutes. He just rode for 54 minutes. How many minutes does he have left?

   75 - 54 = ☐ minutes biking

6. There were 84 basketballs in the gym. Some of the basketballs were in a bin, and 63 were on the floor. How many basketballs were in the bin?

   84 - ☐ = 63 balls

7. A soccer team scored 58 goals in a game. They scored some goals in the first half of the game, and 25 goals in the second half. How many goals did they score in the first half of the game?

   58 - ☐ = 25 goals

8. Jenny wants to jump rope 66 times. She has already jumped 24 times. How many more jumps does she need to do?

   66 - 24 = ☐ jumps

9. There were 97 hula hoops in the gym. Some were hanging on the wall, and 36 were on the floor. How many hula hoops were hanging on the wall?

   97 - ☐ = 36 hula hoops

10. 59 students were playing freeze tag. Some of the students were frozen, and 47 of the students were still running. How many students were frozen?

    59 - ☐ = 47 students

14.3 Two-Digit Subtraction Without Regrouping

Name: _____   Date: _____

Find the Mistake!

There is a regrouping error in each of these problems! Can you find the mistakes? Circle the mistake on the left. Then use the boxes on the right to find the difference.

Example: (6) ̶7̶ 13   5 ̶7̶ 13
          − 3 5   − 3 5
          ───────── ─────────
              3 8   2 8

1. 4 ̶5̶ 12   ☐ 4 2
   − 1 9   − 1 9
   ───────── ─────────
       3 3   ☐☐

2. 4 ̶1̶ 3   ☐ 5 3
   − 2 6   − 2 6
   ───────── ─────────
       2 3   ☐☐

3. 5 ̶7̶ 4   ☐ 6 4
   − 3 15   − 3 5
   ───────── ─────────
       2 11   ☐☐

4. 8 ̶8̶ 15   ☐ 7 5
   − 4 7   − 4 7
   ───────── ─────────
       4 8   ☐☐

5. 8 ̶0̶ 2   ☐ 9 2
   − 8 9   − 8 9
   ───────── ─────────
       0 7   ☐☐

Challenge: Which subtraction sentence can we use for the word problem below? Write it in the boxes and find the difference. Don't forget to regroup!

Riley and her friends want to build another leaf fort. They need 96 leaves. They have used 67 of them. How many more leaves do they need to make the fort?

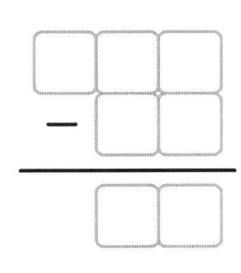

☐☐
− ☐☐
─────
☐☐

177   14.4 Two-Digit Subtraction With Regrouping

Name: _____ Date: _____

Input/Output Table

Can you show the numbers in the output column? Follow along in the lesson to check your work.

Input	Output
65	
70	
75	
80	
Rule: -10	

14.5 Input/Output Tables (Subtract)

Name: _____ Date: _____

What Are the Missing Numbers?

Use the spaces next to each input/output table to show your subtraction work.

Example:

Input	Output
53	40
54	41
55	42
56	43

Rule -13

```
  53      54
- 13    - 13
  ――      ――
  40      41

  55      56
- 13    - 13
  ――      ――
  42      43
```

Input	Output
83	
85	
87	
89	

Rule -41

Input	Output
62	
64	
66	
68	

Rule -22

14.5 Input/Output Tables (Subtract)

Input	Output
33	
37	
41	
45	
Rule -15	

Input	Output
55	
56	
57	
58	
Rule -25	

Input	Output
92	
94	
96	
98	
Rule -34	

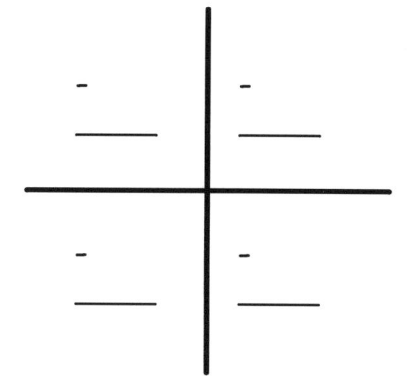

14.5 Input/Output Tables (Subtract)

Name: _____ Date: _____

Fact-Family Subtraction

Can you use the triangles to subtract? Find the whole and parts. Then fill out the subtraction sentences in the middle of the triangle.

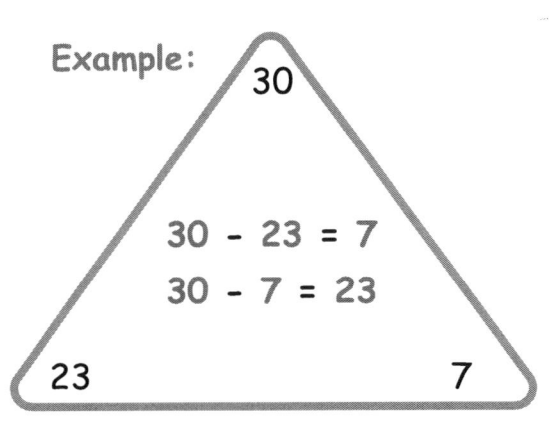

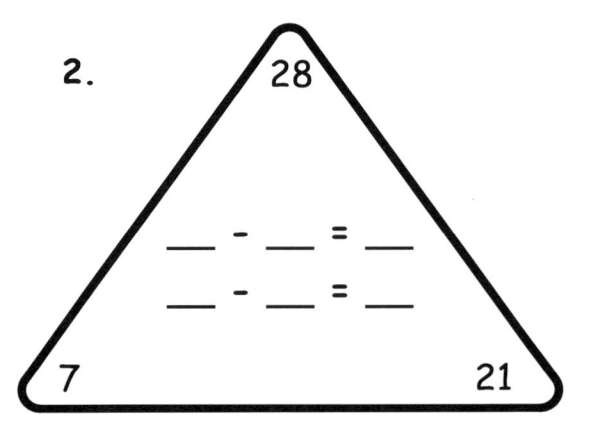

Example:

30
30 - 23 = 7
30 - 7 = 23
23   7

1.
17
__ - __ = __
__ - __ = __
3   14

2.
28
__ - __ = __
__ - __ = __
7   21

3.
30
__ - __ = __
__ - __ = __
5   25

4.
50
__ - __ = __
__ - __ = __
20   30

15.1 Two-Digit Fact Families

5. Triangle: 70 (top), 30 (bottom-left), 40 (bottom-right)
___ - ___ = ___
___ - ___ = ___

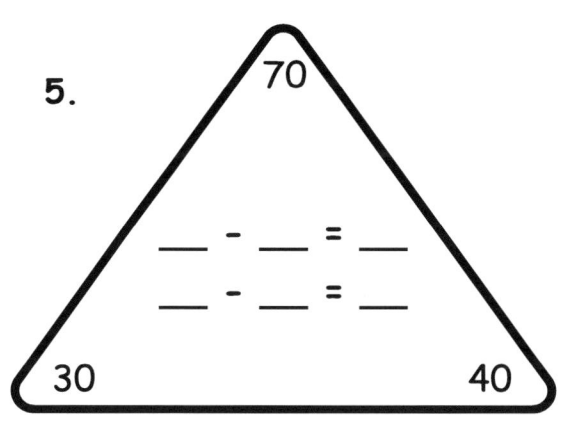

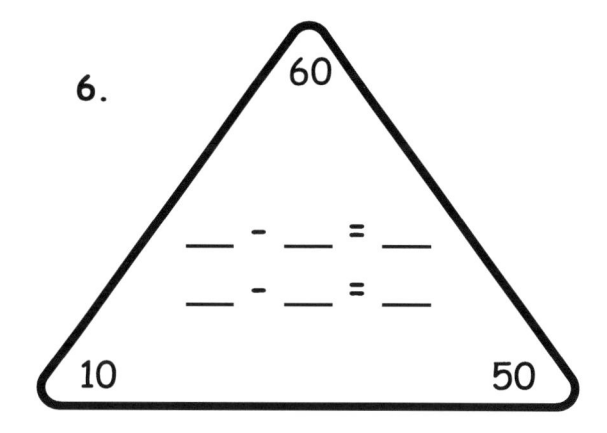

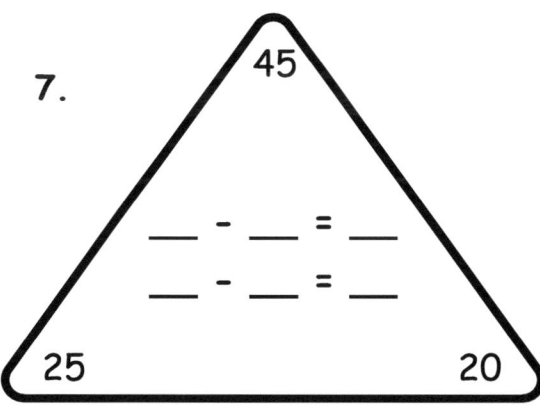

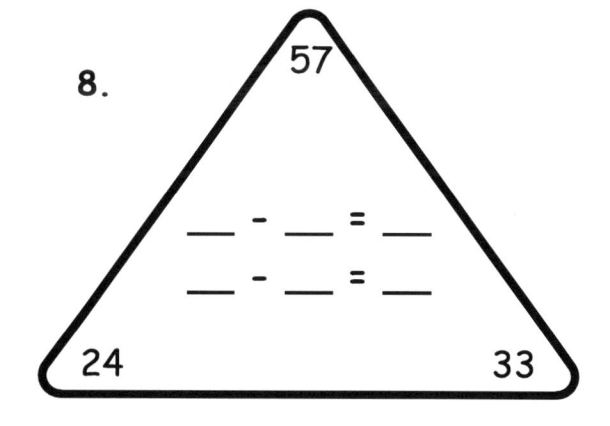

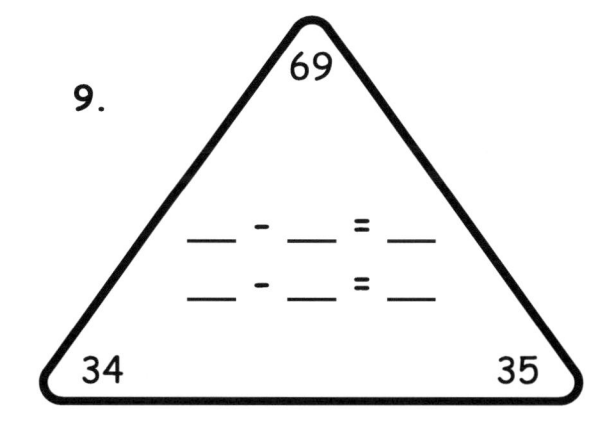

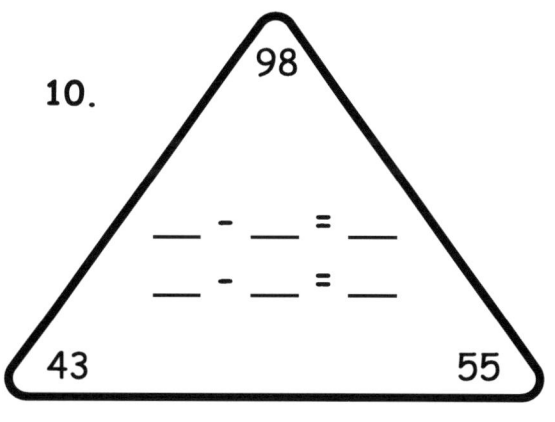

6. Triangle: 60 (top), 10 (bottom-left), 50 (bottom-right)
___ - ___ = ___
___ - ___ = ___

7. Triangle: 45 (top), 25 (bottom-left), 20 (bottom-right)
___ - ___ = ___
___ - ___ = ___

8. Triangle: 57 (top), 24 (bottom-left), 33 (bottom-right)
___ - ___ = ___
___ - ___ = ___

9. Triangle: 69 (top), 34 (bottom-left), 35 (bottom-right)
___ - ___ = ___
___ - ___ = ___

10. Triangle: 98 (top), 43 (bottom-left), 55 (bottom-right)
___ - ___ = ___
___ - ___ = ___

Think About It!
Why does this fact family have only one subtraction sentence?
Write and/or draw to show what you think!

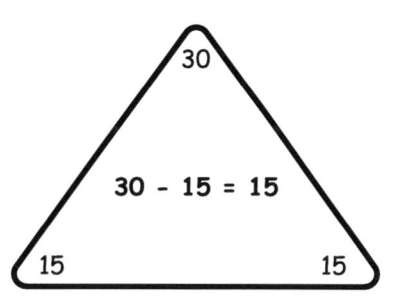

Triangle: 30 (top), 15 (bottom-left), 15 (bottom-right)
30 - 15 = 15

15.1 Two-Digit Fact Families

Name: _____   Date: _____

Mentally Subtract Two-Digit Numbers

Can you subtract these numbers in your head?
Match each difference with its color.
Then, have fun coloring!

Example:
80 - 70 = 10

60 - 30 = ___   70 - 20 = ___

90 - 20 = ___   80 - 40 = ___   61 - 1 = ___

88 - 8 = ___   46 - 3 = ___   99 - 9 = ___

24 - 2 = ___   20 - 10 = ___

Coloring Key

50, 30   40, 60, 70   80, 90, 43   10, 22

183   15.2 Mentally Subtract Two-Digit Numbers

Name: _____ Date: _____

Fill In!

Can you subtract in parts? Fill in the missing numbers. Then find the difference!

Example:

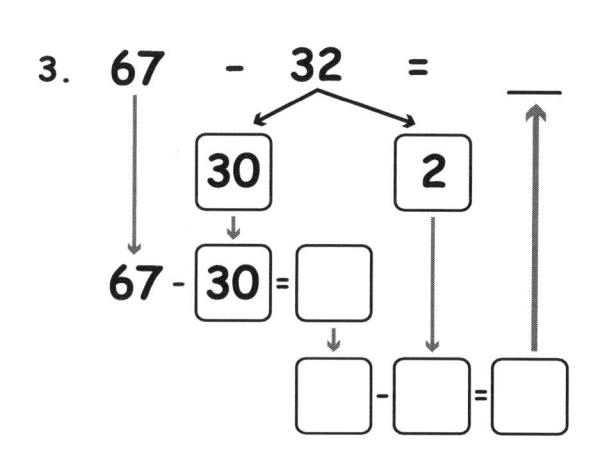

95 − 33 = 62

30, 3

95 − 30 = 65

65 − 3 = 62

1. 75 − 25 = ___

20, 5

75 − 20 = 55

☐ − ☐ = ☐

2. 85 − 65 = ___

60, 5

85 − 60 = 25

☐ − ☐ = ☐

3. 67 − 32 = ___

30, 2

67 − 30 = ☐

☐ − ☐ = ☐

4. 88 − 54 = ___

50, 4

88 − 50 = ☐

☐ − ☐ = ☐

5. 96 − 41 = ___

40, 1

96 − 40 = ☐

☐ − ☐ = ☐

15.3 Take Apart Tens to Subtract

Subtracting Page

Use this page to help you solve the problems shown.

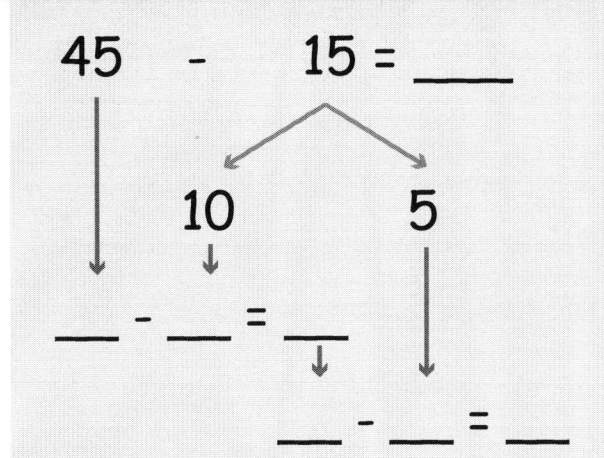

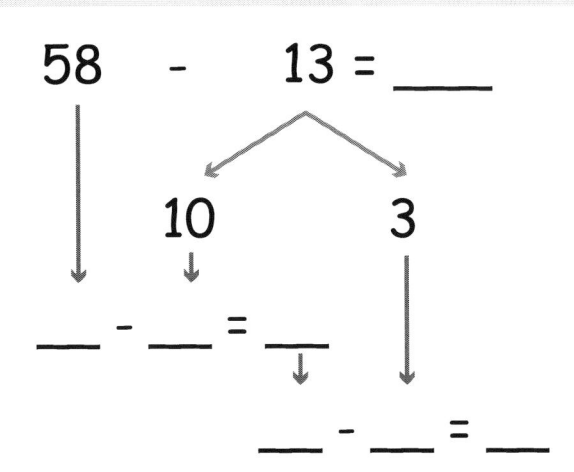

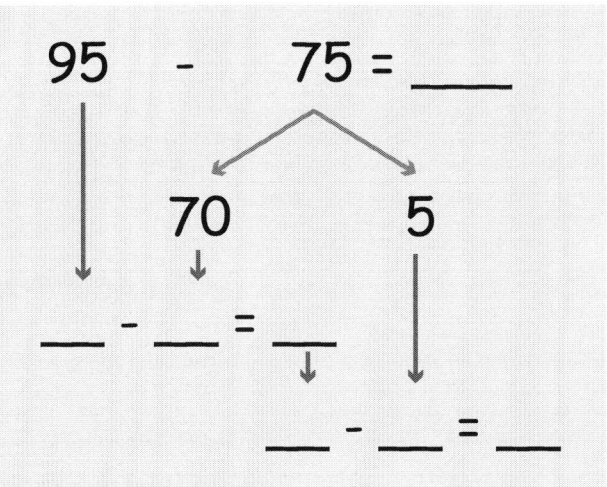

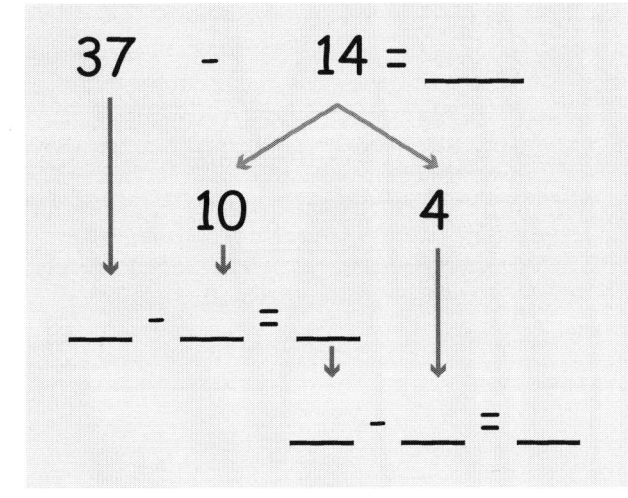

45 - 15 = ___

10   5

___ - ___ = ___

___ - ___ = ___

62 - 32 = ___

30   2

___ - ___ = ___

___ - ___ = ___

58 - 13 = ___

10   3

___ - ___ = ___

___ - ___ = ___

95 - 75 = ___

70   5

___ - ___ = ___

___ - ___ = ___

37 - 14 = ___

10   4

___ - ___ = ___

___ - ___ = ___

15.3 Take Apart Tens to Subtract

Name: _____ Date: _____

Fill In!

Can you subtract in parts?
Use the numbers in the box to fill in the parts.
Then write the difference on the line.

Example:

75 - 34 = 41

(30) (4)

Box: 75 30 45 4 41

75 - 30 = **45**

45 - 4 = 41

1. **56 - 22 = ___**

(20) (2)

Box: 2 20 36 34 56

___ - ___ = **36**

___ - ___ = ___

2. **68 - 35 = ___**

(30) (5)

Box: 38 5 30 68 33

___ - ___ = **38**

___ - ___ = ___

15.4 Apply the Take Apart Strategy

186

Next page

3. 79 - 54 = ___
      ↙   ↘
    (50) (4)

   ___ - ___ = 29

   ___ - ___ = ___

   | 29 4 79 |
   | 50 25 |

4. 87 - 46 = ___
      ↙   ↘
    (40) (6)

   ___ - ___ = 47

   ___ - ___ = ___

   | 6 40 87 |
   | 41 47 |

5. 95 - 43 = ___
      ↙   ↘
    (40) (3)

   ___ - ___ = 55

   ___ - ___ = ___

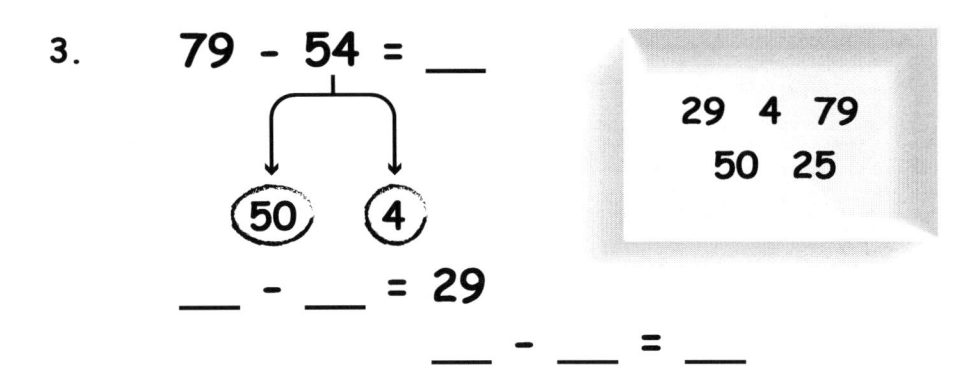

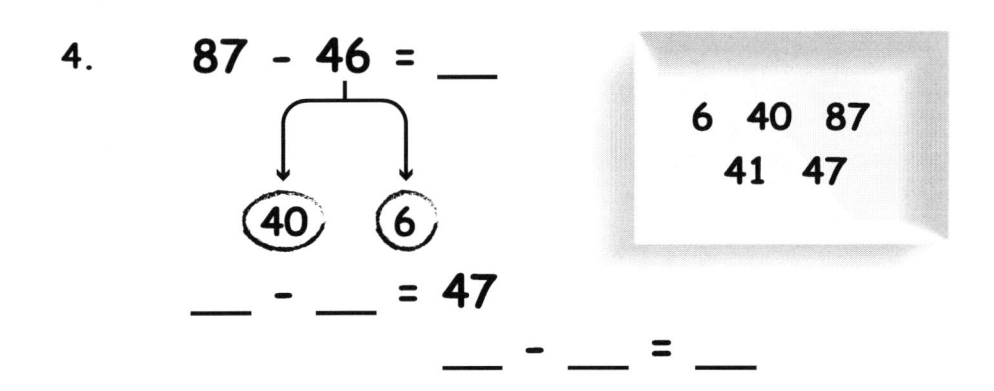

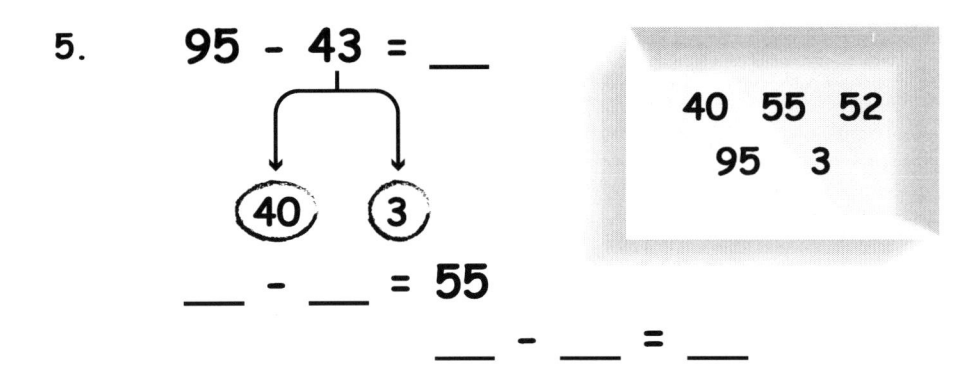

   | 40 55 52 |
   | 95 3 |

Write About It!: Why is subtracting in parts a helpful strategy? Draw a picture or write to show what you think! Use the problem below to help you!

75 - 34 = 41
    ↙   ↘
  (30) (4)
75 - 30 = 45
      45 - 4 = 41

| 75 30 45 |
| 4 41 |

187   15.4 Apply the Take Apart Strategy

Name: _____ Date: _____

Make Ten to Subtract

Can you make ten to subtract?

Example:

$35 - 9 = \underline{26}$

$-\boxed{5} - \boxed{5}$
$\overline{\boxed{30} - \boxed{4} = \boxed{26}}$

1. $52 - 14 = \underline{}$

$-\boxed{2} - \boxed{2}$
$\overline{\boxed{} - \boxed{} = \underline{}}$

2. $83 - 9 = \underline{}$

$-\boxed{3} - \boxed{3}$
$\overline{\boxed{} - \boxed{} = \underline{}}$

3. $67 - 17 = \underline{}$

$-\boxed{7} - \boxed{7}$
$\overline{\boxed{} - \boxed{} = \underline{}}$

5. $56 - 8 = \underline{}$

$-\boxed{} - \boxed{}$
$\overline{\boxed{} - \boxed{} = \underline{}}$

6. $34 - 19 = \underline{}$

$-\boxed{} - \boxed{}$
$\overline{\boxed{} - \boxed{} = \underline{}}$

15.5 Make Ten to Subtract

Name: _____ Date: _____

Hundred Chart Check

Use a subtraction strategy to find the difference. Then check your work using the hundred chart. Color up and to the left with a green crayon. Circle the difference and see if it matches your first answer!

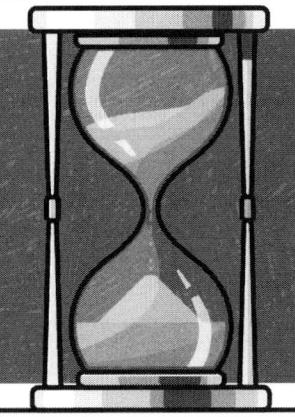

Example:

53 - 11 = 42

```
  53
- 11
----
  42
```

1. 29 - 12 = ___

```
  29
- 12
----
```

189

16.1 Subtract on a Hundred Chart

2. 58 - 34 = ___

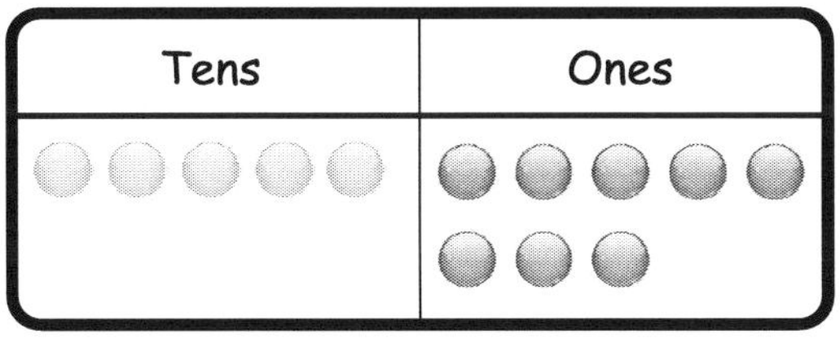

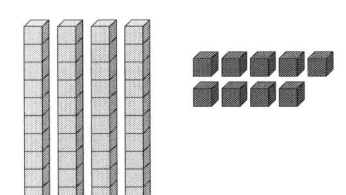

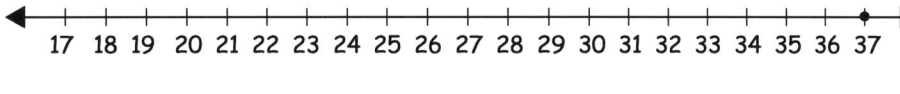

3. 49 - 16 = ___

4. 37 - 15 = ___

16.1 Subtract on a Hundred Chart

190

5. 86 - 55 = __

$$\begin{array}{r}86\\-55\\\hline\end{array}$$

__

1	2	3	4	5	6	7	8	9	10
11	12	13	14	15	16	17	18	19	20
21	22	23	24	25	26	27	28	29	30
31	32	33	34	35	36	37	38	39	40
41	42	43	44	45	46	47	48	49	50
51	52	53	54	55	56	57	58	59	60
61	62	63	64	65	66	67	68	69	70
71	72	73	74	75	76	77	78	79	80
81	82	83	84	85	86	87	88	89	90
91	92	93	94	95	96	97	98	99	100

Write About It!

Which strategy do you like the best? Draw and write to explain why!

Three-Digit Number Puzzle

Can you subtract from a three-digit number? Find the difference and write your answer on each blank.

```
  7 0 0
- 4 0 0
———————
  □ □ □
```

```
    □ □
  4 0 0
-   4 0
———————
  □ □ □
```

```
    □ □
  9 0 0
-   8 0
———————
  □ □ □
```

```
  8 0 0
- 3 0 0
———————
  □ □ □
```

```
    □ □
  2 0 0
-   9 0
———————
  1 1 0
```

```
    □ □
  5 0 0
-   1 0
———————
  □ □ □
```

16.2 Subtract from a Three-Digit Number

Name: _____ Date: _____

Subtract Three-Digit Numbers

Can you solve these subtraction problems? Color in your answer on the holiday lights.

Example:

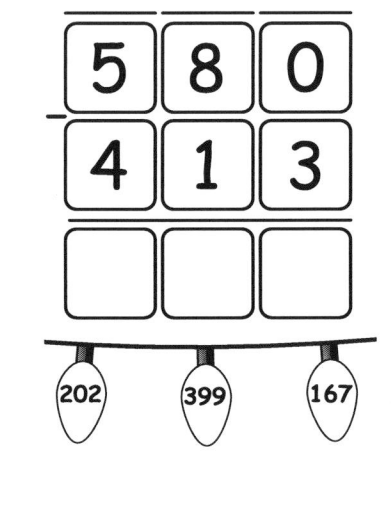

```
    4 17
  5 5̸ 7̸
-  2 3 9
  ───────
  3 1 8
```
(500) (318) (239)

```
  9 2 4
- 7 0 8
  ─────
```
(216) (422) (912)

```
  5 8 0
- 4 1 3
  ─────
```
(202) (399) (167)

```
  2 4 3
- 1 3 6
  ─────
```
(112) (107) (85)

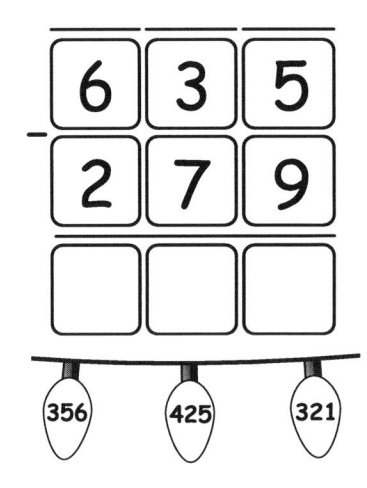

```
  6 3 5
- 2 7 9
  ─────
```
(356) (425) (321)

```
  8 4 8
- 6 4 9
  ─────
```
(465) (527) (199)

193

16.3 Subtract Three-Digit Numbers

Name: _____ Date: _____

Subtraction Page

Work through the word problem in the lesson and write the subtraction sentence.

What are the whole and the part?

$$\underline{} - \underline{} = \underline{?}$$
    Whole   Part

16.4 Write a Subtraction Sentence   194

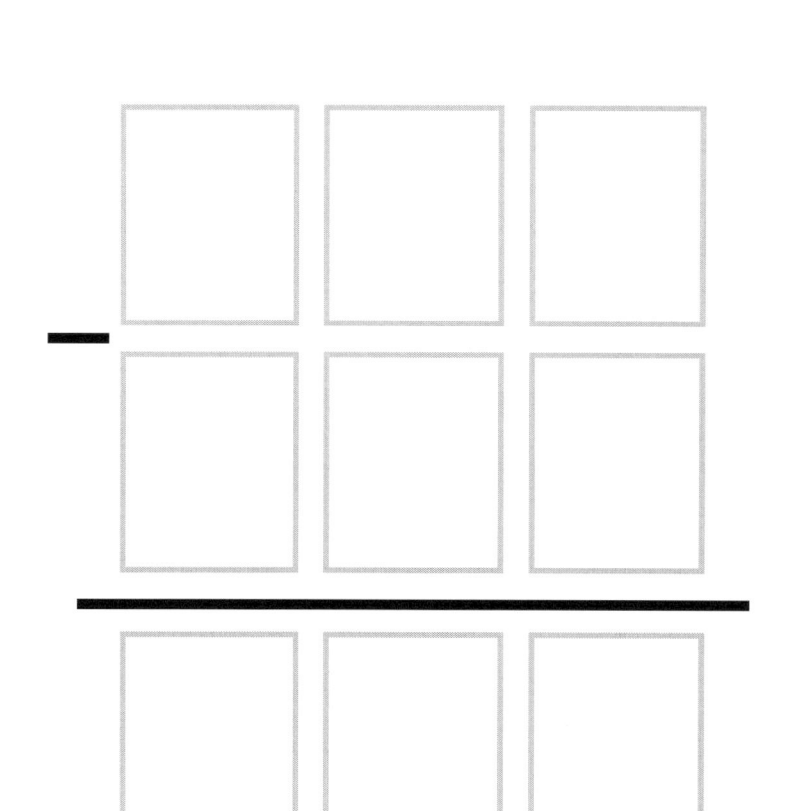

Name: _____ Date: _____

Missing Numbers
Use the guess-and-check strategy to find the missing numbers.

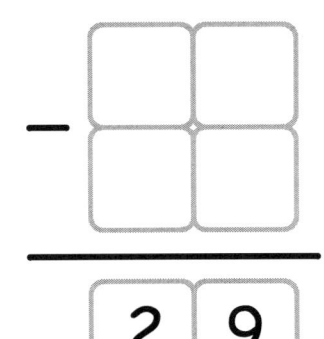

Example:

$$\begin{array}{r} 8\,8 \\ -\ 3\,1 \\ \hline 5\,7 \end{array}$$

Missing digits: 1 3 8 8

1.

$$\begin{array}{r} \square\,\square \\ -\ \square\,\square \\ \hline 2\,9 \end{array}$$

Missing digits: 1 4 8 9

2.

$$\begin{array}{r} \square\,\square \\ -\ \square\,\square \\ \hline 4\,8 \end{array}$$

Missing digits: 0 2 4 9

195   16.5 Find the Numbers

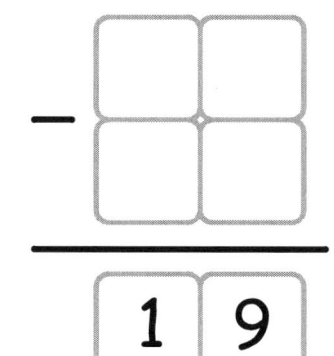

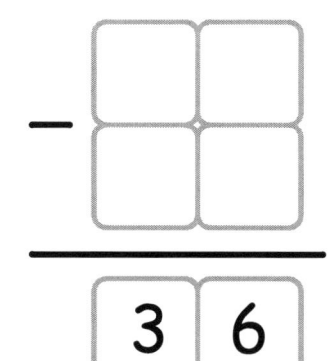

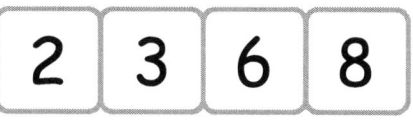

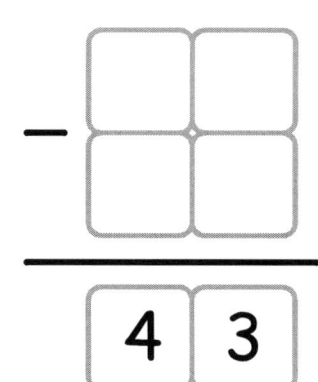

3.

$$\begin{array}{r} \square\square \\ -\ \square\square \\ \hline 1\ 9 \end{array}$$

Missing digits: 6 7 8 8

4.

$$\begin{array}{r} \square\square \\ -\ \square\square \\ \hline 3\ 6 \end{array}$$

Missing digits: 2 3 6 8

5.

$$\begin{array}{r} \square\square \\ -\ \square\square \\ \hline 4\ 3 \end{array}$$

Missing digits: 5 6 9 9

16.5 Find the Numbers

Name: _____ Date: _____

Measurement Time!

Let's measure these objects using non-standard units of measurement.

1. Measure the height of these objects.

The snowman is ___ pencils tall.

This ice skate is ___ craft sticks tall.

The guitar is ___ pencils tall.

2. Measure the length of these objects.

The ice skate is ___ paper clips long.

The guitar is ___ craft sticks long.

The snowman is ___ craft sticks wide.

17.1 Non-standard Units of Measure

3. Draw lines to the long, longer, and longest toys.

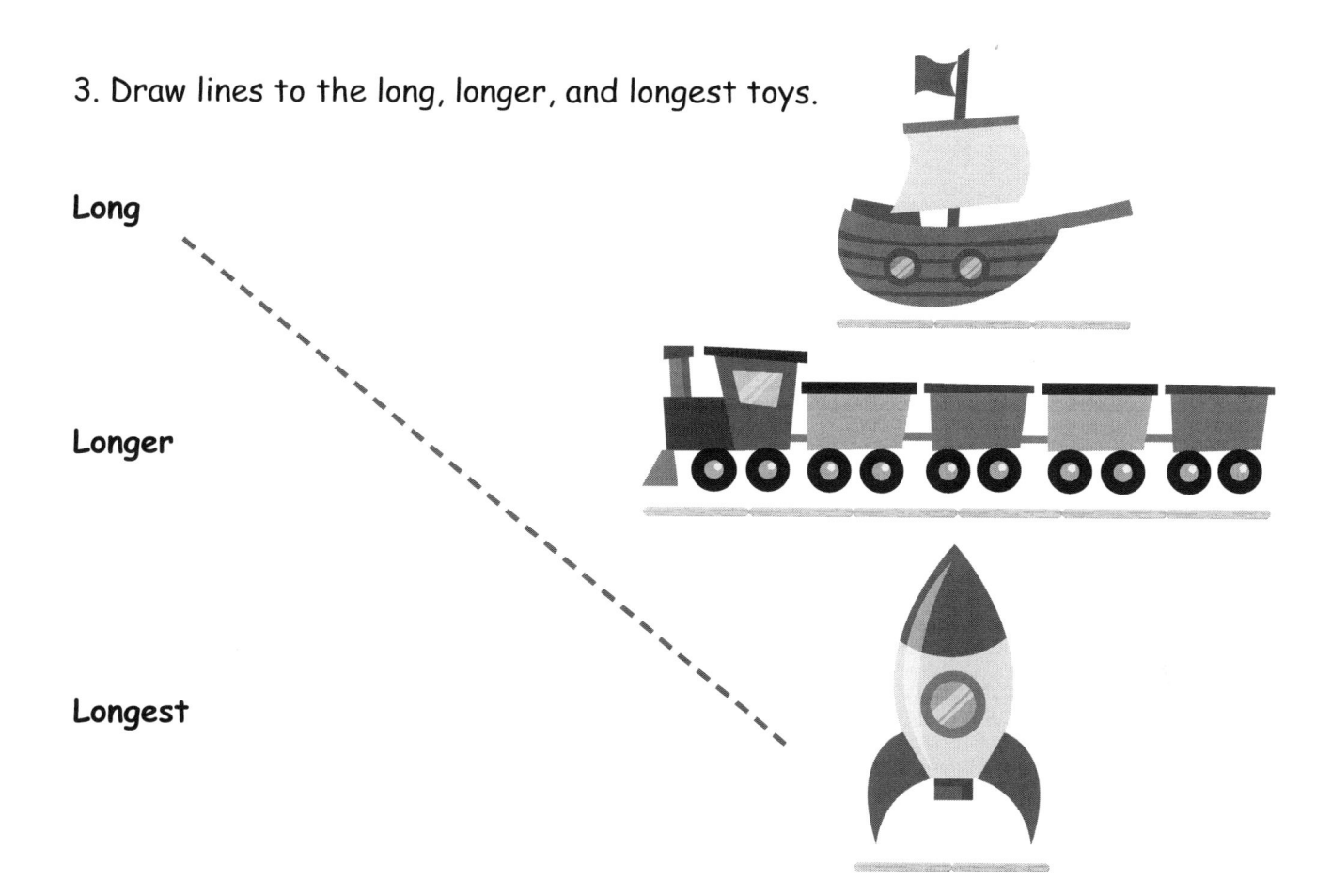

Long

Longer

Longest

4. Draw lines to the short, shorter, and shortest toys.

Short

Shorter

Shortest

17.1 Non-standard Units of Measure

Name: _____ Date: _____

Inches, Feet, and Yards
Let's measure these objects using inches, feet, and yards.

1. Measure the height of these objects.

The mug is ___ inches tall.

199

17.2 Inches, Feet and Yards

Next pa

This snowman is ___ feet tall.

17.2 Inches, Feet and Yards

The tree is ___ yards tall.

201

17.2 Inches, Feet and Yards

The ice skate is ___ inches long.

17.2 Inches, Feet and Yards

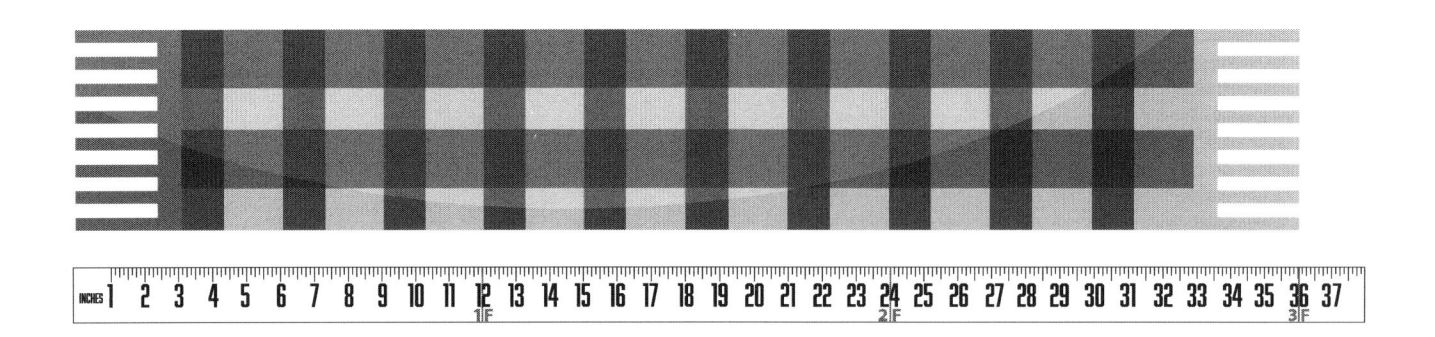

The scarf is ___ feet long.

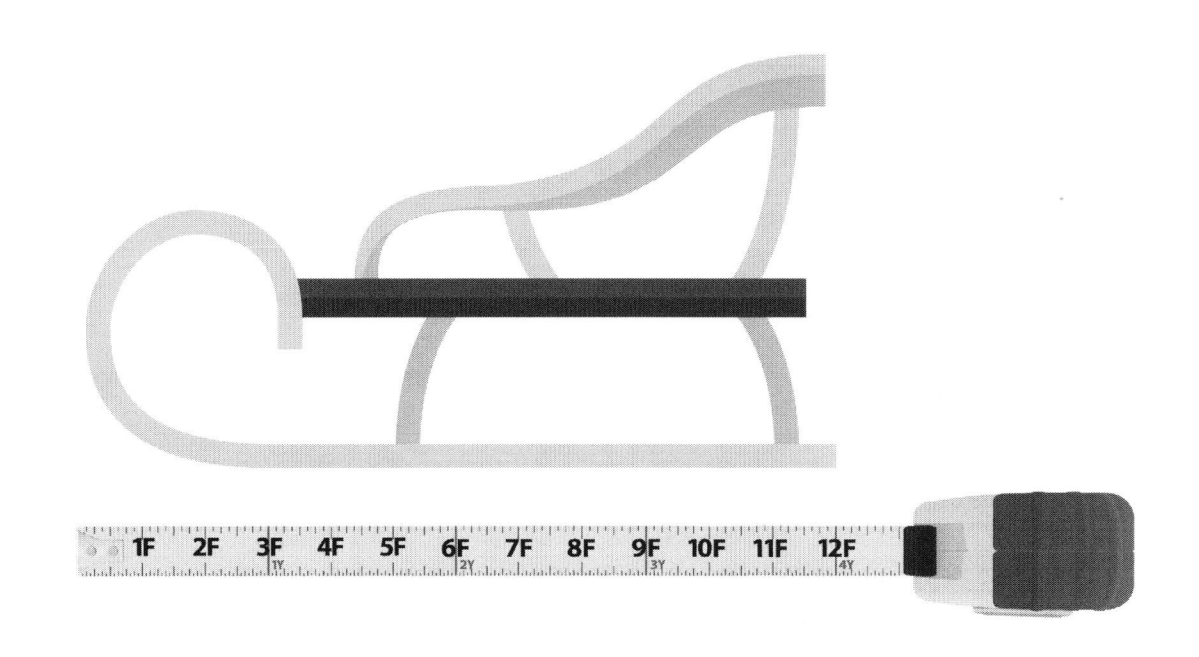

The sled is ___ yards long.

This snowflake is 1 inch tall. Check mark the measuring tool you would use to measure this snowflake.

☐ Ruler

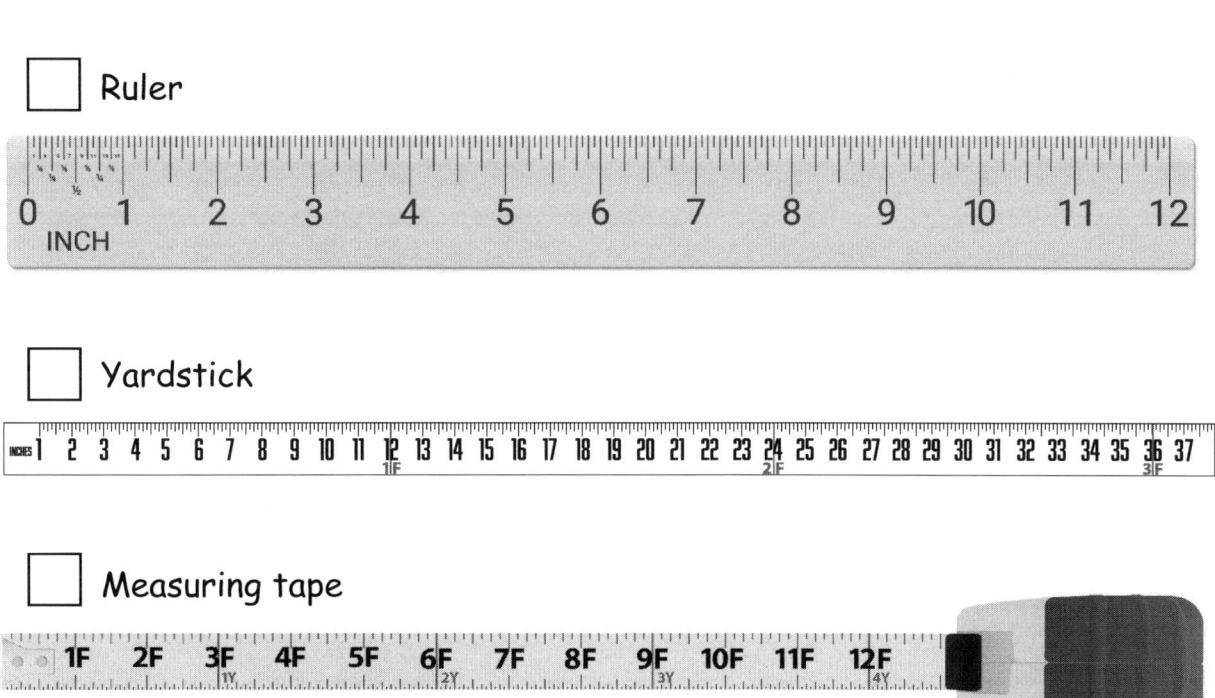

☐ Yardstick

☐ Measuring tape

204

This tree is 1 yard tall. Check mark the measuring tool you would use to measure this tree.

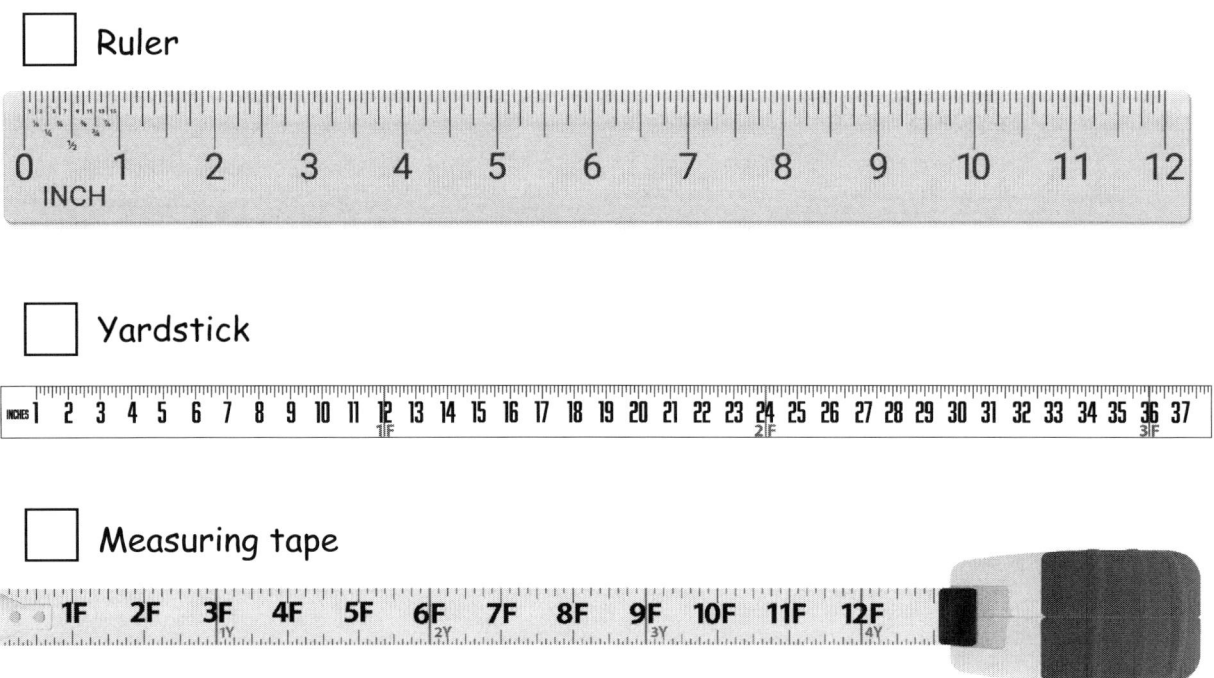

☐ Ruler

☐ Yardstick

☐ Measuring tape

205

17.2 Inches, Feet and Yards

Use a ruler to measure your shoe. How many inches long is your shoe?

_____ inches

Use a measuring tape to measure a door. How many inches tall is the door?

_____ inches

Name: _____ Date: _____

Centimeters and Meters

Let's practice measuring objects in centimeters and meters.

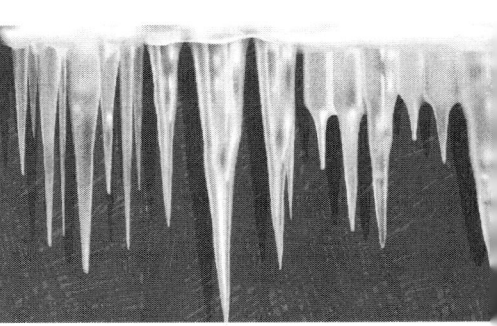

Example:

<u>26</u> cm

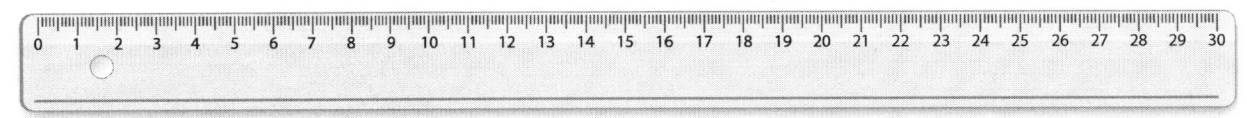

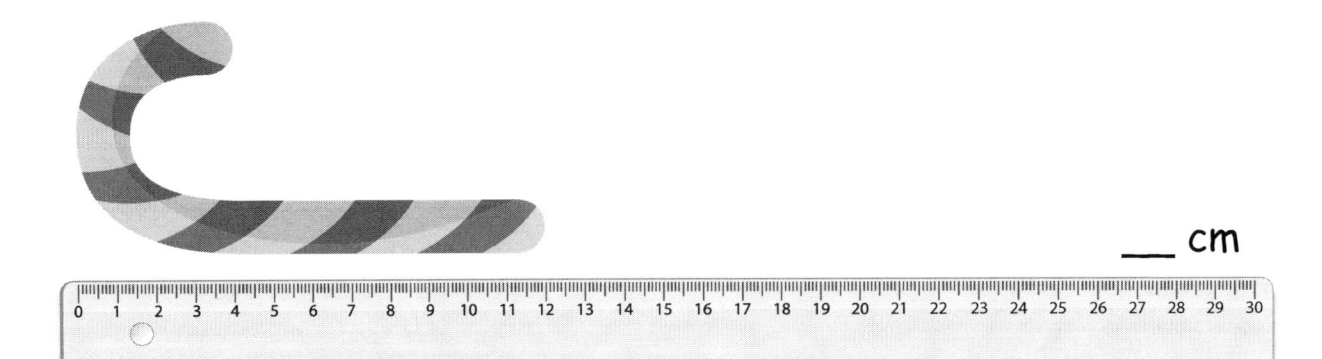

___ cm

207

17.3 Centimeters and Meters

Next pa

___ cm

___ cm

___ cm

17.3 Centimeters and Meters

208

Next page

___ cm

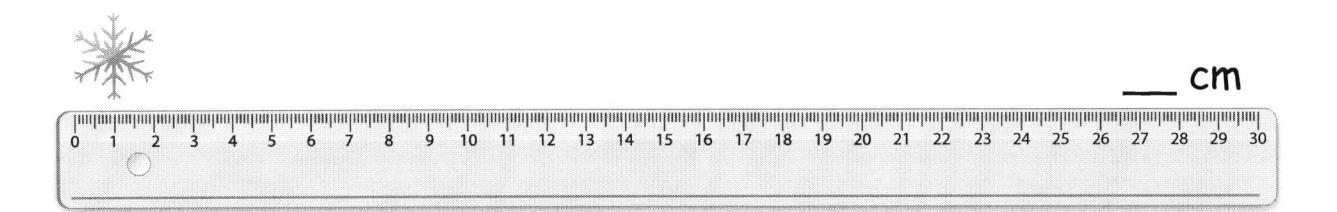

___ cm

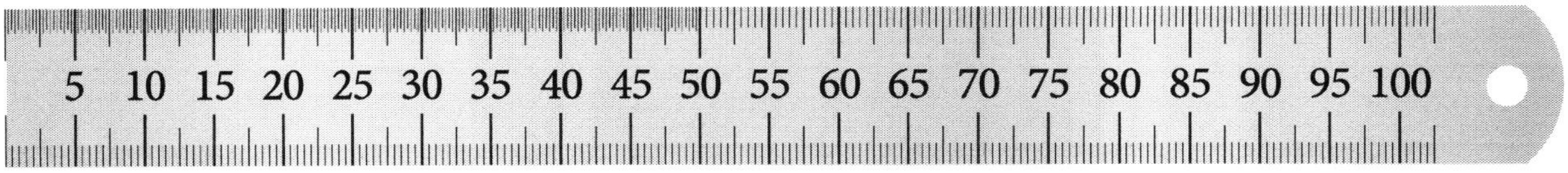

___ cm

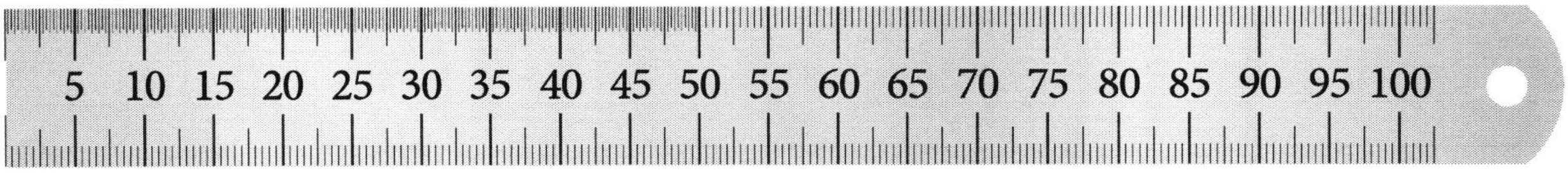

___ cm

209 17.3 Centimeters and Meters

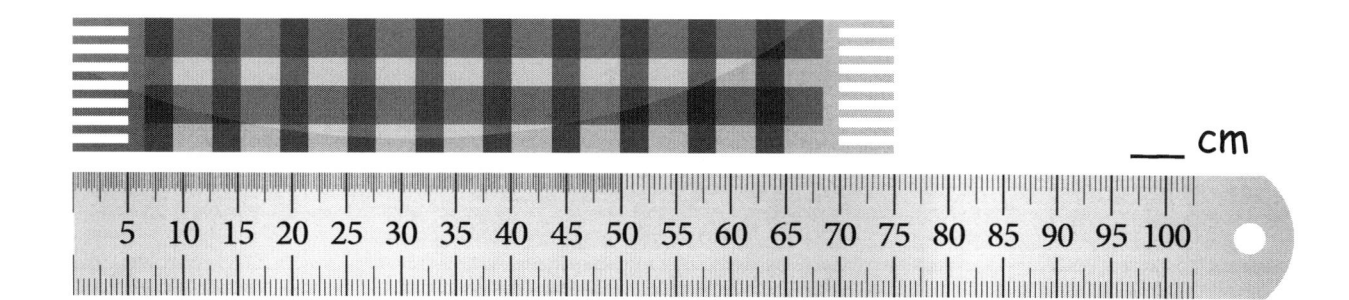

____ cm

____ cm

17.3 Centimeters and Meters

Name: _____ Date: _____

Relate Inches, Feet, and Yards

What standard unit of measurement would you use to measure these objects?

What would you use to measure this dollar bill?

☐ Ruler
☐ Yardstick

What would you use to measure this car?

☐ Ruler
☐ Yardstick

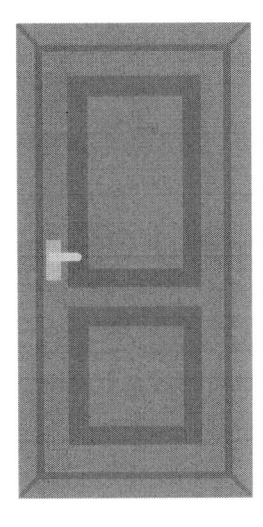

What is the unit of measurement?

This door is 8 _____ tall.

What is the unit of measurement?

This swimming pool is 25 _____ long.

211

17.4 Relate Inches, Feet and Yards

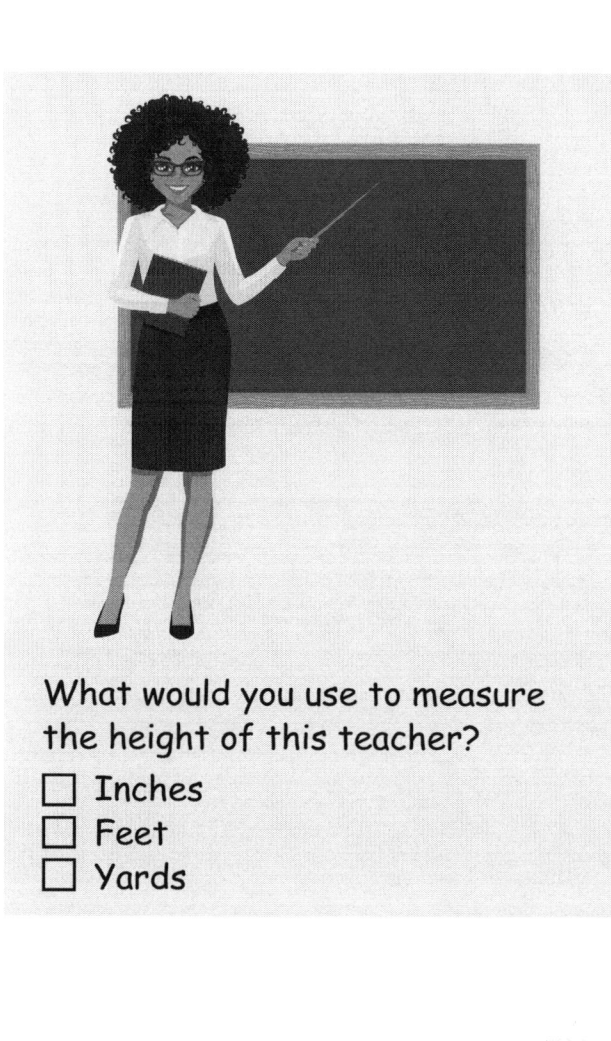

What would you use to measure the height of this teacher?
- [ ] Inches
- [ ] Feet
- [ ] Yards

What would you use to measure the length of this phone?
- [ ] Inches
- [ ] Feet
- [ ] Yards

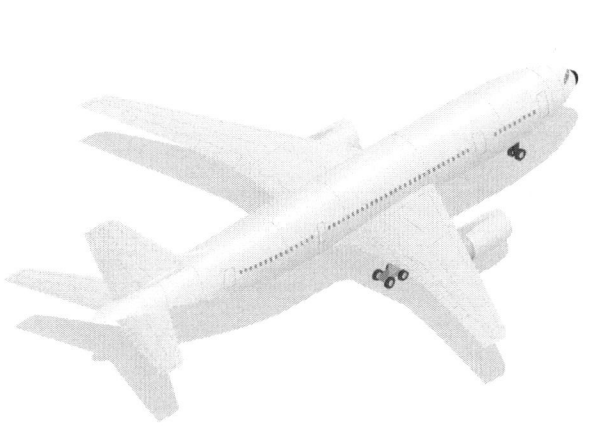

What would you use to measure this airplane?
- [ ] Ruler
- [ ] Yardstick

What would you use to measure this cup?
- [ ] Ruler
- [ ] Yardstick

17.4 Relate Inches, Feet and Yards

What would you use to measure the length of this field?

☐ Inches   ☐ Feet   ☐ Yards

What would you use to measure the length of this pencil?

☐ Inches   ☐ Feet   ☐ Yards

Name: _____ Date: _____

Relate Centimeters and Meters

Circle the better measurement for each object.

1. How long is this school bus?

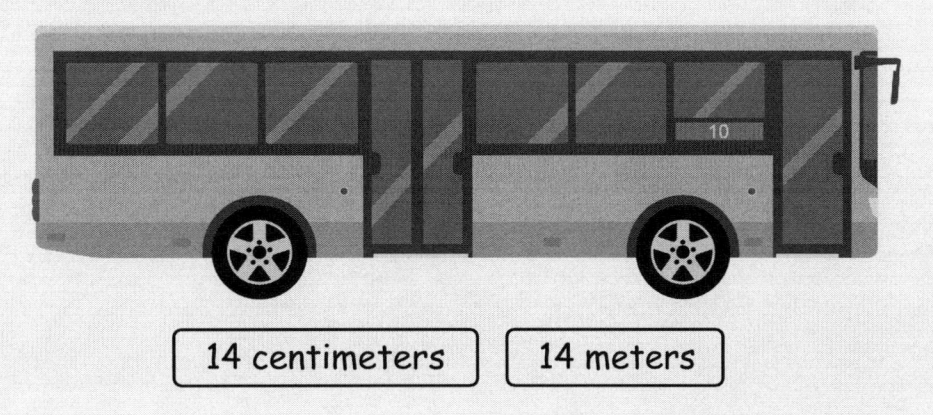

14 centimeters   14 meters

2. How long is this whale?

25 centimeters   25 meters

3. What is the missing unit of measurement?

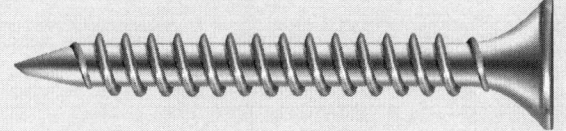

This screw is 8 _____ long.

centimeters   meters

17.5 Relate Centimeters and Meters

214

Next page

4. What is the missing unit of measurement?

This skating rink is 60 _____ long

centimeters   meters

5. How tall are this glasses?

5 centimeters   5 meters

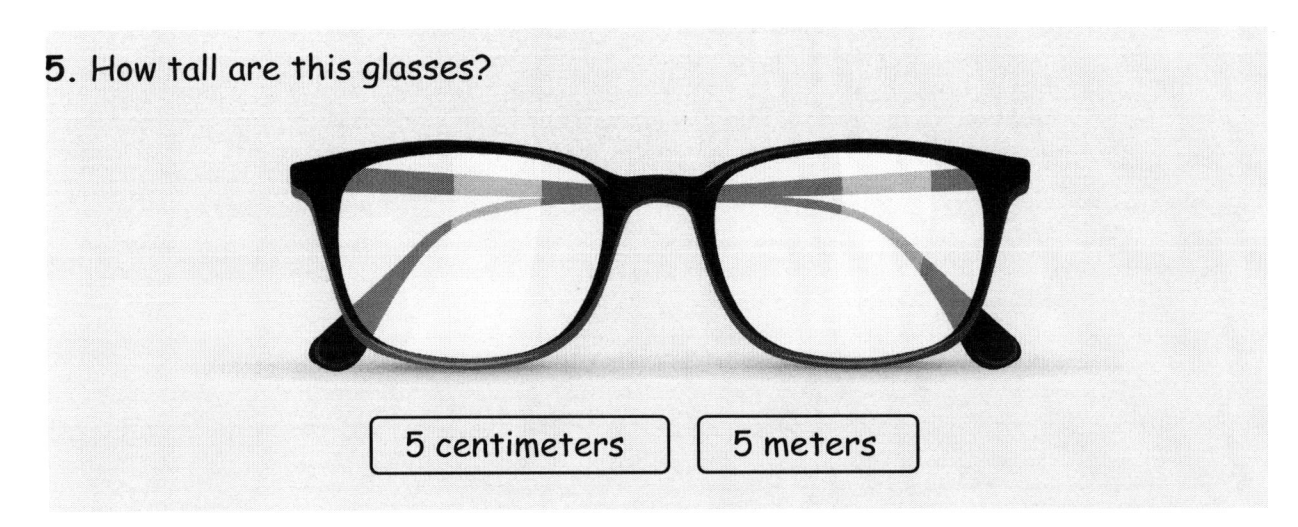

6. How tall is this laptop?

30 centimeters

30 meters

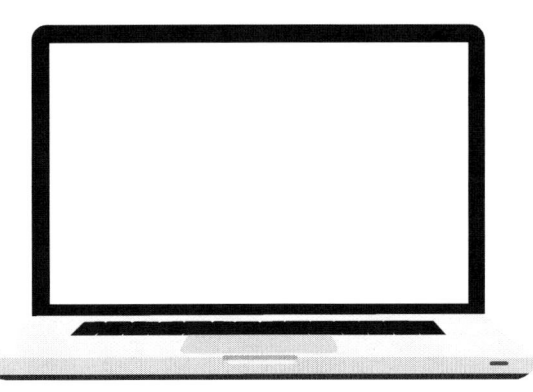

215

17.5 Relate Centimeters and Meters

7. What would you use to measure the height of this mountain?

ruler   meter stick

8. What would you use to measure the height of this glass?

ruler

meter stick

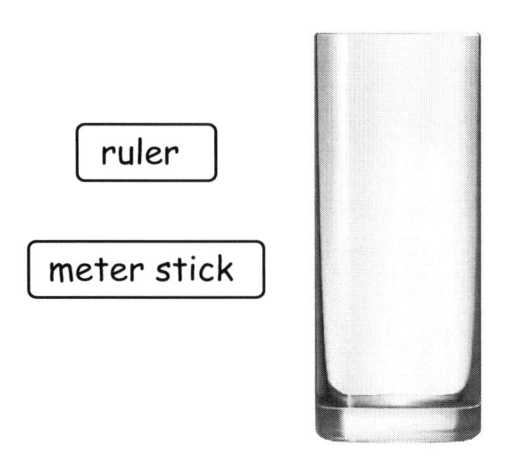

9. What would you use to measure the height of this boot?

centimeters

meters

10. What would you use to measure the length of this school?

centimeters

meters

17.5 Relate Centimeters and Meters

Name: _____ Date: _____

Estimate Using Inches, Feet, and Yards

Circle the best measurement for each object.

1. Would you measure the length of this book in inches, feet, or yards?

- inches
- feet
- yards

2. Would you measure the height of this basketball hoop in inches, feet, or yards?

- inches
- feet
- yards

3. Would you measure the length of this toy train in inches, feet, or yards?

inches | feet | yards

4. Would you measure the height of this baseball in inches, feet, or yards?

inches | feet | yards

217

18.1 Estimate Using Inches, Feet and Yards

5. Would you measure the height of this scooter in inches, feet, or yards?

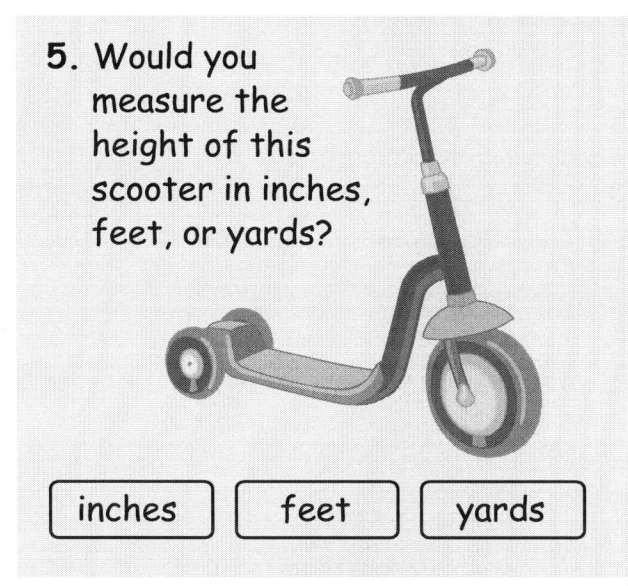

[inches]　[feet]　[yards]

6. How long is this jump rope?

[about 2 inches]
[about 7 feet]
[about 20 yards]

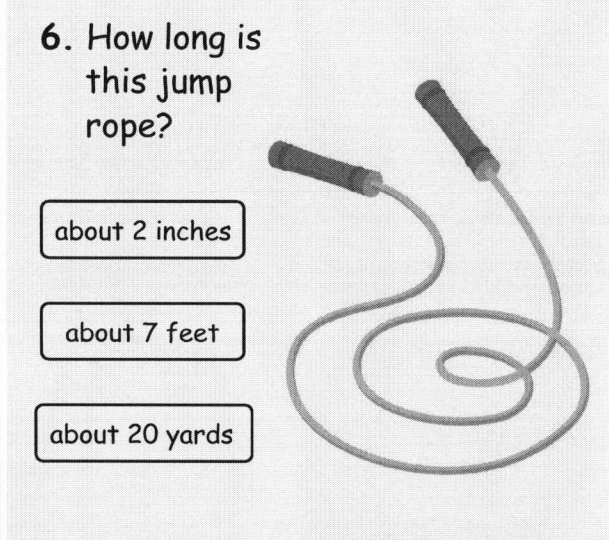

7. How long is this trampoline?

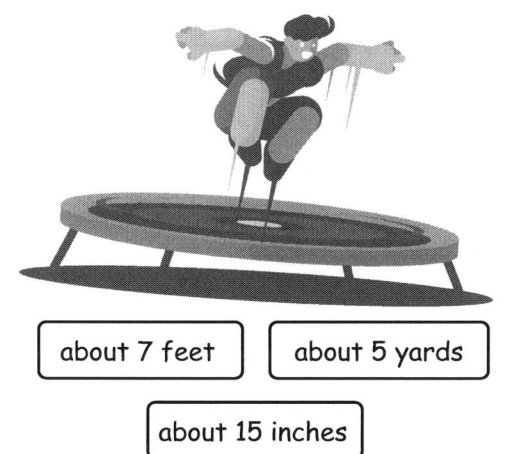

[about 7 feet]　[about 5 yards]
[about 15 inches]

8. How tall is this cell phone?

[about 6 inches]
[about 4 feet]
[about 17 yards]

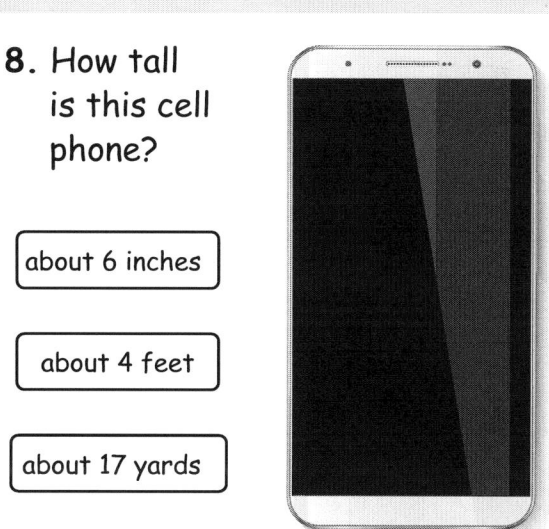

9. How long is this box of toys?

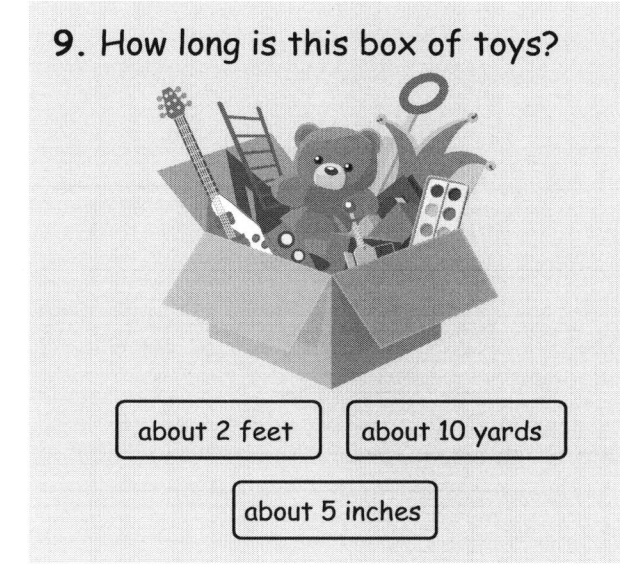

[about 2 feet]　[about 10 yards]
[about 5 inches]

10. How wide is this track?

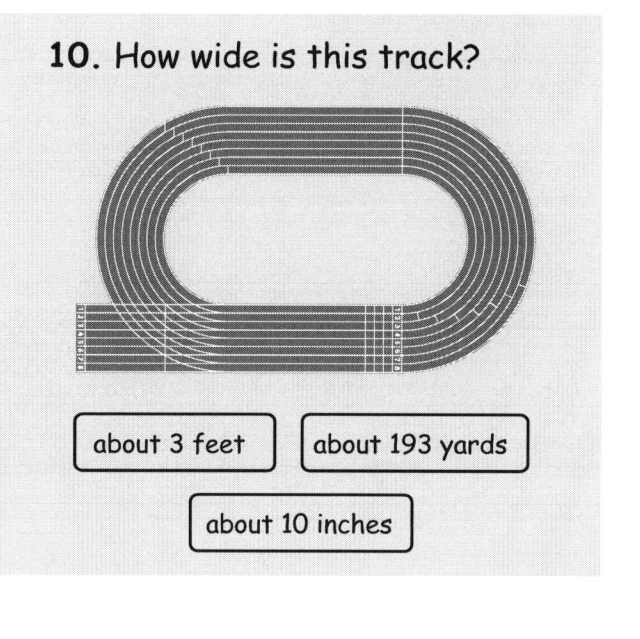

[about 3 feet]　[about 193 yards]
[about 10 inches]

18.1 Estimate Using Inches, Feet and Yards

Name: _____ Date: _____

Estimate Using Centimeters and Meters

Circle the best measurement for each object.

1. Would you measure the height of this slide in centimeters or meters?

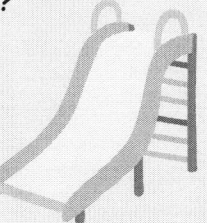

   centimeters   meters

2. Would you measure the height of this puzzle piece in centimeters or meters?

   centimeters   meters

3. Would you measure the length of this toy duck in centimeters or meters?

   centimeters   meters

4. How tall is this bouncy house?

   3 centimeters   5 meters
   15 centimeters

5. How long is this diving board?

   2 centimeters   6 meters
   12 centimeters

6. How long is this football?

   1 centimeters   4 meters
   25 centimeters

219

18.2 Estimate Using Inches, Feet and Yards

Draw a line to match each toy with its estimated measurement.

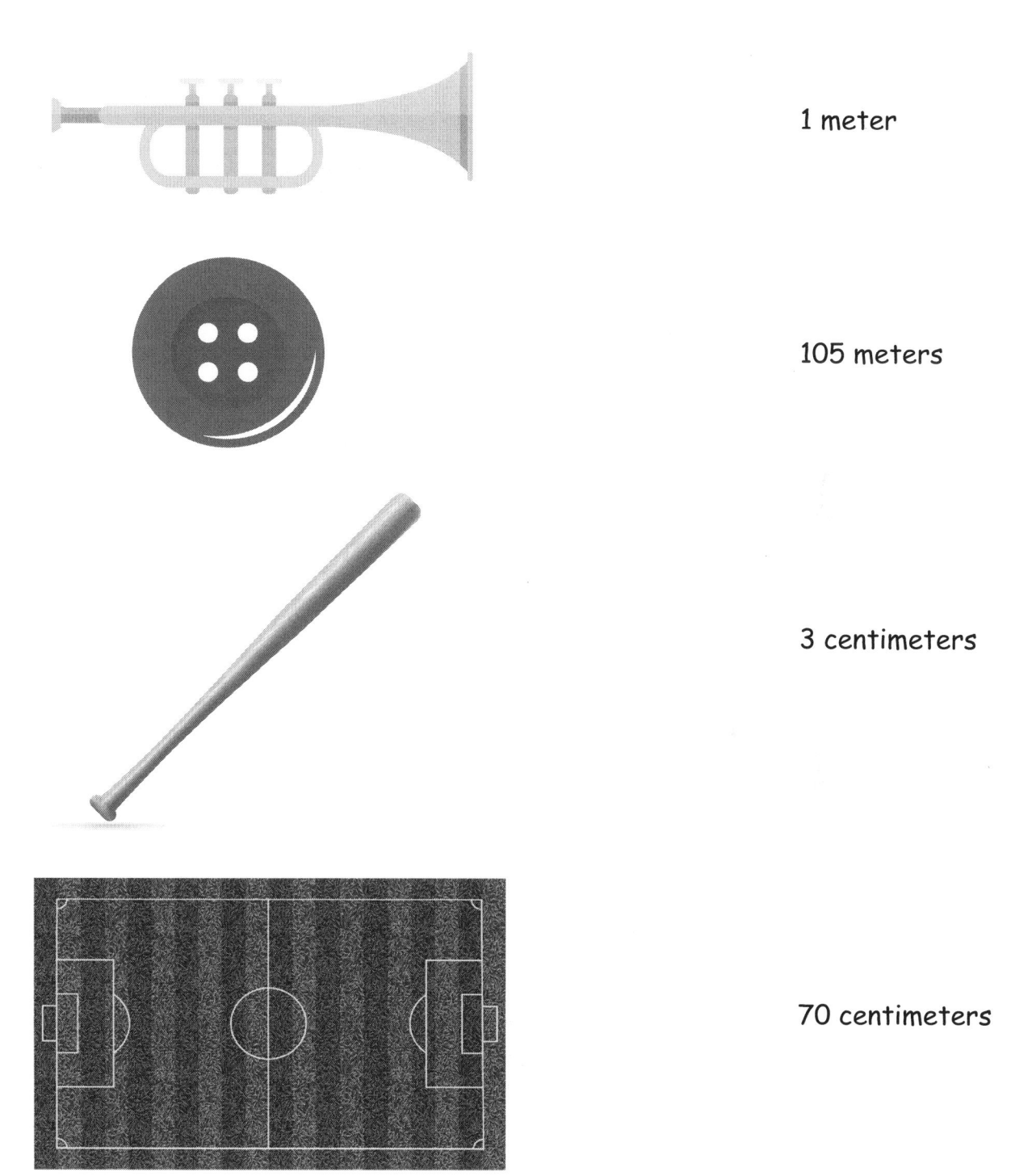

1 meter

105 meters

3 centimeters

70 centimeters

18.2 Estimate Using Centimeters and Meters

Name: _____   Date: _____

Compare Customary Lengths

Can you compare the lengths of these toys?
First, record the length or height of each toy.
Then, use subtraction to compare them.

Example:

__11__ inches

__5__ inches

__11__ - __5__ = __6__

The train is __6__ inches longer than the block tower.

221

18.3 Compare Customary Lengths

___ inches   ___ inches

___ - ___ = ___

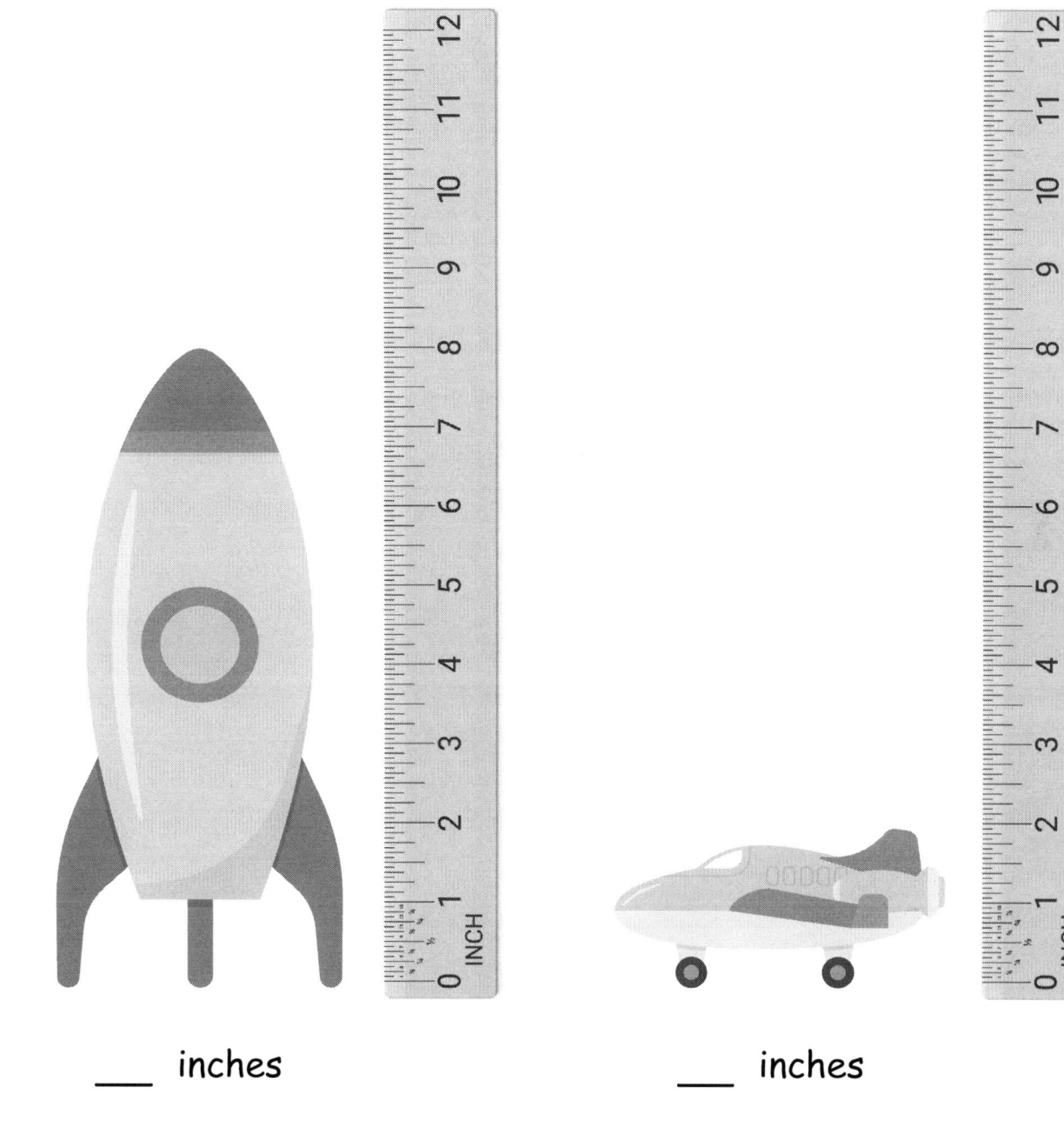

The toy rocket is ___ inches taller than the toy plane.

18.3 Compare Customary Lengths

___ feet

___ foot

___ - ___ = ___

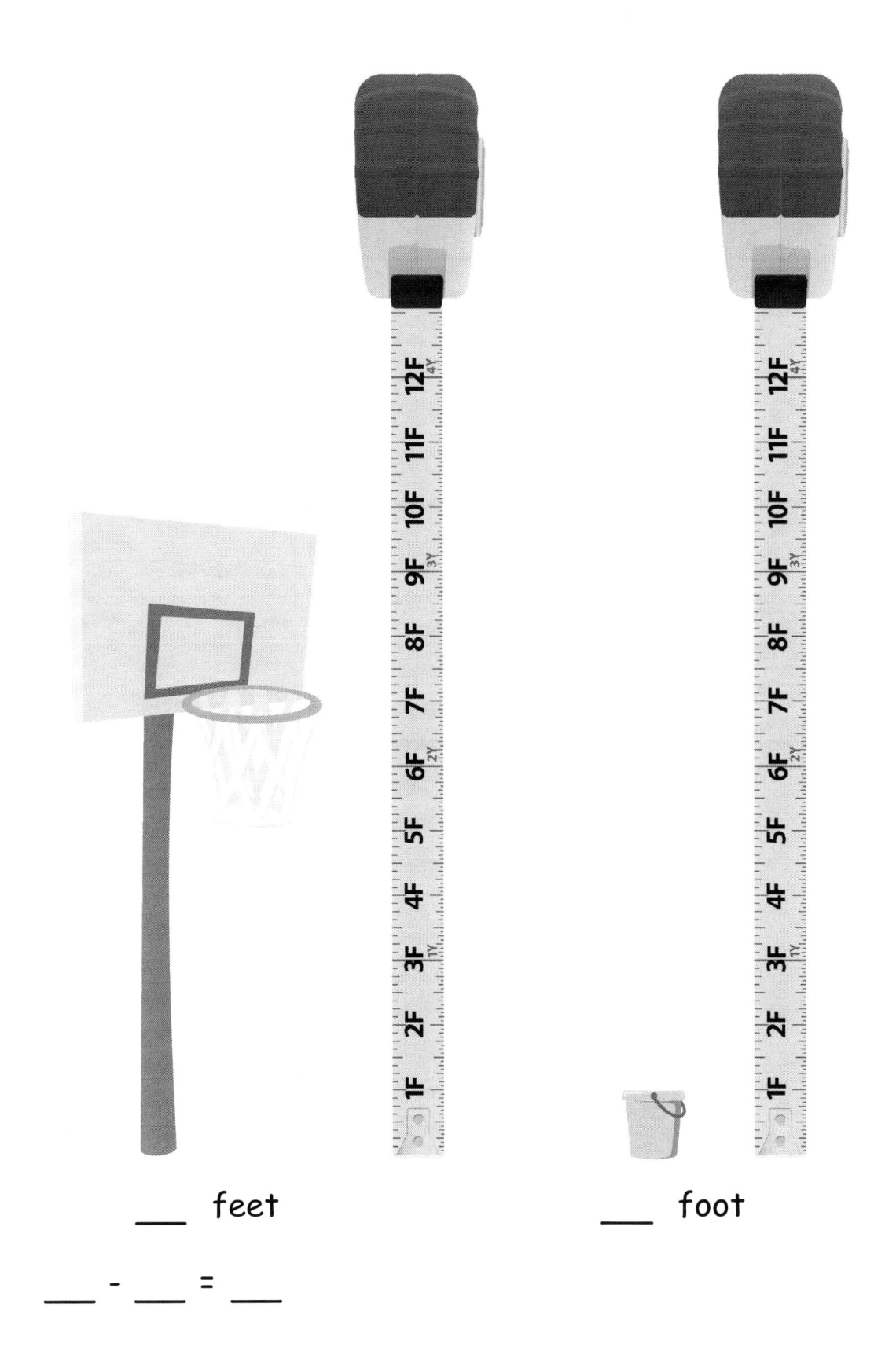

The basketball hoop is ____ feet taller than the bucket.

223

18.3 Compare Customary Lengths

___ inches

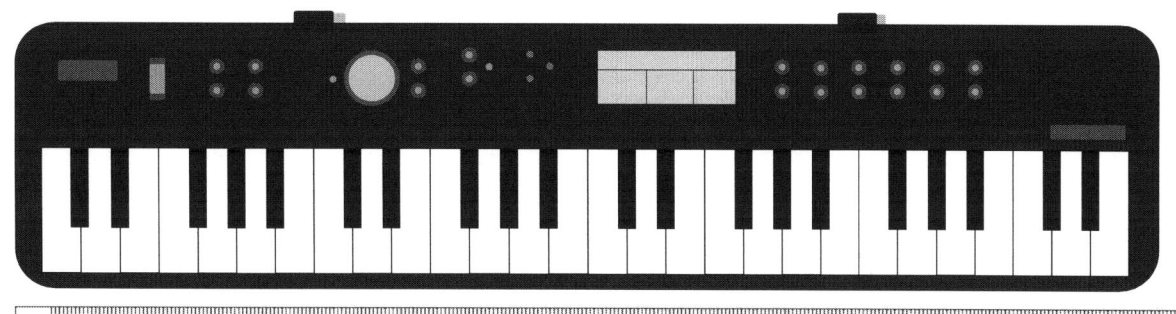

___ inches

___ - ___ = ___

The keyboard is _____ inches longer than the baseball card.

___ inches

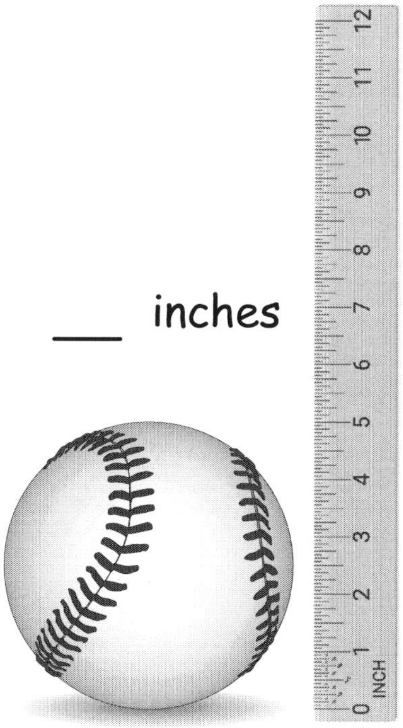

___ inches

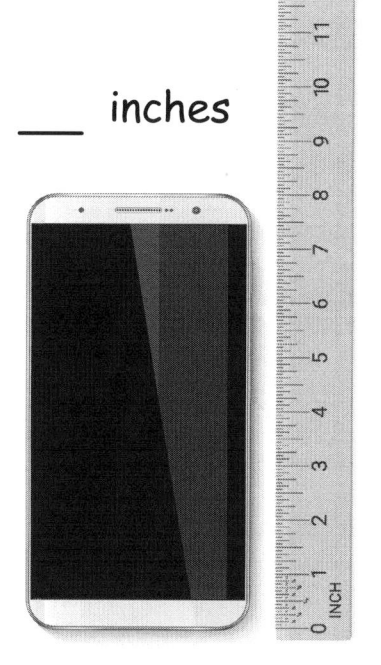

___ - ___ = ___

The cell phone is _____ inches taller than the baseball.

18.3 Compare Customary Lengths

___ yards   ___ yards

___ - ___ = ___

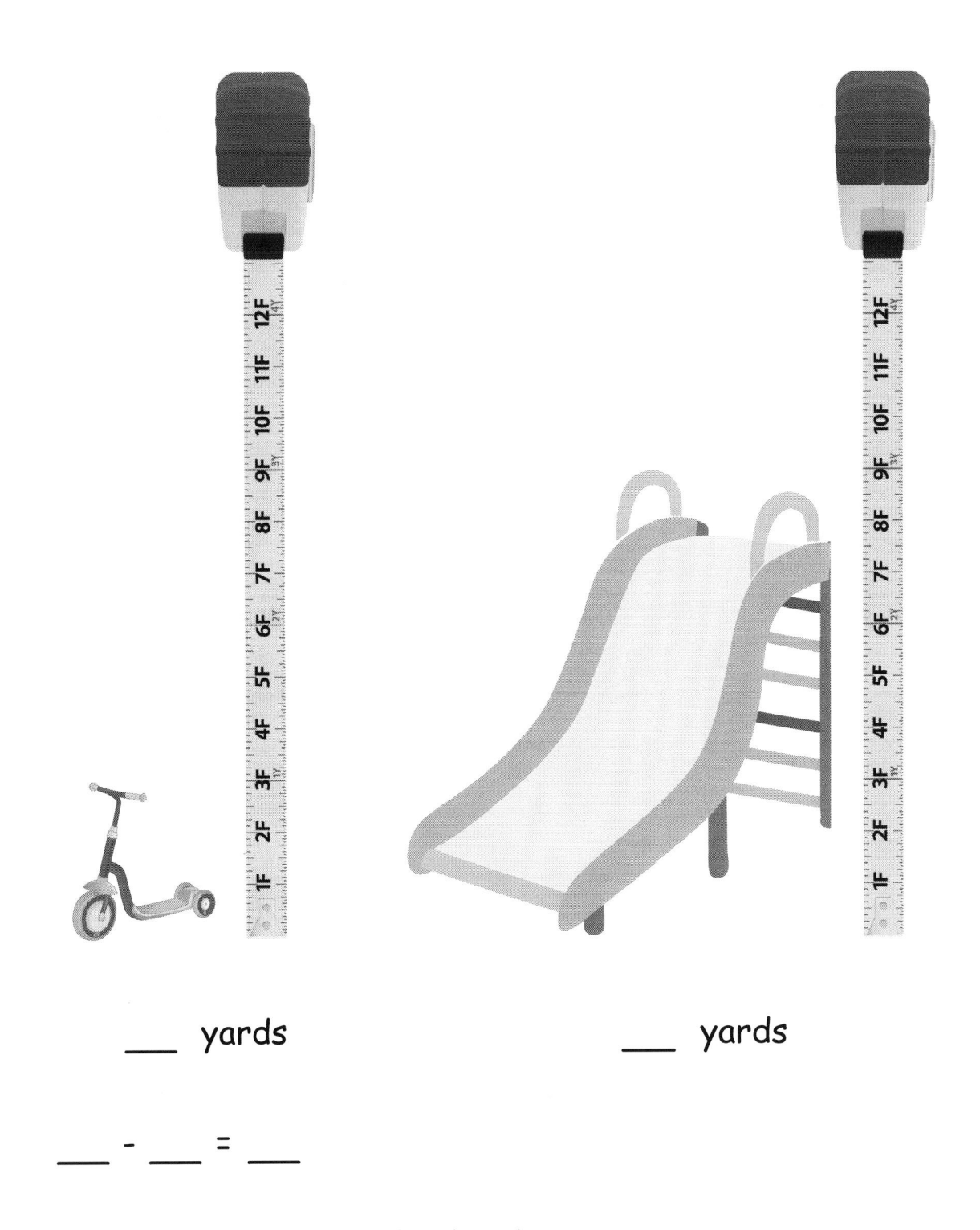

The slide is ____ yards taller than the scooter.

225   18.3 Compare Customary Lengths

Name: _____ Date: _____

Compare Metric Lengths

Can you compare the lengths of these toys using centimeters and meters? Record the length or height of each toy, and use subtraction to compare them.

Example:

How much longer is the trombone than the trumpet?

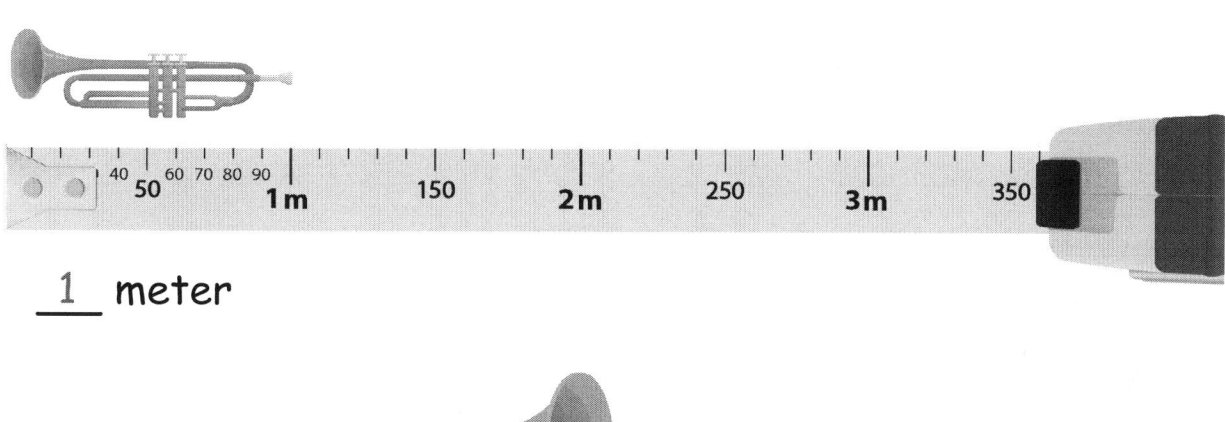

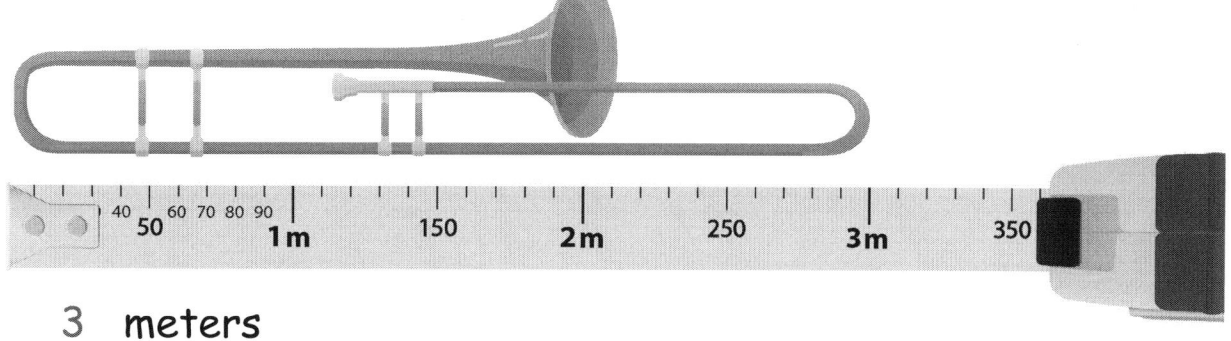

__1__ meter

__3__ meters

__3__ - __1__ = __2__

The trombone is __2__ meters longer than the trumpet.

18.4 Compare Metric Lengths

226

Next page

1. How much longer is the hockey glove than the hockey puck?

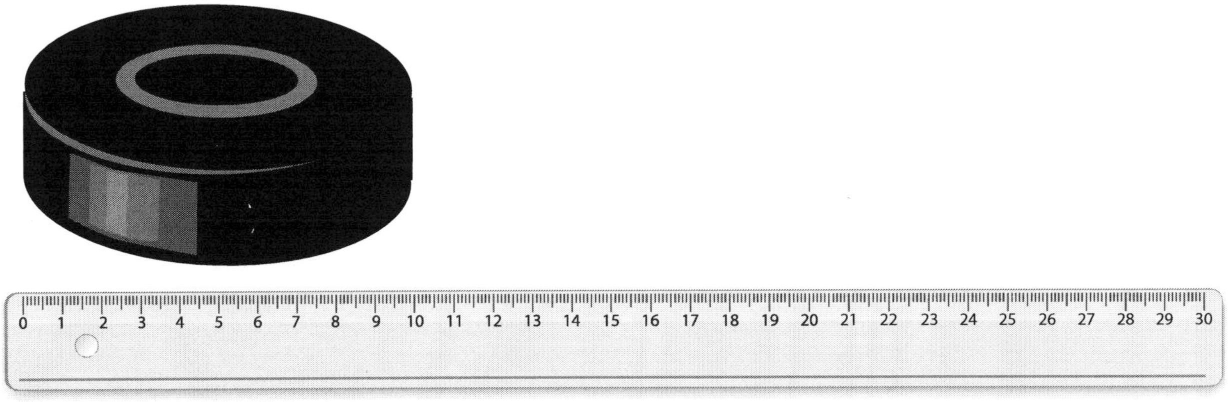

___ centimeters

___ centimeters

___ ___ ___

The hockey glove is ___ centimeters longer than the hockey puck.

2. How much longer is the baseball bat than the baseball?

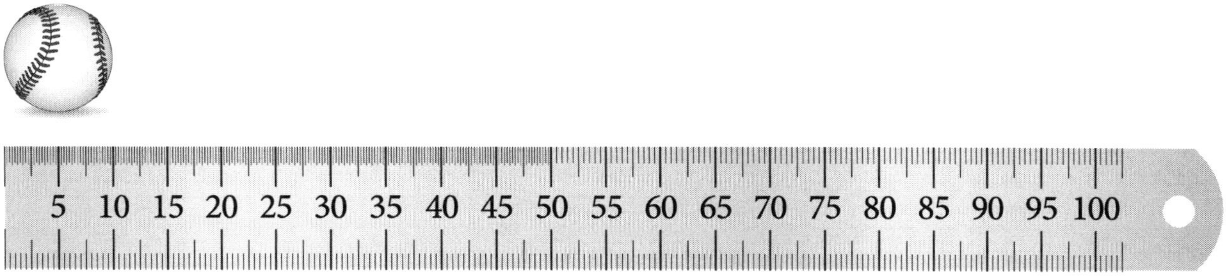

___ centimeters

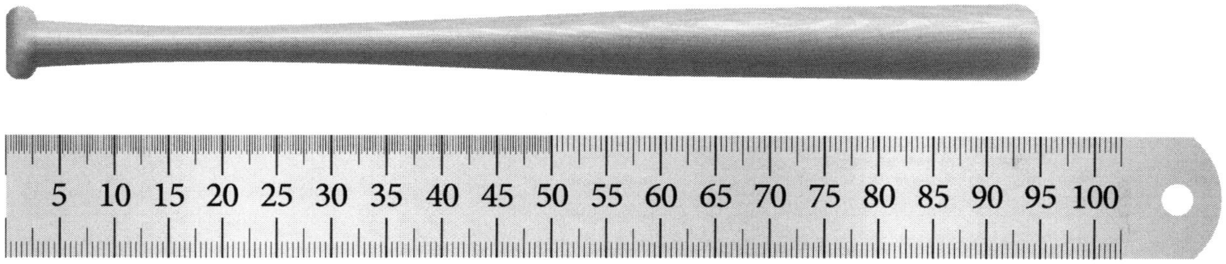

___ centimeters

___ ___ ___

The baseball bat is ____ centimeters longer than the baseball.

18.4 Compare Metric Lengths

Next page

3. How much taller is the TV than the remote?

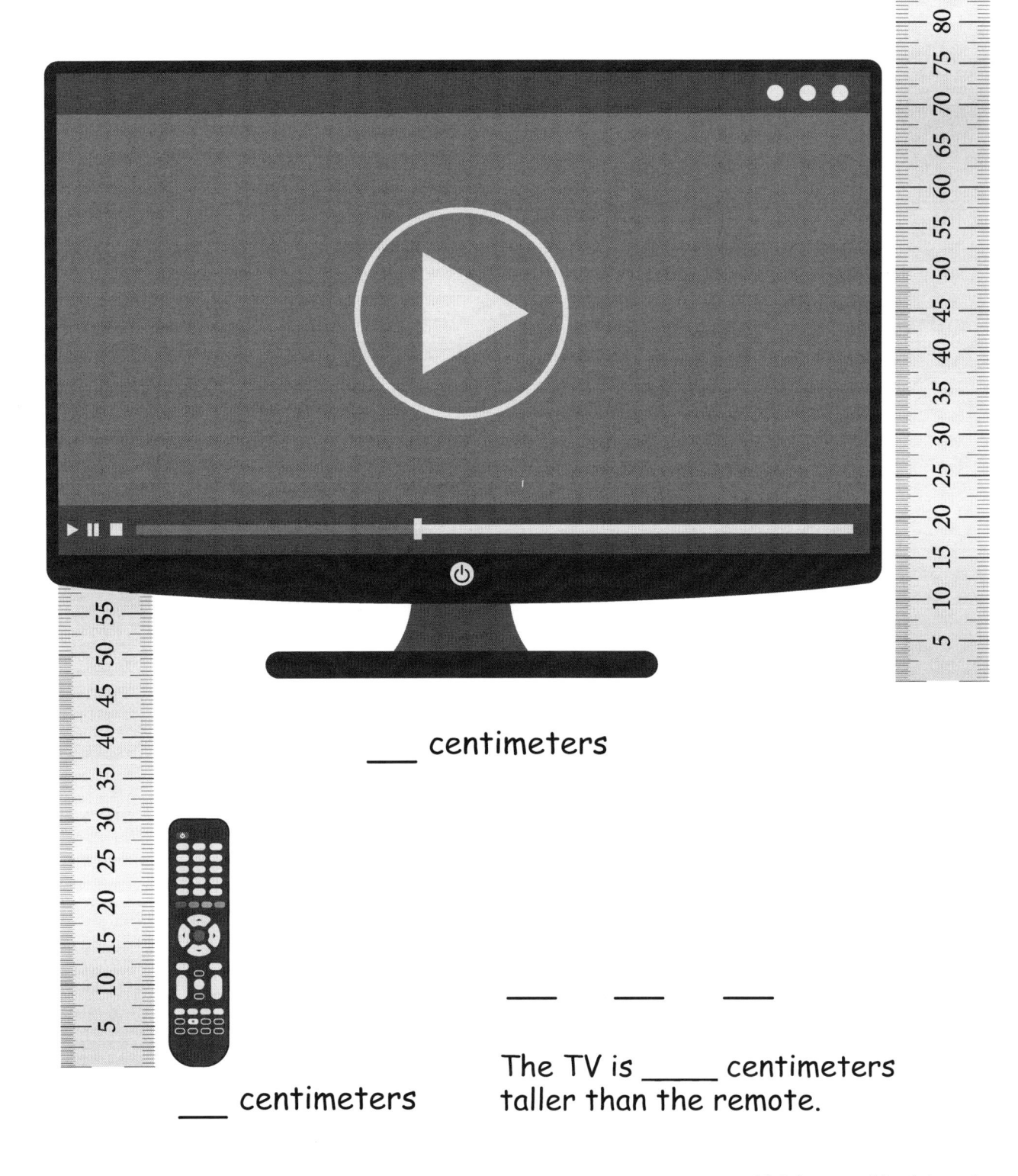

___ centimeters

___ centimeters

___ ___ ___

The TV is ____ centimeters taller than the remote.

229

18.4 Compare Metric Lengths

3. How much taller is the gray bear than the brown bear?

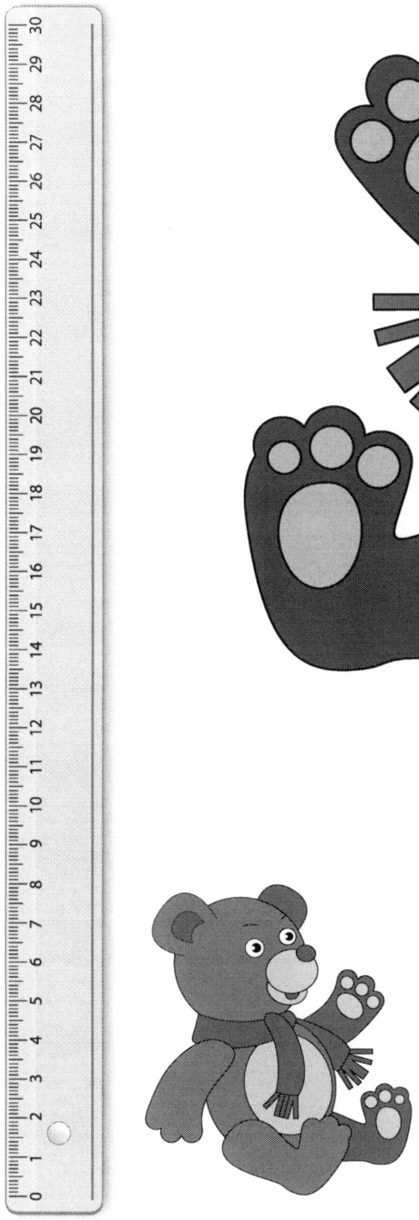

___ centimeters

___ ___ ___

The gray bear is ____ centimeters taller than the brown bear.

___ centimeters

18.4 Compare Metric Lengths

Name: _____ Date: _____

Compare Measurements

Which toy is bigger? Use the measuring tools to find out. Then color in the bigger toy!

Example:

_5_ inches

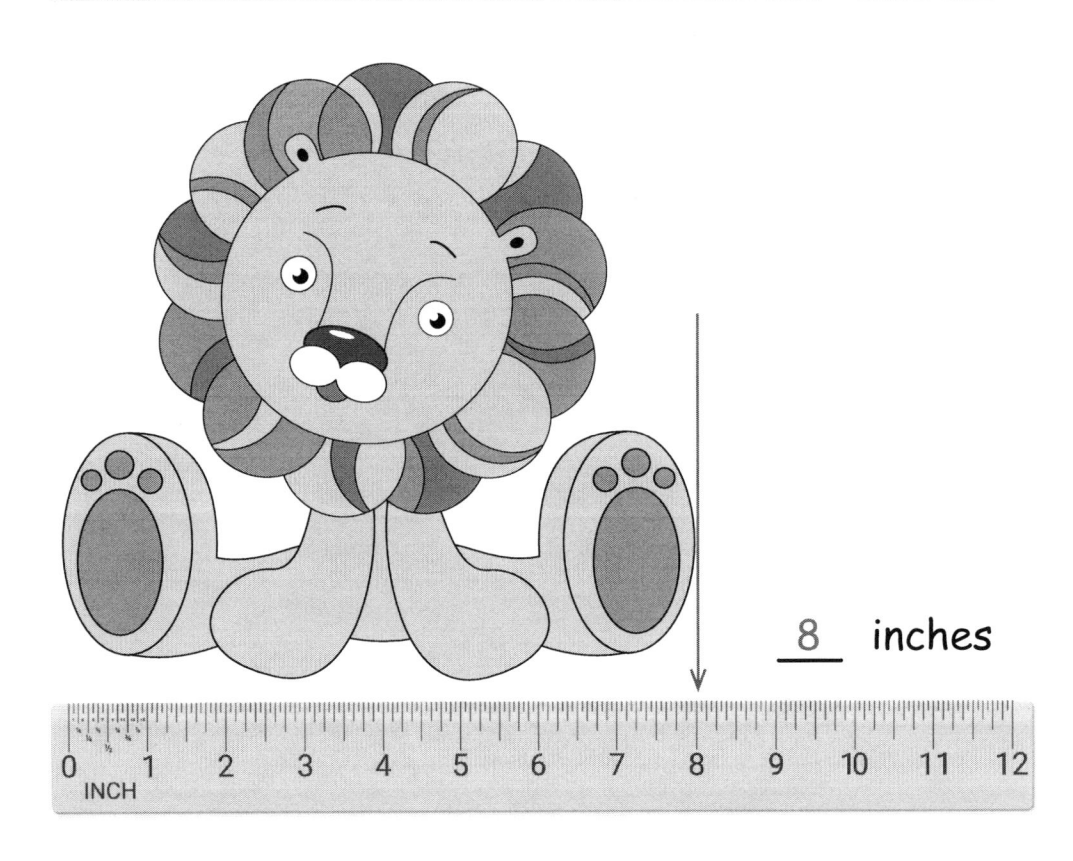

_8_ inches

231 18.5 Select and Use Customary and/or Metric Tools

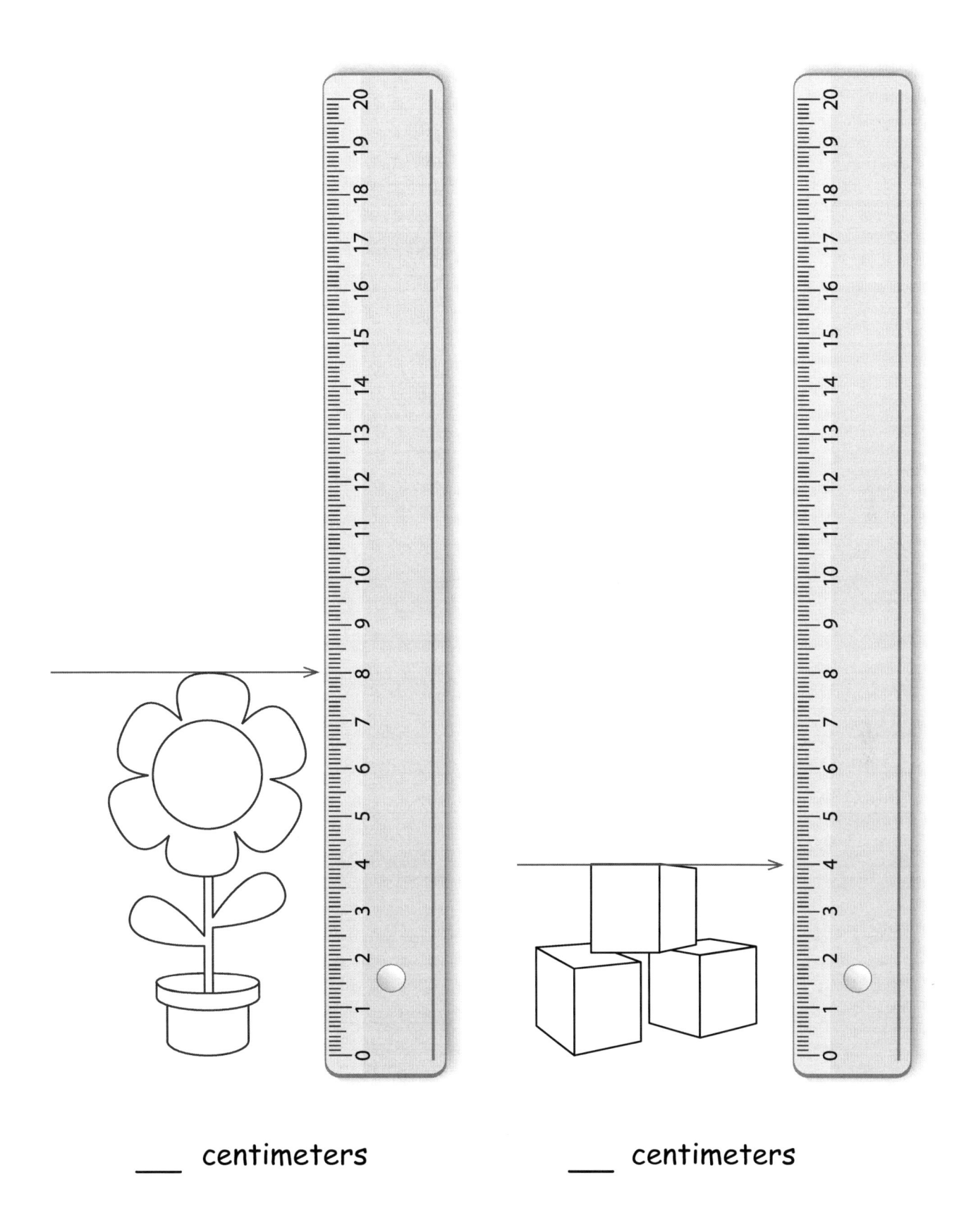

___ centimeters   ___ centimeters

18.5 Select and Use Customary and/or Metric Tools

232

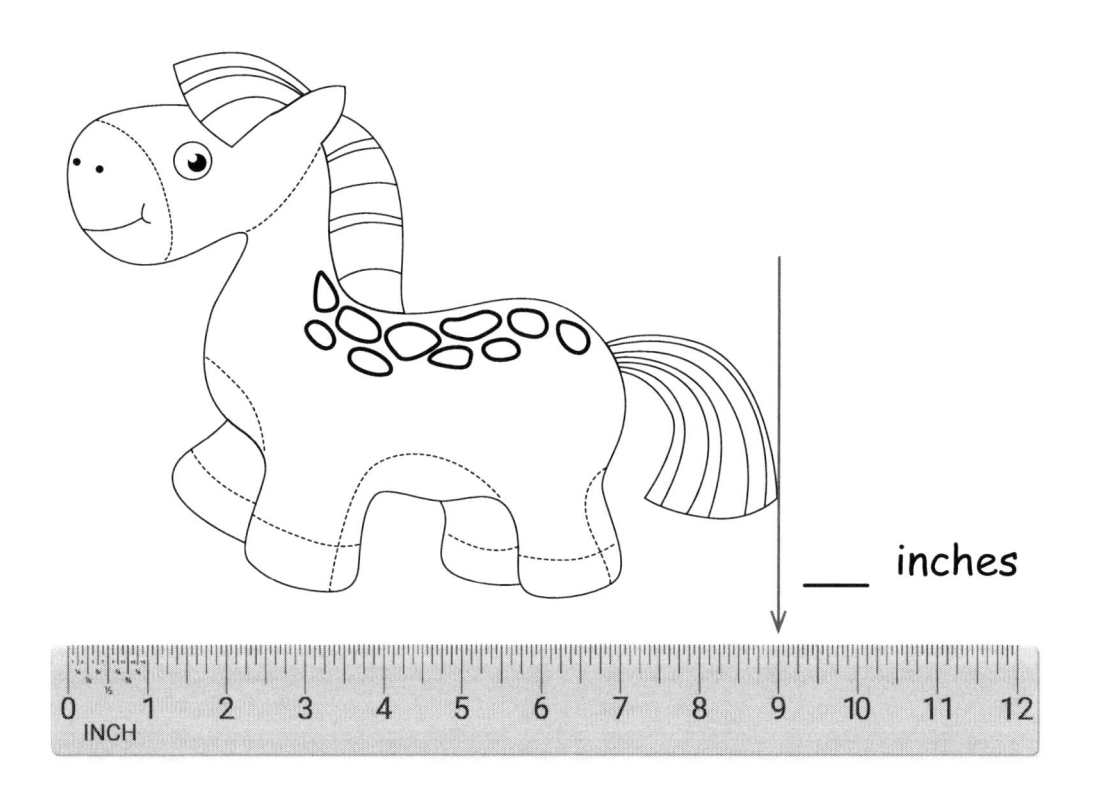

___ inches

___ inches

233   18.5 Select and Use Customary and/or Metric Tools

___ feet

___ feet

18.5 Select and Use Customary and/or Metric Tools

234

Next page

___ meter

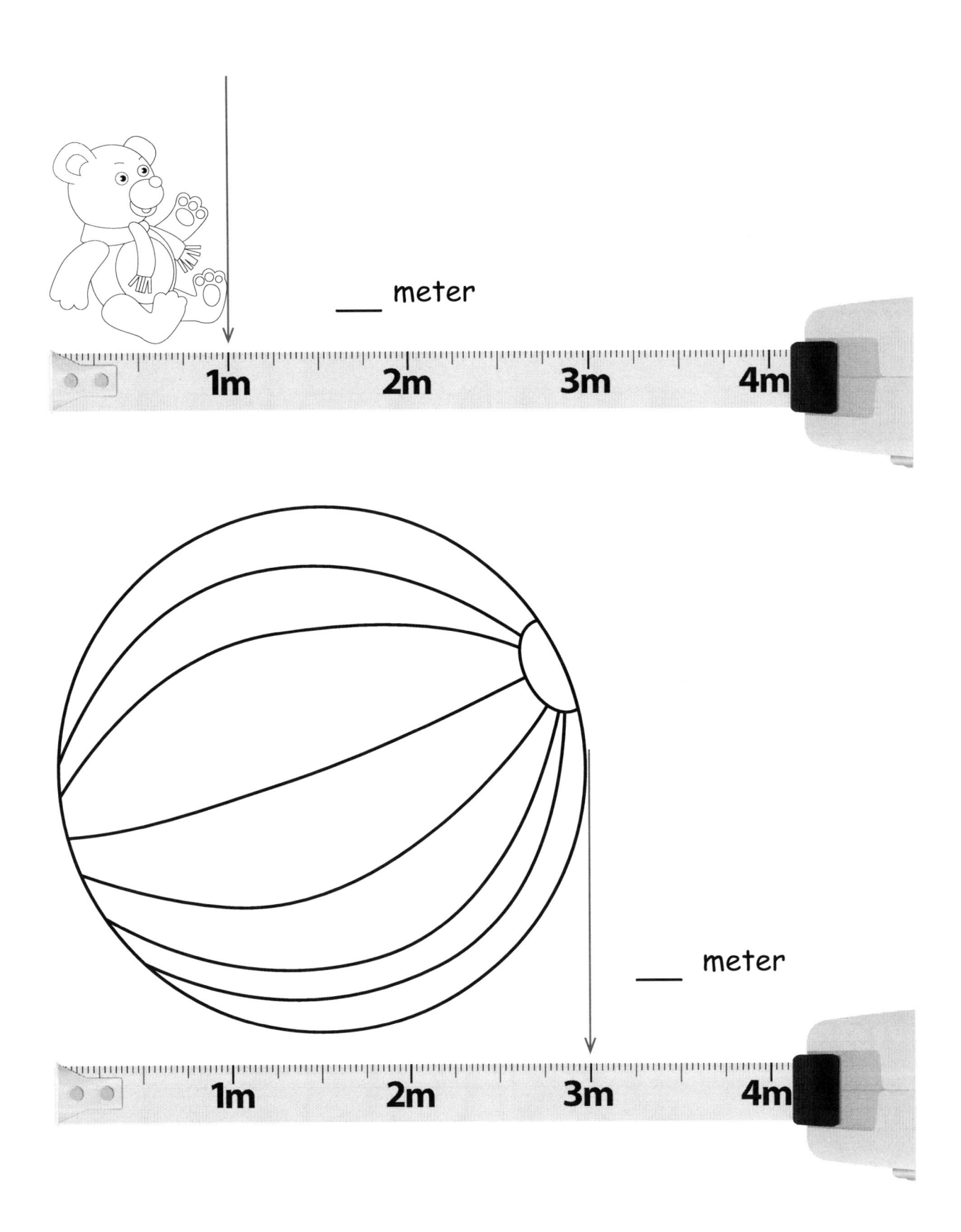

___ meter

235 18.5 Select and Use Customary and/or Metric Tools

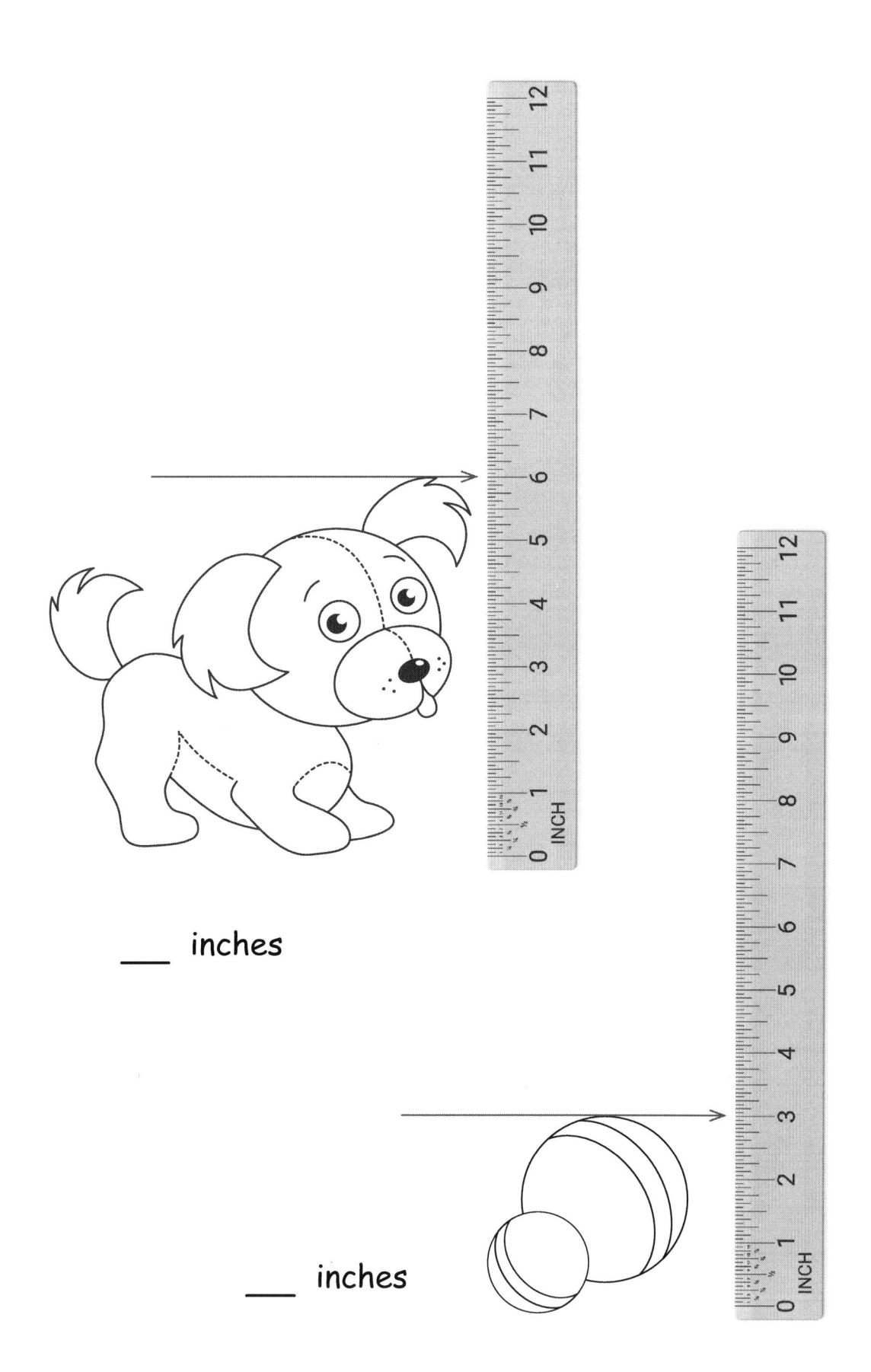

___ inches

___ inches

18.5 Select and Use Customary and/or Metric Tools

Challenge: Measure this toy in inches and centimeters. How do you know that inches are bigger than centimeters? Write and draw to show what you think!

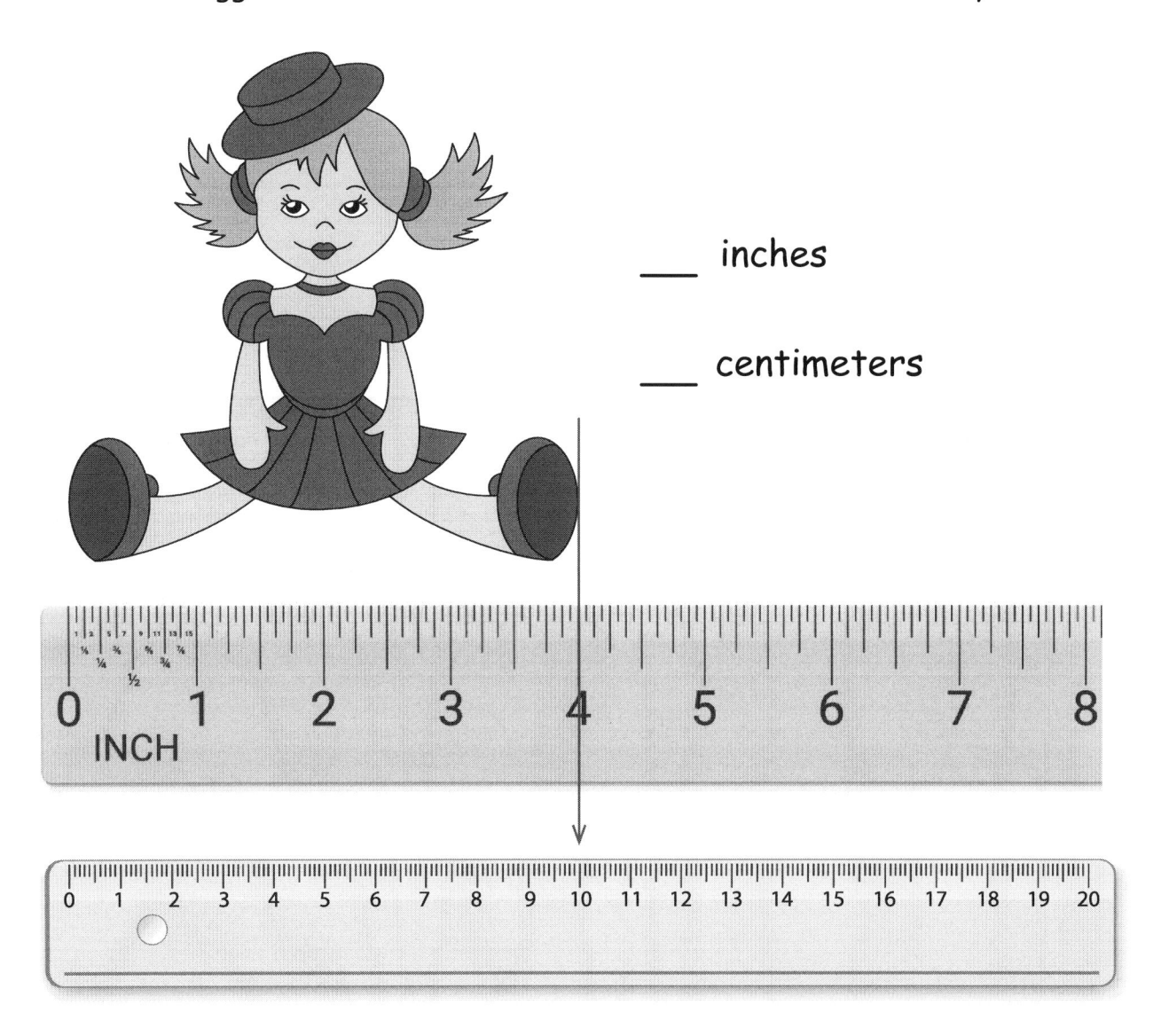

___ inches

___ centimeters

Cutout Worksheets

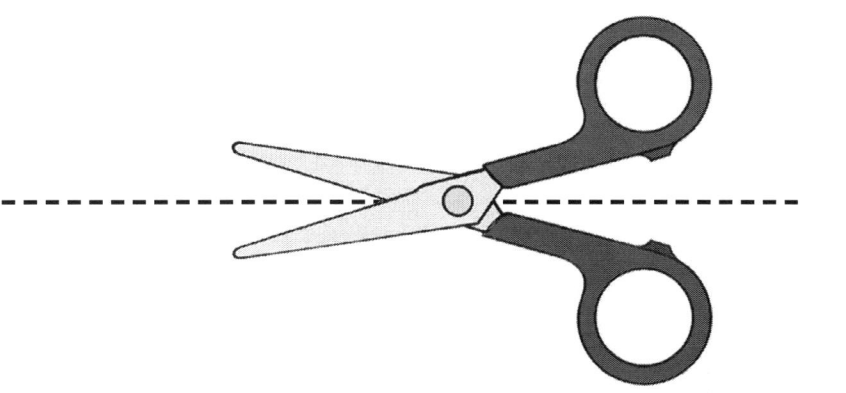

Name: _____ Date: _____

Addition Properties Flashcards

Cut out the flashcards for extra practice at home.

2 + 3 =	7 + 5 =	2 + 6 =
3 + 7 =	5 + 8 =	9 + 6 =
7 + 4 =	4 + 5 =	9 + 2 =
3 + 4 =	8 + 6 =	5 + 10 =
4 + 8 =	3 + 5 =	1 + 19 =

1.1 Addition Properties

240

Next page

8	12	5
15	13	10
11	9	11
15	14	7
20	8	12

Name: _____ Date: _____

Practice: Add to 20

Ask an adult for scissors and cut along the dotted lines. Follow the directions on the next page to glue the unicorns in their unicorn pens.

Lily

- 6 + 6 = 12
- 7 + 8 = 15
- 7 + 2 = 9
- 16 + 4 = 20
- 6 + 7 = 13
- 9 + 5 = 14
- 13 + 3 = 16
- 4 + 3 = 7
- 4 + 4 = 8
- 10 + 5 = 15

3.1 Add To (Up to 20)

Next page

These unicorn pens are labeled with different addition strategies. Place each unicorn in the strategy you think would be best to use when solving the addition sentence.

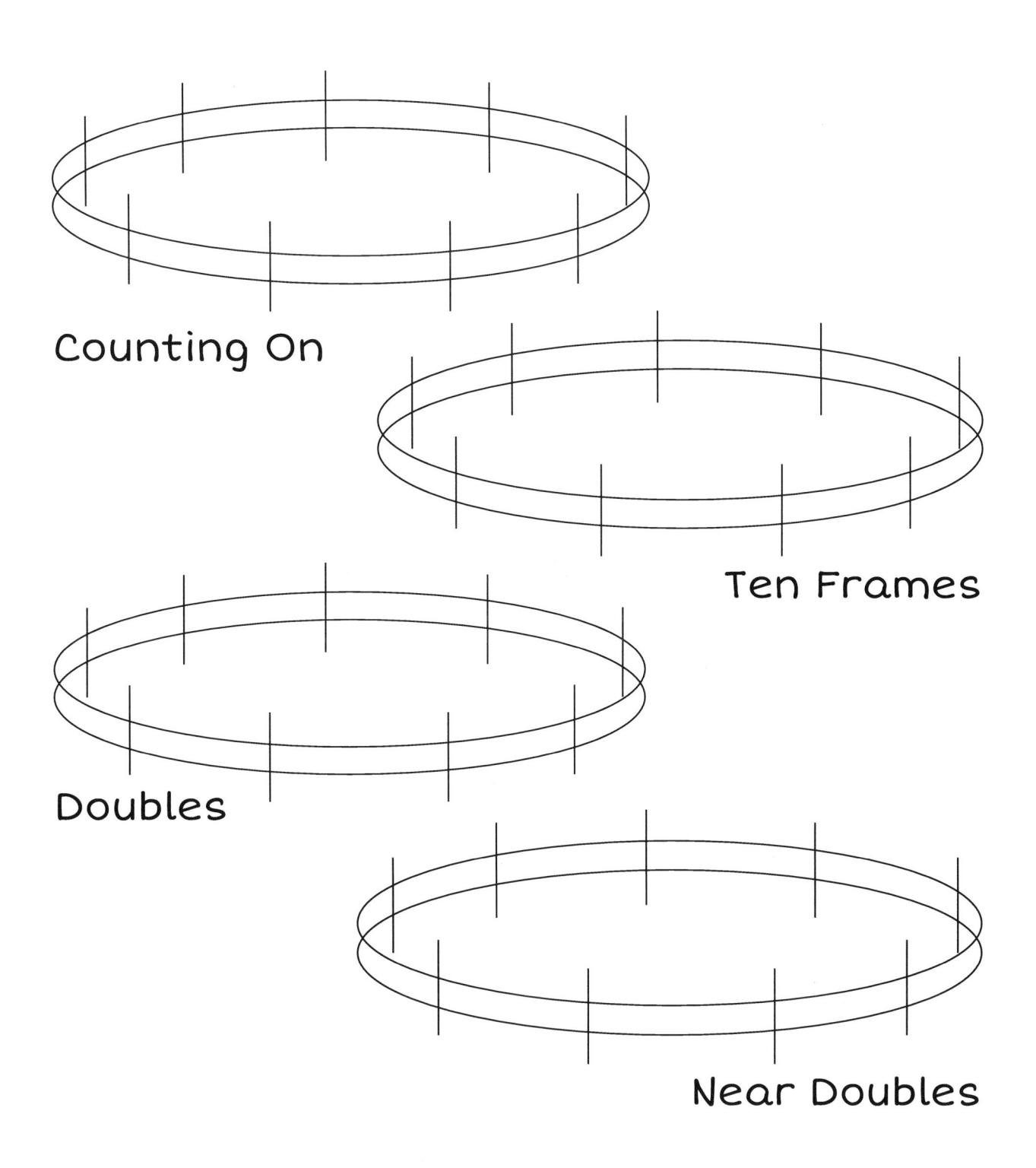

Counting On

Ten Frames

Doubles

Near Doubles

3.1 Add To (Up to 20)

Name: _____ Date: _____

Practice: Write Addition Sentences

Levi found so many lucky charms on his walk through the enchanted forest! Read each problem and find the key words and numbers. Put them in the "Key Words" box. Then, cut out and glue the pictures to show Levi's lucky charms all together in the "Picture" box. Lastly, write out the addition sentence in the "Addition Sentence" box.

Example: Levi had 4 gold coins in his pocket, then he found 10 more. How many gold coins does he have in all?

Picture	Key Words
	1. in all
	2. 4
	3. 10
	Addition Scentence
	4 + 10 = 14

1. Levi had 6 gold coins in his pocket, then he found 7 more. How many gold coins does he have in all?

Picture	Key Words
	Addition Scentence
	☐ + ☐ = ☐

3.2 Write Addition Sentences

246

Next page

2. Levi had 9 horseshoes in his pocket, he found 5 more. How many horseshoes does he have altogether?

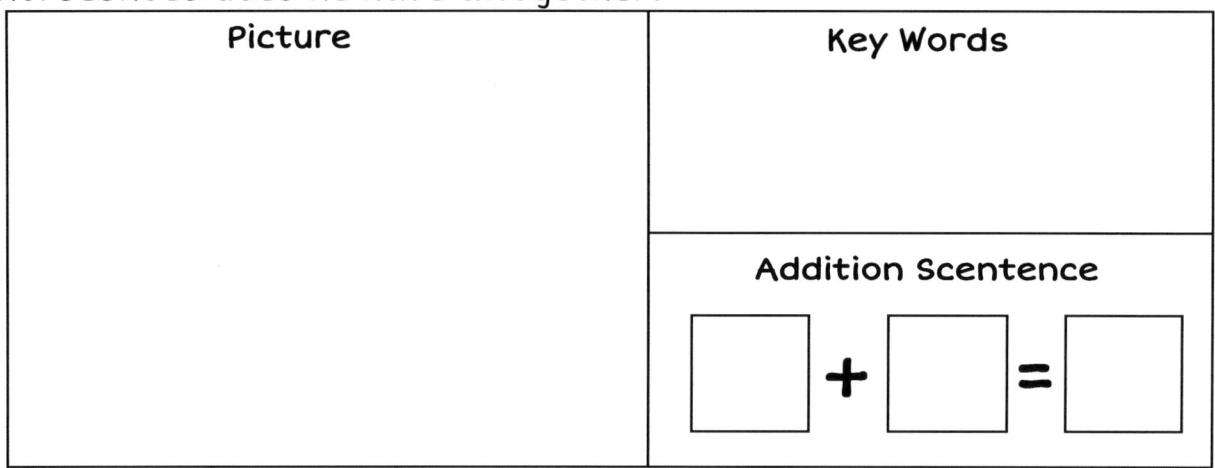

Picture	Key Words
	Addition Scentence $\square + \square = \square$

3. Levi had 10 ladybugs in his pocket, then he found 2 more. How many ladybugs does he have in total?

Picture	Key Words
	Addition Scentence $\square + \square = \square$

4. Levi had 8 bamboo sticks in his pocket. Then he found 6 acorns. How many bamboo sticks and acorns does Levi have in all?

Picture	Key Words
	Addition Scentence $\square + \square = \square$

3.2 Write Addition Sentences

5. Levi had 9 shooting stars in his pocket. Then he found 4 rainbow charms. How many shooting stars and rainbow charms does Levi have altogether?

Picture	Key Words
	Addition Scentence ☐ + ☐ = ☐

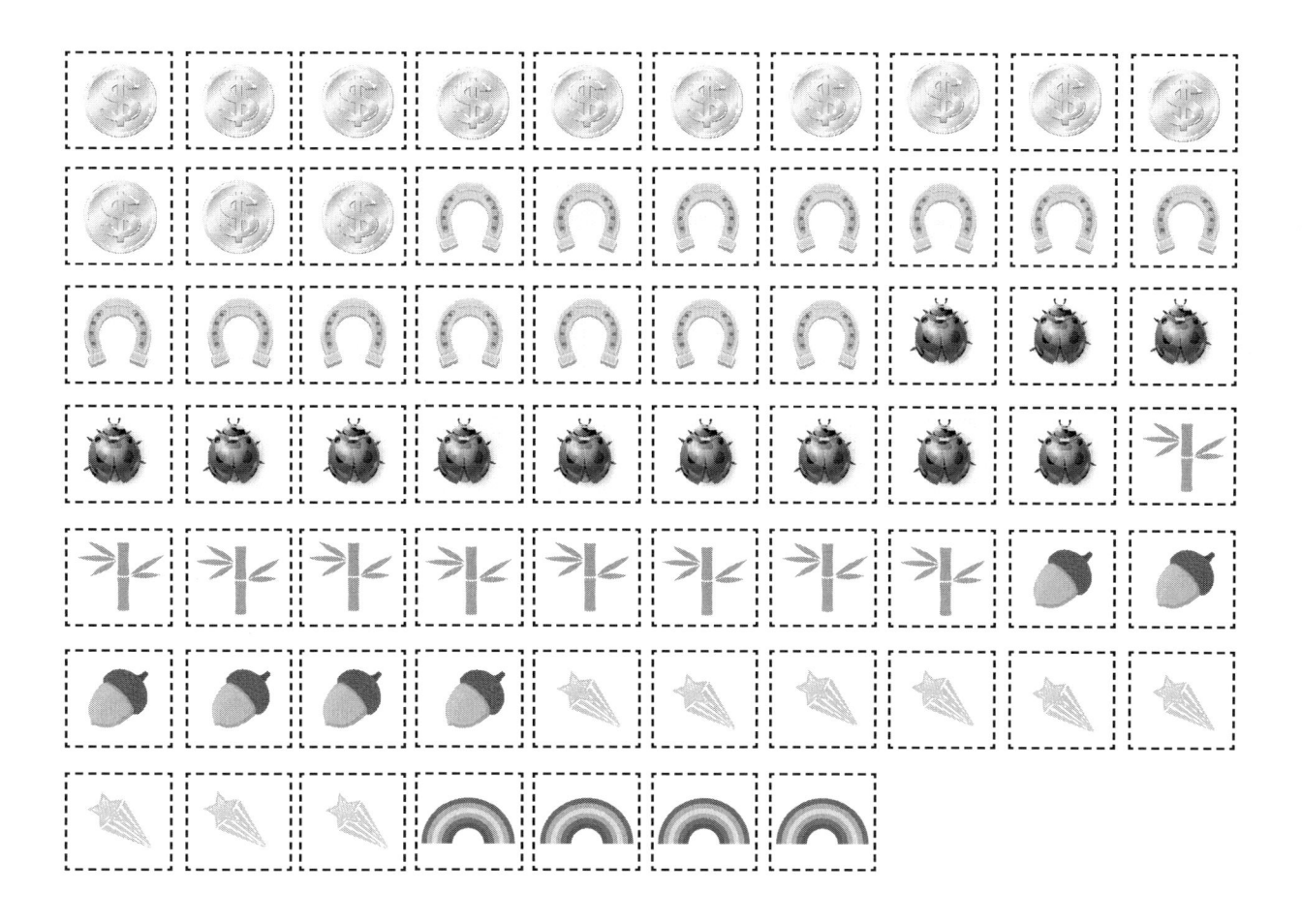

3.2 Write Addition Sentences

Name: _____ Date: _____

Practice: Find the Missing Whole by Adding

Follow the directions below to play the game. Make sure to use the game cards, game board, and worksheet to play.

1. Cut out the subtraction sentences on the dotted lines so that you have 25 subtraction cards. Shuffle the cards and set aside.
2. Flip the cards face down. Then flip the first card so that you can read the subtraction sentence.
3. Match the number on the card with the number on the recording page. Find the missing whole by completing the part-part-whole chart, and writing the addition sentence that helps you find the whole.
4. After you've found the whole, find that same number on your game board. Then cover it with a counter.
5. Win the game by covering 5 wholes in a row! **This means you may not need to find the missing whole of every subtraction sentence.**

Example:

Subtraction Card

1.
___ − 12 = 8

Game Board

13	18	14	16	17
17	(20)			16
6	17	14	10	15
20	15	9	16	15
19	13	20	13	17

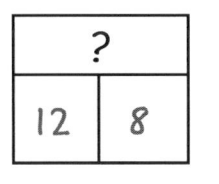

1.		
? − 12 = 8	? / 12 / 8	12 + 8 = (20)

4.3 Missing Numbers

250

Next page

Cut out the subtraction sentences on the dotted lines so that you have 25 subtraction cards. Shuffle the cards and set aside.

1. ___ − 12 = 8	2. ___ − 5 = 10	3. ___ − 4 = 2	4. ___ − 11 = 6	5. ___ − 6 = 8
6. ___ − 10 = 9	7. ___ − 4 = 16	8. ___ − 7 = 11	9. ___ − 7 = 9	10. ___ − 5 = 10
11. ___ − 6 = 7	12. ___ − 7 = 10	13. ___ − 14 = 2	14. ___ − 11 = 7	15. ___ − 5 = 9
16. ___ − 6 = 10	17. ___ − 13 = 4	18. ___ − 5 = 8	19. ___ − 10 = 3	20. ___ − 1 = 10
21. ___ − 9 = 8	22. ___ − 4 = 5	23. ___ − 10 = 10	24. ___ − 3 = 12	25. ___ − 8 = 2

4.3 Missing Numbers

Next page

This is your game board. Do not cut these squares. These numbers represent the missing wholes. You can cover each number with a counter once you complete the problem and find the missing whole. Get 5 in a row to win!

13	18	14	16	17
17	20	11	18	16
6	17	14	10	15
20	15	9	16	15
19	13	20	13	17

4.3 Missing Numbers

Next page

This is your worksheet. Find the missing whole by adding the parts together. Once you know the whole, cover that same number with a counter on your gameboard. 5 counters in a row wins!

1.	? − 12 = 8	? / ☐ ☐	__ + __ = __
2.	? − 5 = 10	? / ☐ ☐	__ + __ = __
3.	? − 4 = 2	? / ☐ ☐	__ + __ = __
4.	? − 11 = 6	? / ☐ ☐	__ + __ = __
5.	? − 6 = 8	? / ☐ ☐	__ + __ = __
6.	? − 10 = 9	? / ☐ ☐	__ + __ = __
7.	? − 4 = 16	? / ☐ ☐	__ + __ = __

4.3 Missing Numbers

This is your worksheet. Find the missing whole by adding the parts together. Once you know the whole, cover that same number with a counter on your gameboard. 5 counters in a row wins!

8.	? − 7 = 11	?	__ + __ = __
9.	? − 7 = 9	?	__ + __ = __
10.	? − 5 = 10	?	__ + __ = __
11.	? − 6 = 7	?	__ + __ = __
12.	? − 7 = 10	?	__ + __ = __
13.	? − 14 = 2	?	__ + __ = __
14.	? − 11 = 7	?	__ + __ = __

4.3 Missing Numbers

Next page

This is your worksheet. Find the missing whole by adding the parts together. Once you know the whole, cover that same number with a counter on your gameboard. 5 counters in a row wins!

15.	? - 5 = 9	?	__ + __ = __
16.	? - 6 = 10	?	__ + __ = __
17.	? - 13 = 4	?	__ + __ = __
18.	? - 5 = 8	?	__ + __ = __
19.	? - 10 = 3	?	__ + __ = __
20.	? - 1 = 10	?	__ + __ = __
21.	? - 9 = 8	?	__ + __ = __

4.3 Missing Numbers

This is your worksheet. Find the missing whole by adding the parts together. Once you know the whole, cover that same number with a counter on your gameboard. 5 counters in a row wins!

22.	? - 4 = 5	?	__ + __ = __
23.	? - 10 = 10	?	__ + __ = __
24.	? - 3 = 12	?	__ + __ = __
25.	? - 8 = 2	?	__ + __ = __

4.3 Missing Numbers

Name: _____ Date: _____

Fact Families

This family is getting ready for a trip to Mars. Before they take off, we must help them build a rocket. You can help build the rocket by following these steps:

1. Use the numbers at the top of each rocket to create the fact families.

2. Cut out the rectangles next to each rocket. Place a dot of glue on each rocket where it is labeled "glue," and glue the rectangles down like a door over each math sentence on the rocket.

3. After your doors are glued down, cut out each rocket.

4. Glue each rocket to the sides of a tissue box.

Once you are finished with this activity, you will have built a rocket for the family!

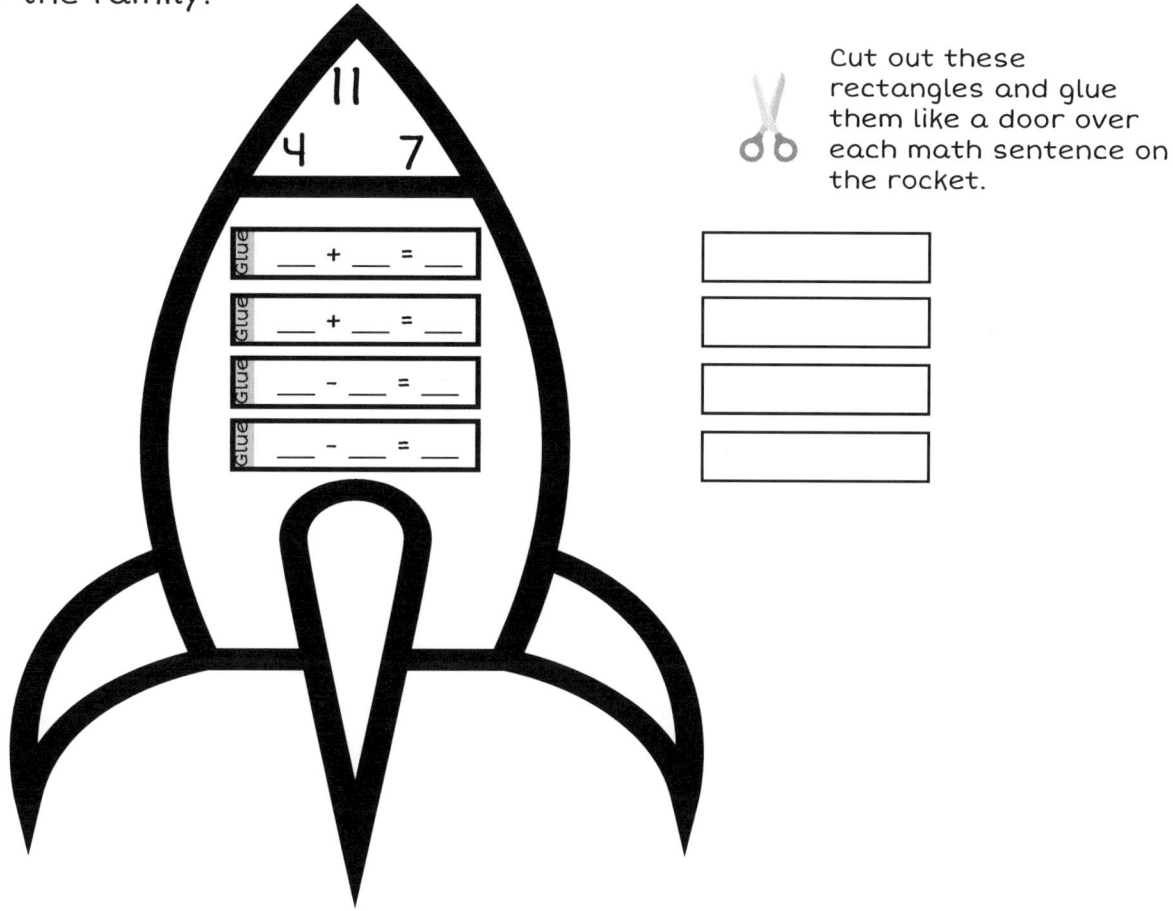

Rocket numbers: 11, 4, 7

___ + ___ = ___
___ + ___ = ___
___ − ___ = ___
___ − ___ = ___

Cut out these rectangles and glue them like a door over each math sentence on the rocket.

4.5 Fact Families

260

Next page

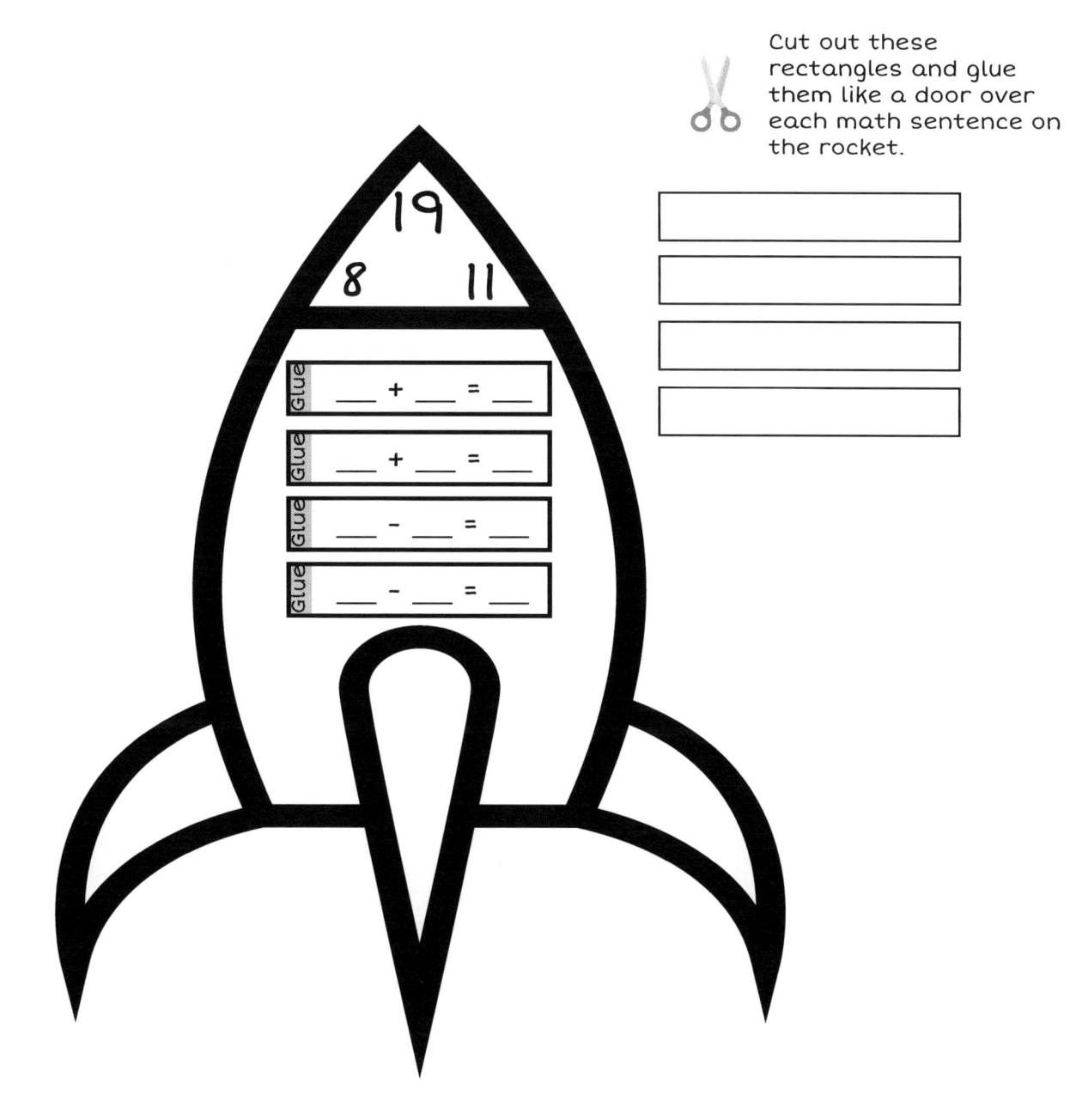

4.5 Fact Families

19
8 11

___ + ___ = ___
___ + ___ = ___
___ - ___ = ___
___ - ___ = ___

Cut out these rectangles and glue them like a door over each math sentence on the rocket.

262

Next page

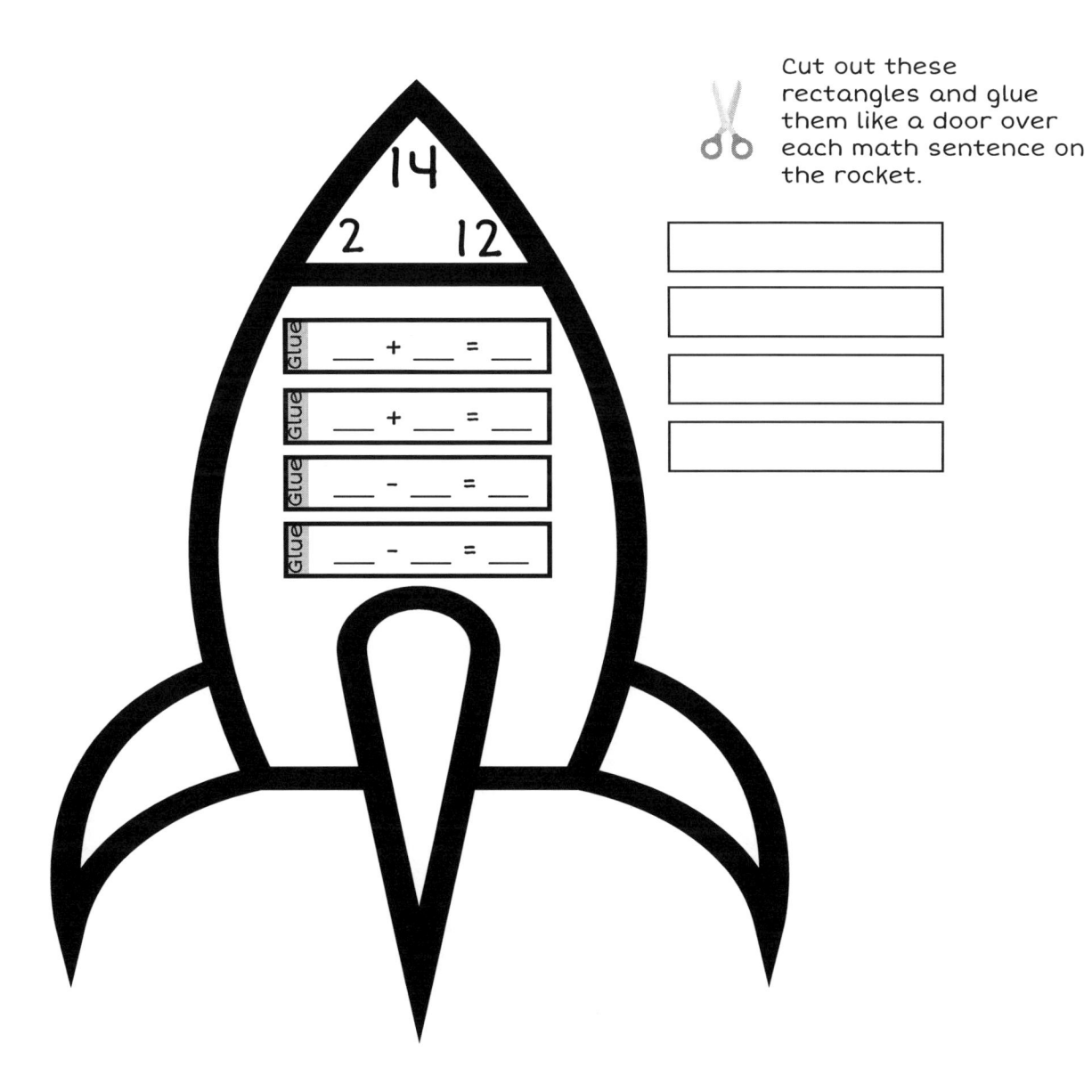

Cut out these rectangles and glue them like a door over each math sentence on the rocket.

14
2   12

___ + ___ = ___

___ + ___ = ___

___ - ___ = ___

___ - ___ = ___

4.5 Fact Families

264

Next page

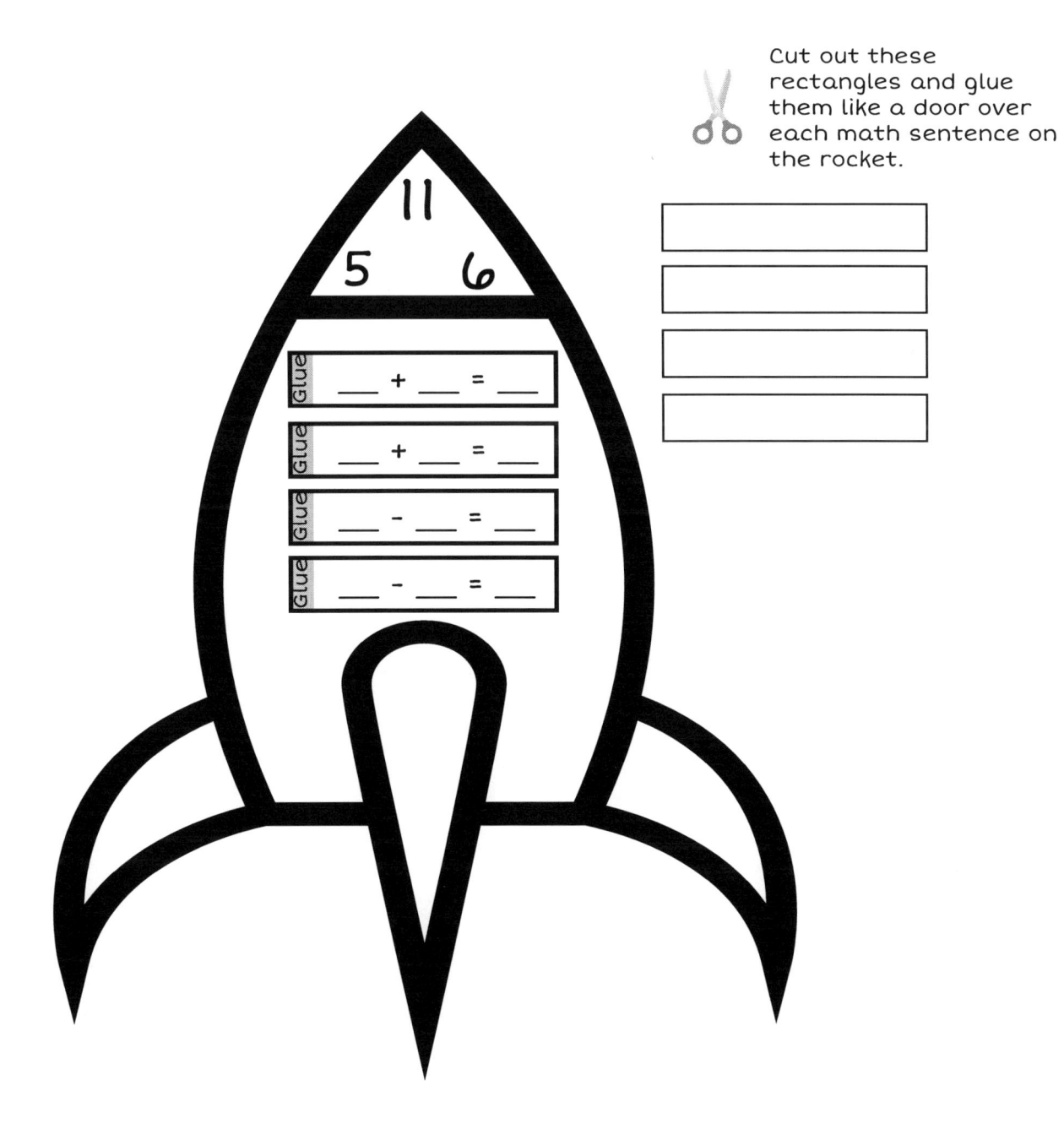

Cut out these rectangles and glue them like a door over each math sentence on the rocket.

11
5   6

Glue | ___ + ___ = ___
Glue | ___ + ___ = ___
Glue | ___ - ___ = ___
Glue | ___ - ___ = ___

4.5 Fact Families

266

Name: _____ Date: _____

Writing Numbers in Base-Ten Notation

Can you write three-digit numbers in base-ten notation?

1. Cut out all of the animals.
2. Glue the animals into each section of the place-value charts.
3. Write down the base-ten notation.

= one

= ten

= hundred

Example:

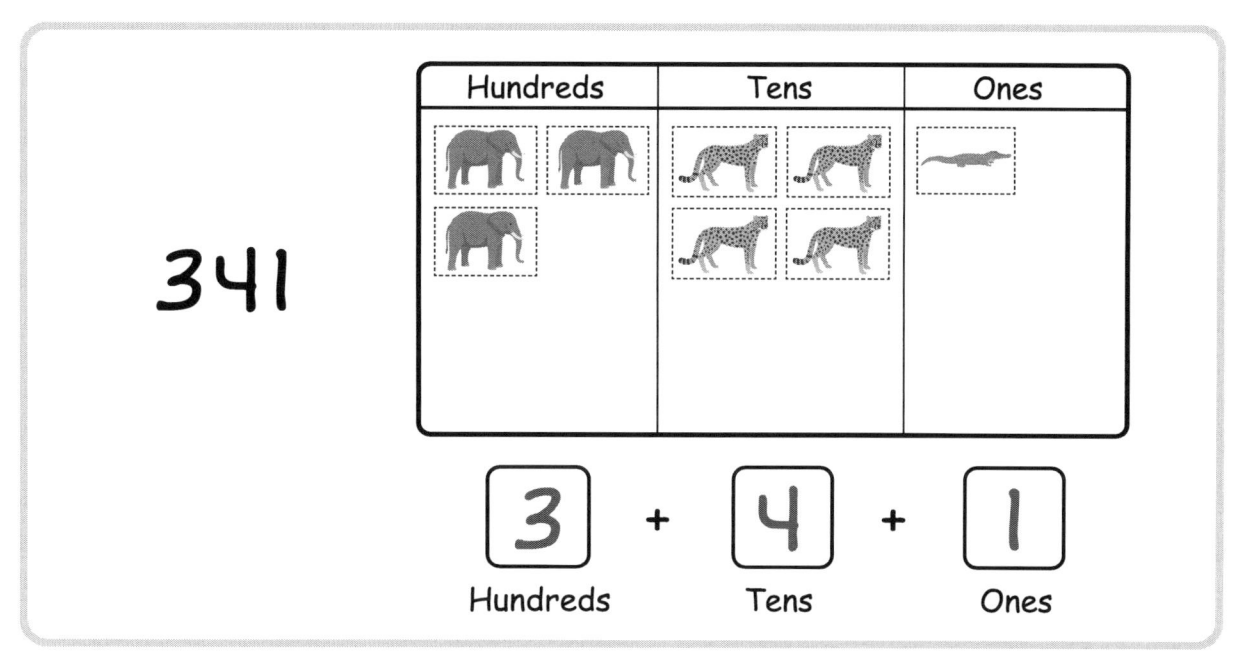

341

Hundreds	Tens	Ones

3 Hundreds + 4 Tens + 1 Ones

5.5 Numbers in Base-Ten Notation

268

Next page

235

Hundreds	Tens	Ones

☐ Hundreds + ☐ Tens + ☐ Ones

614

Hundreds	Tens	Ones

☐ Hundreds + ☐ Tens + ☐ Ones

5.5 Numbers in Base-Ten Notation

170

Hundreds	Tens	Ones

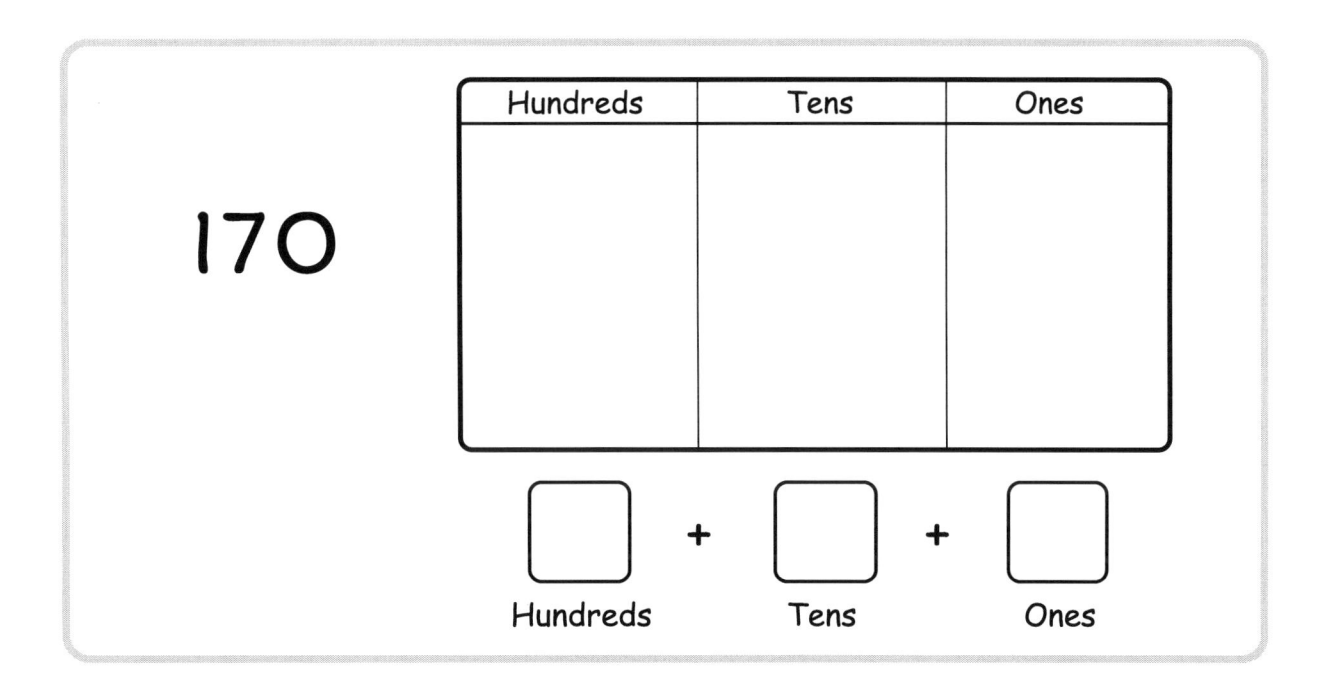

☐ Hundreds + ☐ Tens + ☐ Ones

231

Hundreds	Tens	Ones

☐ Hundreds + ☐ Tens + ☐ Ones

5.5 Numbers in Base-Ten Notation

405

Hundreds	Tens	Ones

☐ + ☐ + ☐
Hundreds   Tens   Ones

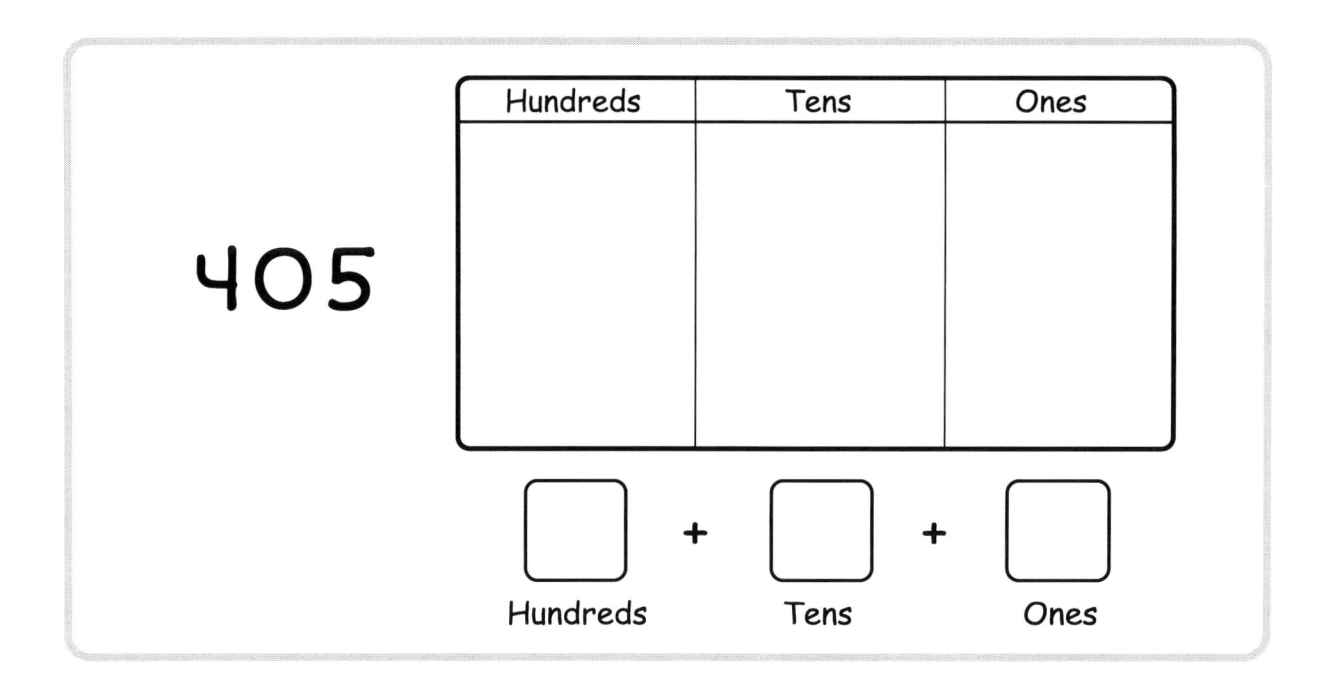

Challenge: The base-ten notation for the number 341 is **3 hundreds + 4 tens + 1 one**. Which of the following is another way to write 341? Circle the answer you think is correct. Then, write or draw to explain why you think the answer you chose is the right one!

a. 400 + 30 + 1

b. 100 + 40 + 3

c. 300 + 40 + 1

5.5 Numbers in Base-Ten Notation

Hundreds	Tens	Ones

5.5 Numbers in Base-Ten Notation

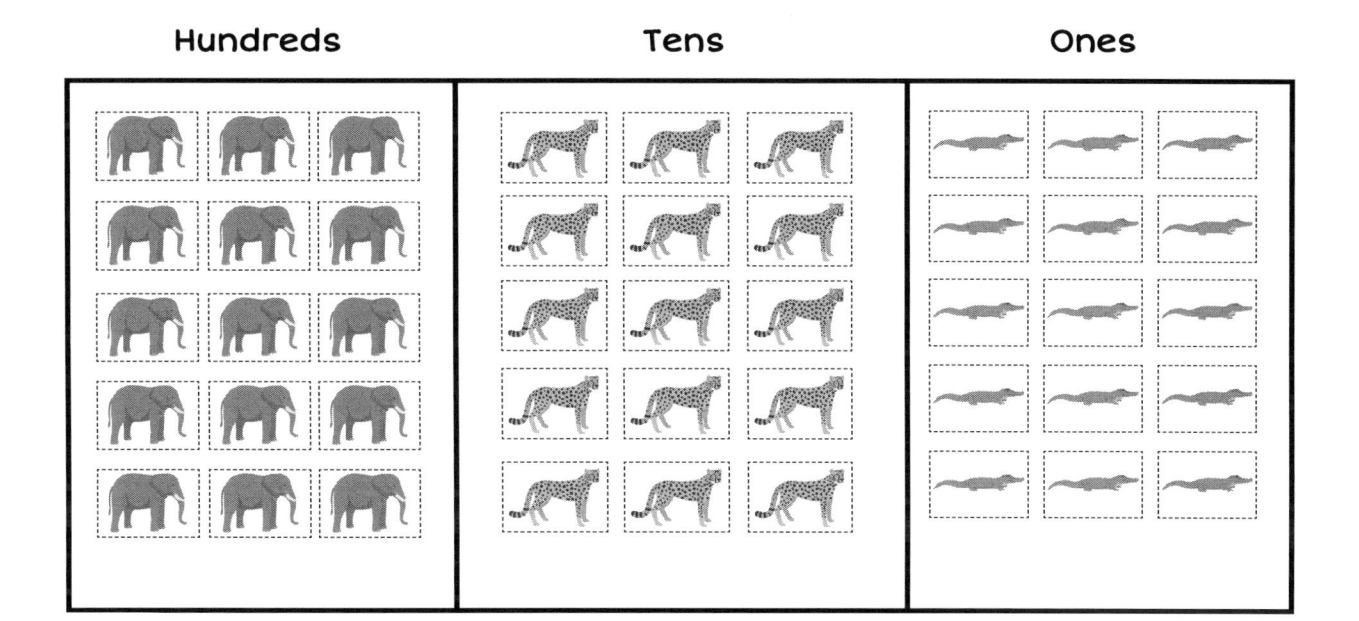

Name: _____   Date: _____

Number Structure Matching Game

Cut out the base-ten block pictures and glue them to their matching numbers.

517	874	149	496	705
320	258	942	371	625

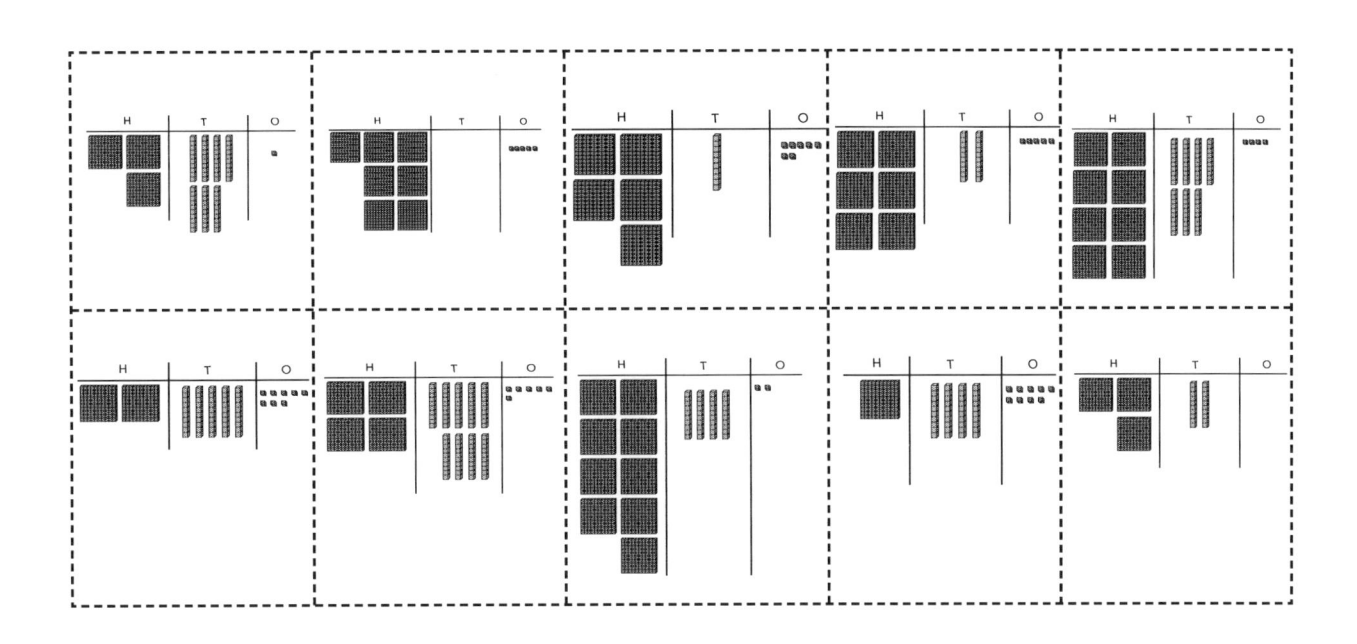

6.2 Number Structure (Hundreds)

Name: _____ Date: _____

Place-Value Number Cards

Cut out the cards on the dotted lines. Follow the directions in the lesson to use these cards to practice showing the hundreds, tens, and ones places in three-digit numbers. Then, use these numbers to complete the Make and Compare Numbers worksheet.

0	0	0	0	0	0	0	0	0	0	0
1	1	1	1	1	1	1	1	1	1	1
2	2	2	2	2	2	2	2	2	2	2
3	3	3	3	3	3	3	3	3	3	3
4	4	4	4	4	4	4	4	4	4	4
5	5	5	5	5	5	5	5	5	5	5
6	6	6	6	6	6	6	6	6	6	6
7	7	7	7	7	7	7	7	7	7	7
8	8	8	8	8	8	8	8	8	8	8
9	9	9	9	9	9	9	9	9	9	9

6.5 Problem Solving Strategy: Reasoning

Name: _____ Date: _____

What's the Number?

Cut out the cards found on the last page of this worksheet. Then glue the cards under each matching set of base-ten blocks.

Example:

Standard Form	Word Form
931	Nine hundred thirty-one

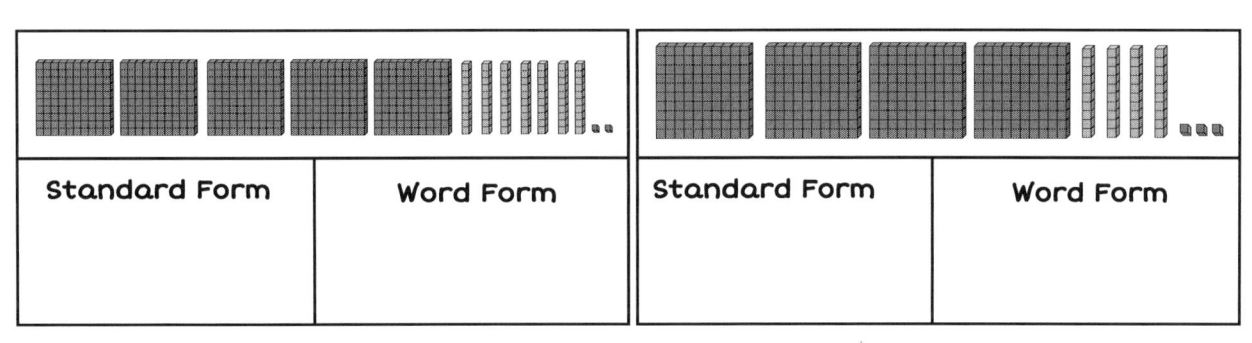

Standard Form	Word Form

Standard Form	Word Form

Standard Form	Word Form

Standard Form	Word Form

Standard Form	Word Form

Standard Form	Word Form

Standard Form	Word Form

7.3 Place Value to 1,000

278

Next page

Standard Form	Word Form

Standard Form	Word Form

Standard Form	Word Form

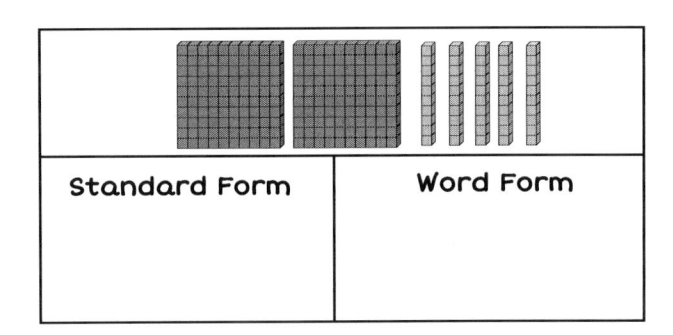

7.3 Place Value to 1,000

250	389	967	194
605	572	836	443
1,000	798	One hundred ninety-four	Nine hundred sixty-seven
Four hundred forty-three	Two hundred fifty	Eight hundred thirty-six	One thousand
Three hundred eighty-nine	Five hundred seventy-two	Six hundred five	Seven hundred ninety-eight

7.3 Place Value to 1,000

Name: _____ Date: _____

Round to the Nearest 10, 100, 1,000

Cut out the numbers below and glue them in the table.

Number	Round to the Nearest 10	Round to the Nearest 100	Round to the Nearest 1,000
6,253		6,300	
1,772			2,000
4,294	4,290		
3,329		3,300	

1,770	4,300	3,000	6,250
6,000	1,800	3,330	4,000

8.4 Round to the Nearest 10, 100, or 1,000

Name: _____ Date: _____

Place-Value Charts

Follow the directions in the lesson to add a one-digit number to a two-digit number using this place-value chart and ten frames.

Tens	Ones

Cut out these ten frames to use on the place-value chart.

9.4 Add a Two-Digit Number to a One-Digit Number

284

Name: _____ Date: _____

Place-Value Chart

Follow the directions in the lesson to use this place-value chart to find the sum of 42 + 46 using counters.

Tens	Ones
____	____

10.2 Rewrite Two-Digit Addition

286

Next page

Place-Value Number Cards

Cut out the cards on the dotted lines. Use these number cards and the Place-Value Chart on the previous page to help you complete the Number Card Addition worksheet.

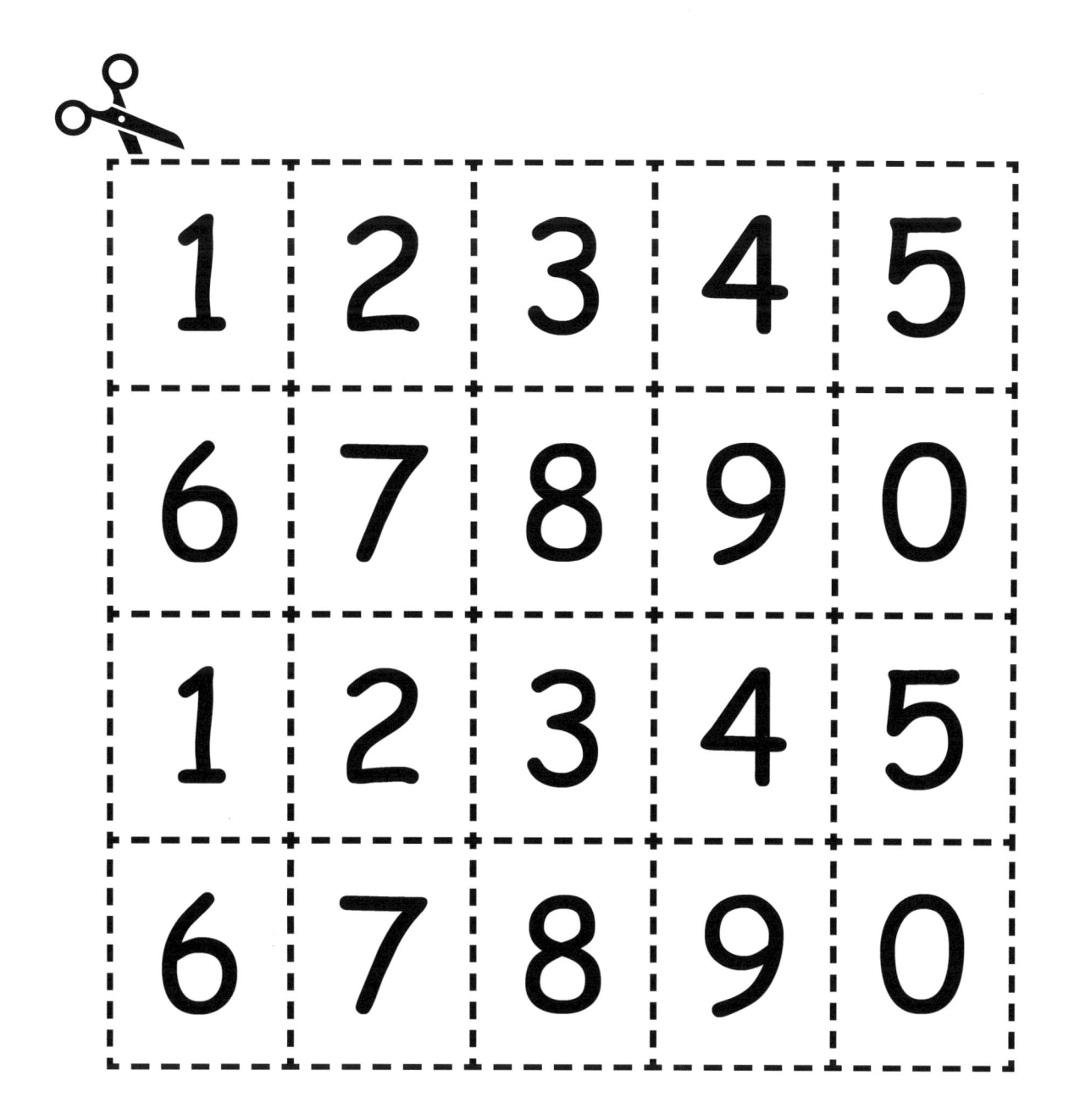

1	2	3	4	5
6	7	8	9	0
1	2	3	4	5
6	7	8	9	0

10.2 Rewrite Two-Digit Addition

Name: _____ Date: _____

Two-Digit Addition Without Regrouping

Cut out the number cards on the next page. Use the number cards and this page by following the directions in your lesson to find the missing addend.

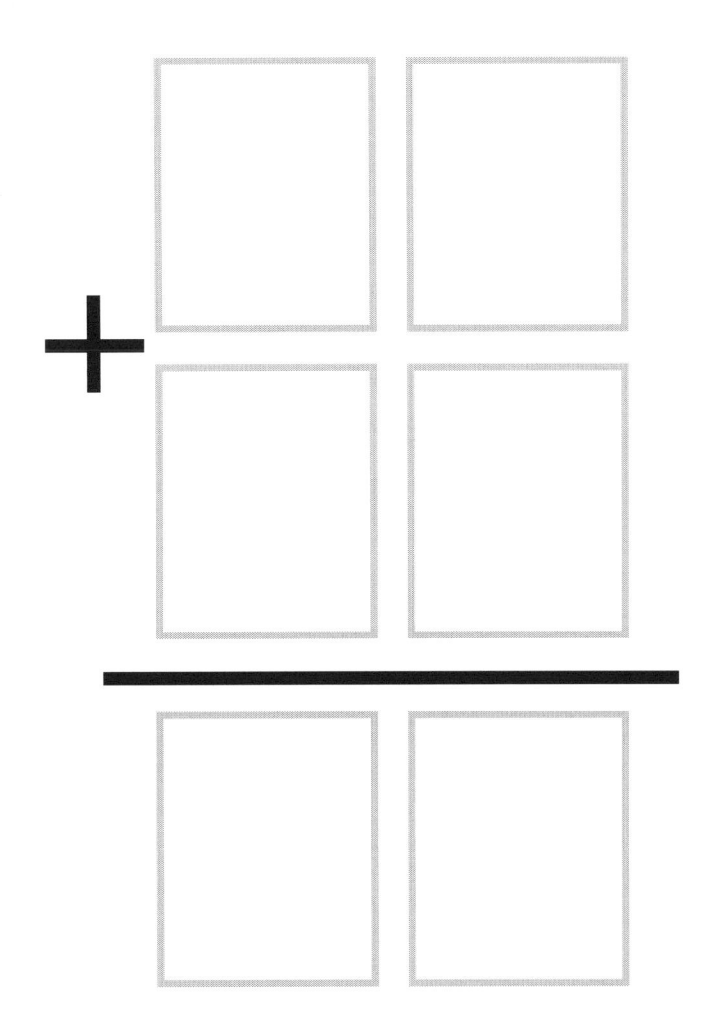

10.3 Two-Digit Addition Without Regrouping

290

Next page

Place-Value Number Cards

Cut out the cards to help you find the missing addend.

1	2	3	4	5
6	7	8	9	0
1	2	3	4	5
6	7	8	9	0

Name: _____ Date: _____

Addition Page

Write the numbers you need and cut out the number cards on the next page. Use the number cards and this page by following the directions in your lesson to regroup and add.

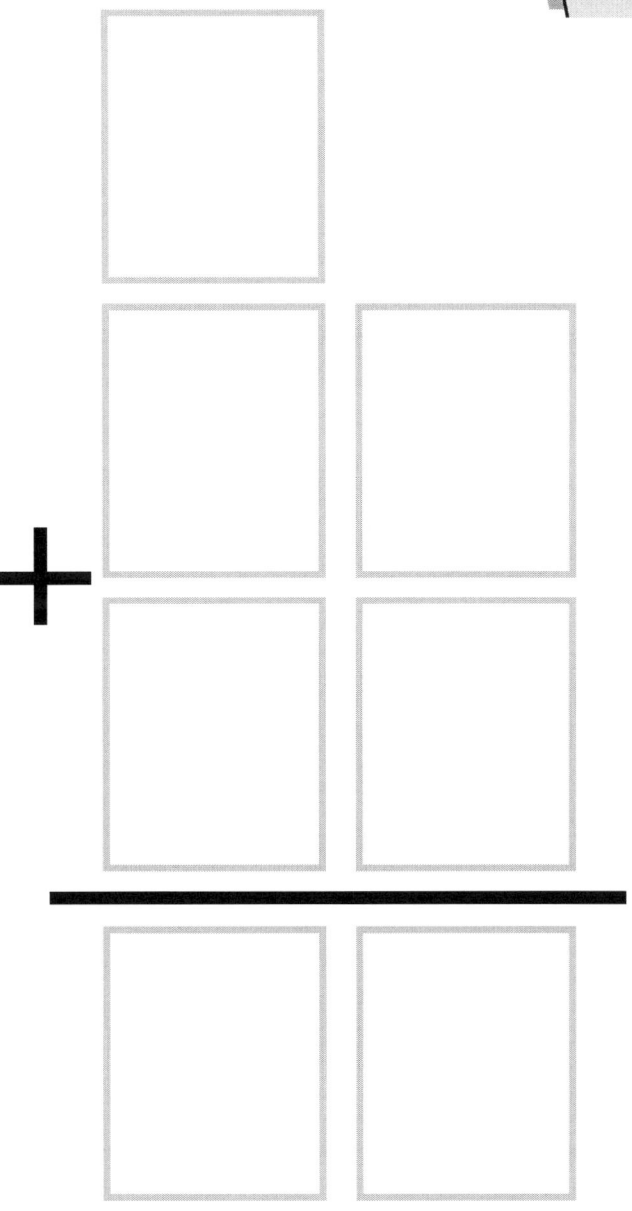

10.4 Two-Digit Addition With Regrouping

294

Next page

Write in the numbers you need. Cut out the cards to regroup and add.

10.4 Two-Digit Addition With Regrouping

Name: _____ Date: _____

Mentally Add Two-Digit Numbers

Cut out the cards on the dotted lines. Follow the directions in the lesson to use the cards to help you practice mental math.

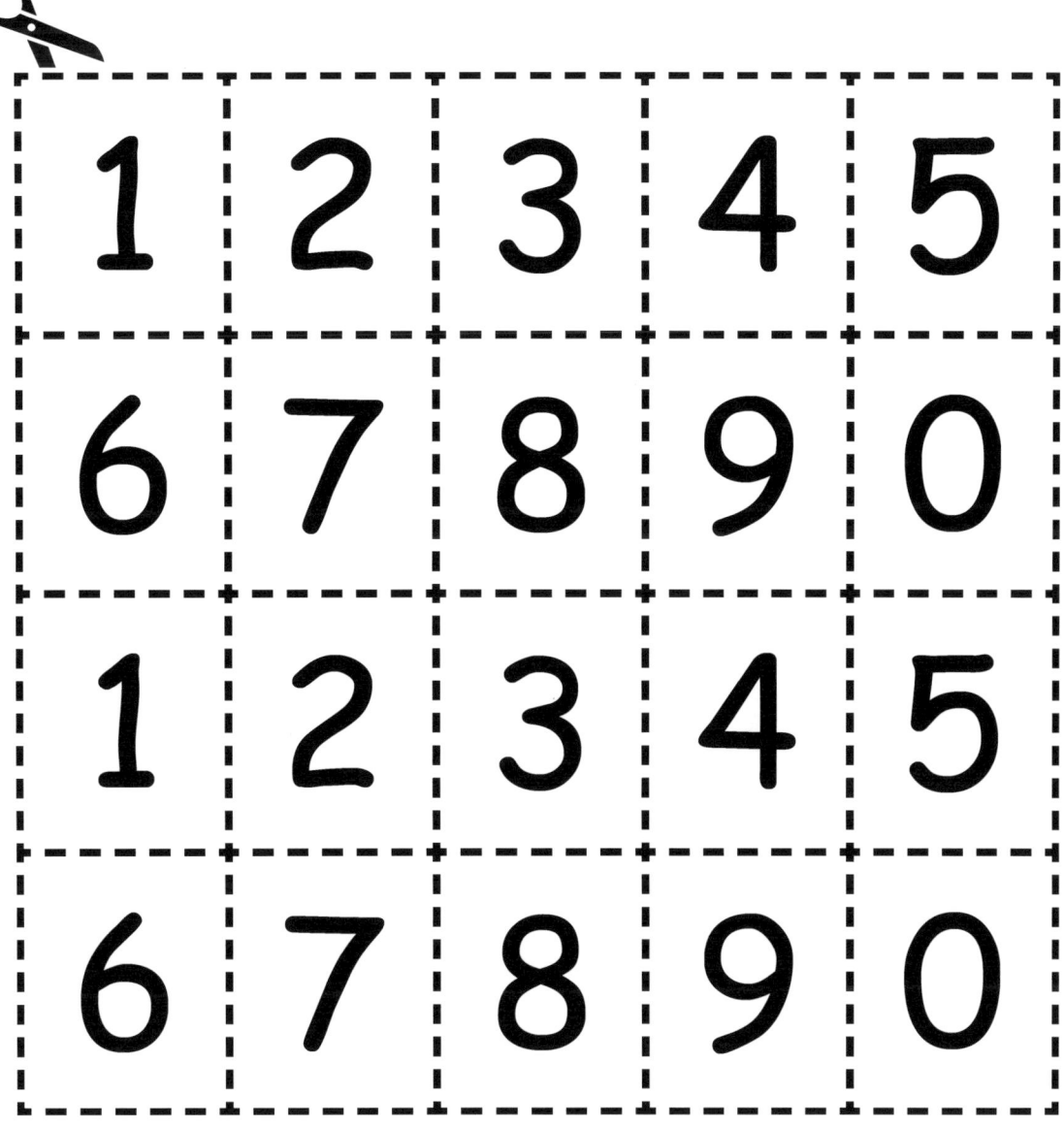

1	2	3	4	5
6	7	8	9	0
1	2	3	4	5
6	7	8	9	0

11.2 Mentally Add Two-Digit Numbers

Name: _____ Date: _____

Adding Sheet

Cut out the whole tens and one-digit number cards. Then, follow the directions in the lesson and use this page to help you add in parts using those number cards. Use the empty lines to help you add on your own.

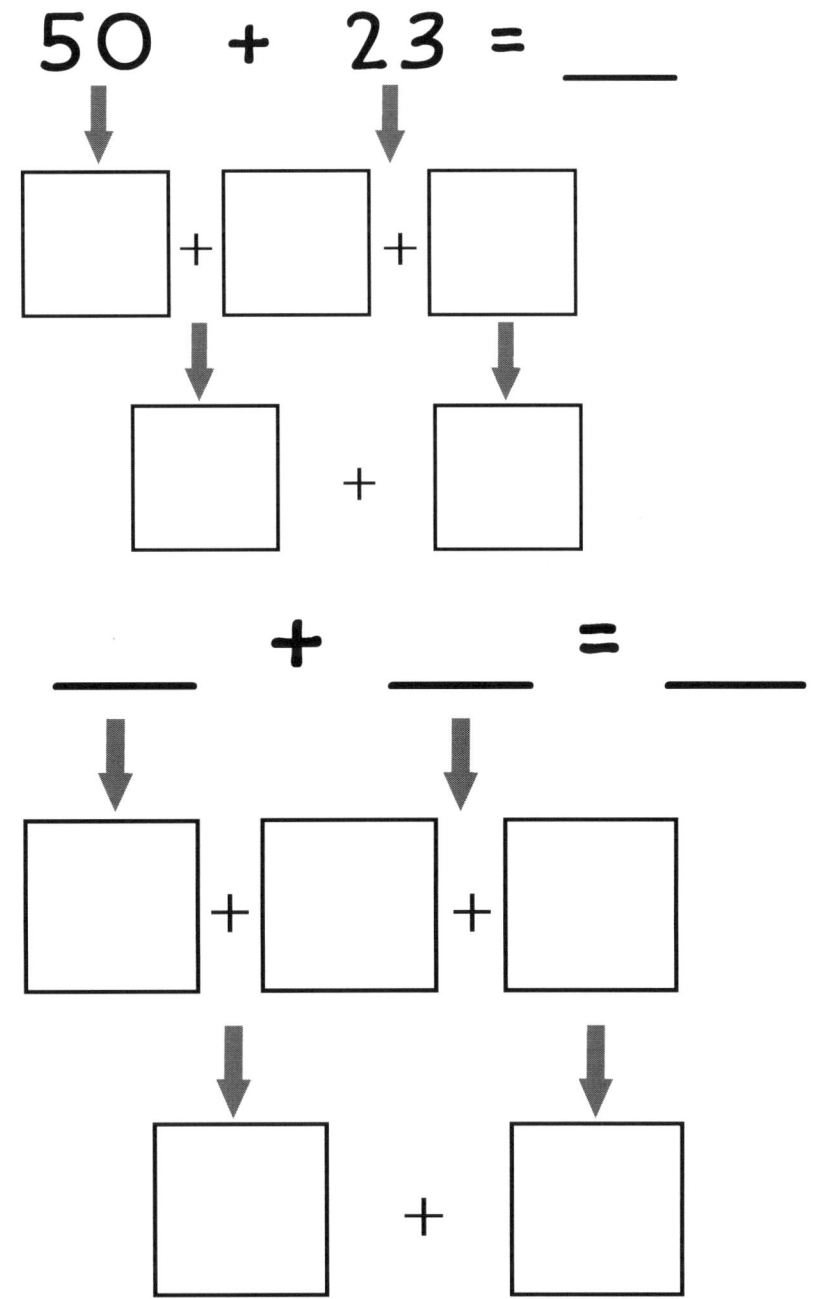

50 + 23 = ___

____ + ____ = ____

11.3 Add in Parts

300

Next page

Whole-Ten Tiles

Cut out the whole tens and one-digit numbers. You will need to use them on the adding sheet!

1	2	3	4	5	6	7
8	9	0	10	20	30	40
50	60	70	80	90		

11.3 Add in Parts

Name: _____ Date: _____

Adding Sheet

Cut out the whole tens and one-digit number cards. Then, follow the directions in the lesson and use this page to help you add in parts using those number cards. Use the empty lines to help you add on your own.

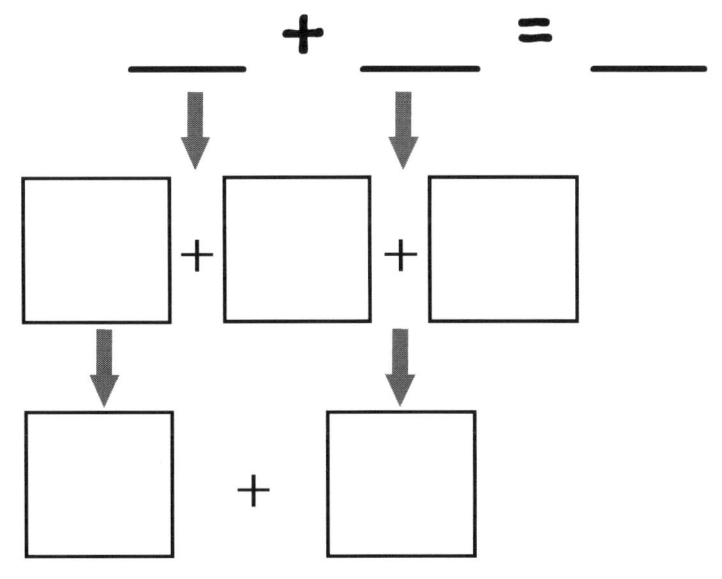

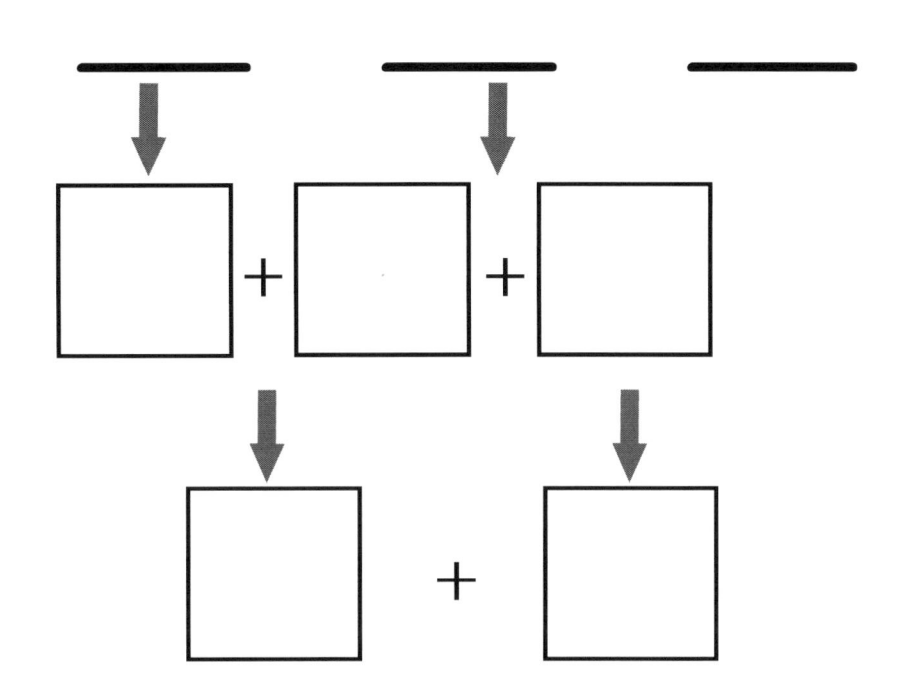

___ + ___ = ___

11.4 Apply the Add in Parts Strategy

304

Next page

Whole-Ten Tiles

Cut out the whole tens and one-digit numbers. You will need to use them on the adding sheet!

1	2	3	4	5	6	7
8	9	0	10	20	30	40
50	60	70	80	90	10	20
30	40	50	60	70	80	90

11.4 Apply the Add in Parts Strategy

Name: _____ Date: _____

Adding Page

Cut out the number cards. Then, follow the directions in the lesson and use this page to help you add four numbers using those number cards.

+

12.3 Add Four Numbers

308

Next page

Number Cards

Cut out the cards to add four numbers.

1	2	3	4	5	6
7	8	9	0	1	2
3	4	5	6	7	8
9	0	1	2	3	4
5	6	7	8	9	0

12.3 Add Four Numbers

Name: _____ Date: _____

Number Line

Cut out the turkey to use with the number line. Then, follow the directions in the lesson and use this page to help you find a missing addend.

___ + ___
Aiden's Food

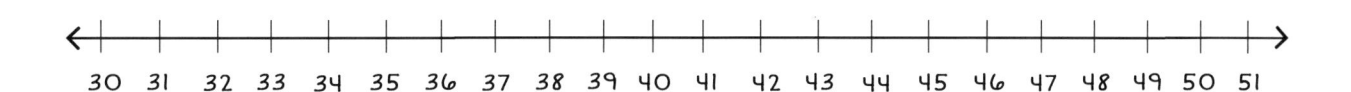

=

___ + ___
Sophia's Food

←|—|—|—|—|—|—|—|—|—|—|—|—|—|—|—|—|—|—|—|—|—|→
30 31 32 33 34 35 36 37 38 39 40 41 42 43 44 45 46 47 48 49 50 51

12.5 Find the Number

Name: _____ Date: _____

Number Line

Cut out the microscope to use with the number line. Then, follow the directions in the lesson and use this page to help you find the difference.

49 - 23 = ☐

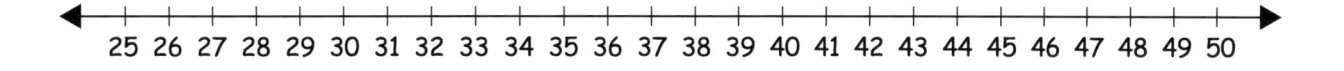

25 26 27 28 29 30 31 32 33 34 35 36 37 38 39 40 41 42 43 44 45 46 47 48 49 50

13.3 Subtract From a Two-Digit Number using a Number Line

314

Name: _____ Date: _____

Place-Value Charts

Cut out the number cards to use in the place-value chart. Then, follow the directions in the lesson and use this page to find the difference of 59 - 13.

Tens	Ones

14.2 Rewrite Two-Digit Subtraction

Next page

Place-Value Number Cards

Cut out the cards to subtract two-digit numbers. You will use these cards to show the tens and ones places on a place-value chart.

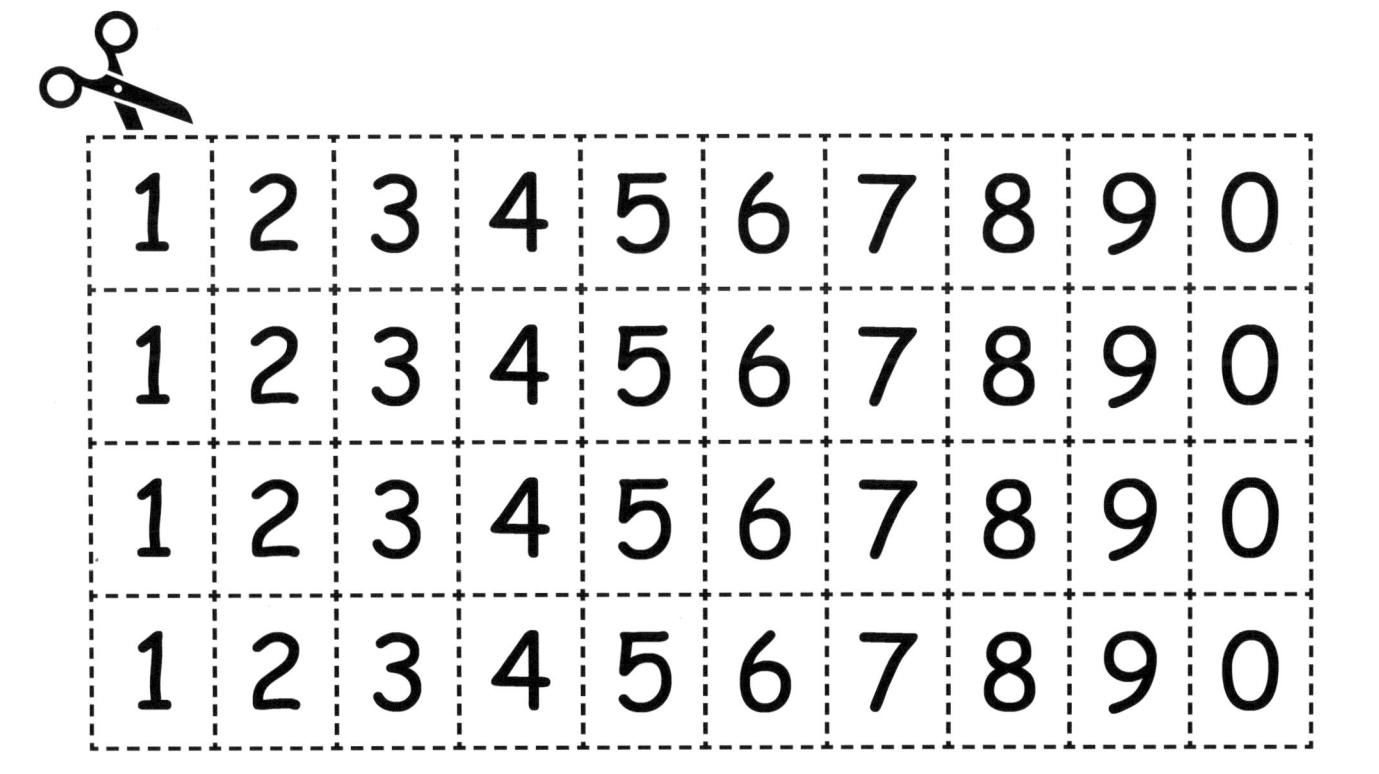

1	2	3	4	5	6	7	8	9	0
1	2	3	4	5	6	7	8	9	0
1	2	3	4	5	6	7	8	9	0
1	2	3	4	5	6	7	8	9	0

14.2 Rewrite Two-Digit Subtraction

Name: _____ Date: _____

Two-Digit Subtraction Without Regrouping

Cut out the number cards. Then, follow the directions in the lesson and use this page to help you find the missing part.

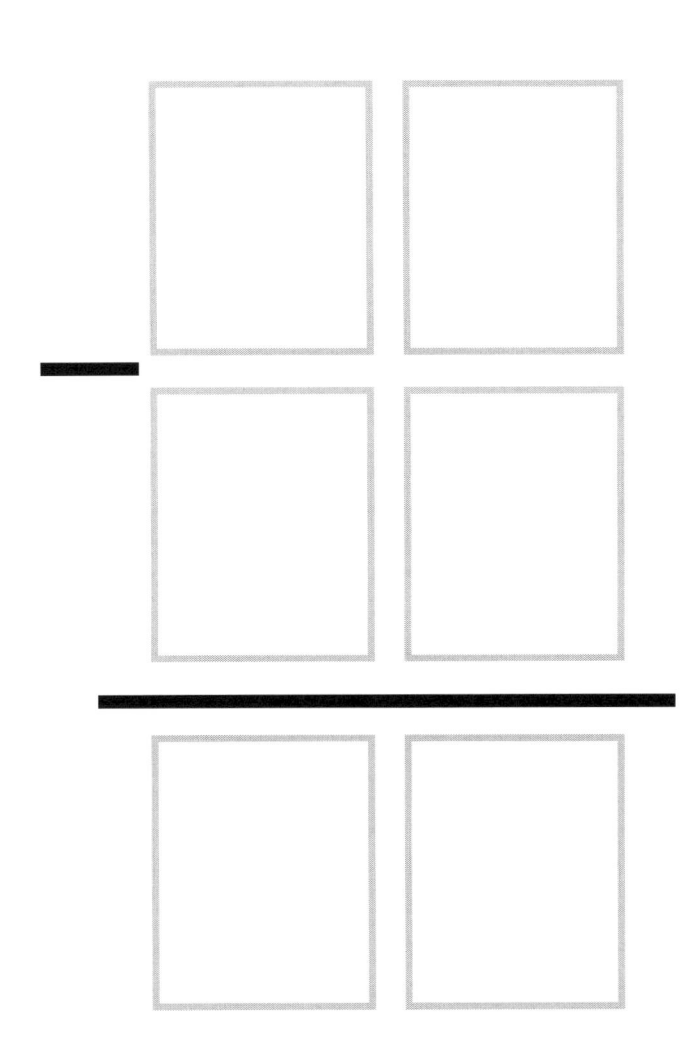

14.3 Two-Digit Subtraction Without Regrouping

Place-Value Number Cards

Cut out the cards to subtract two-digit numbers. You will use these cards to show the tens and ones places on a place-value chart.

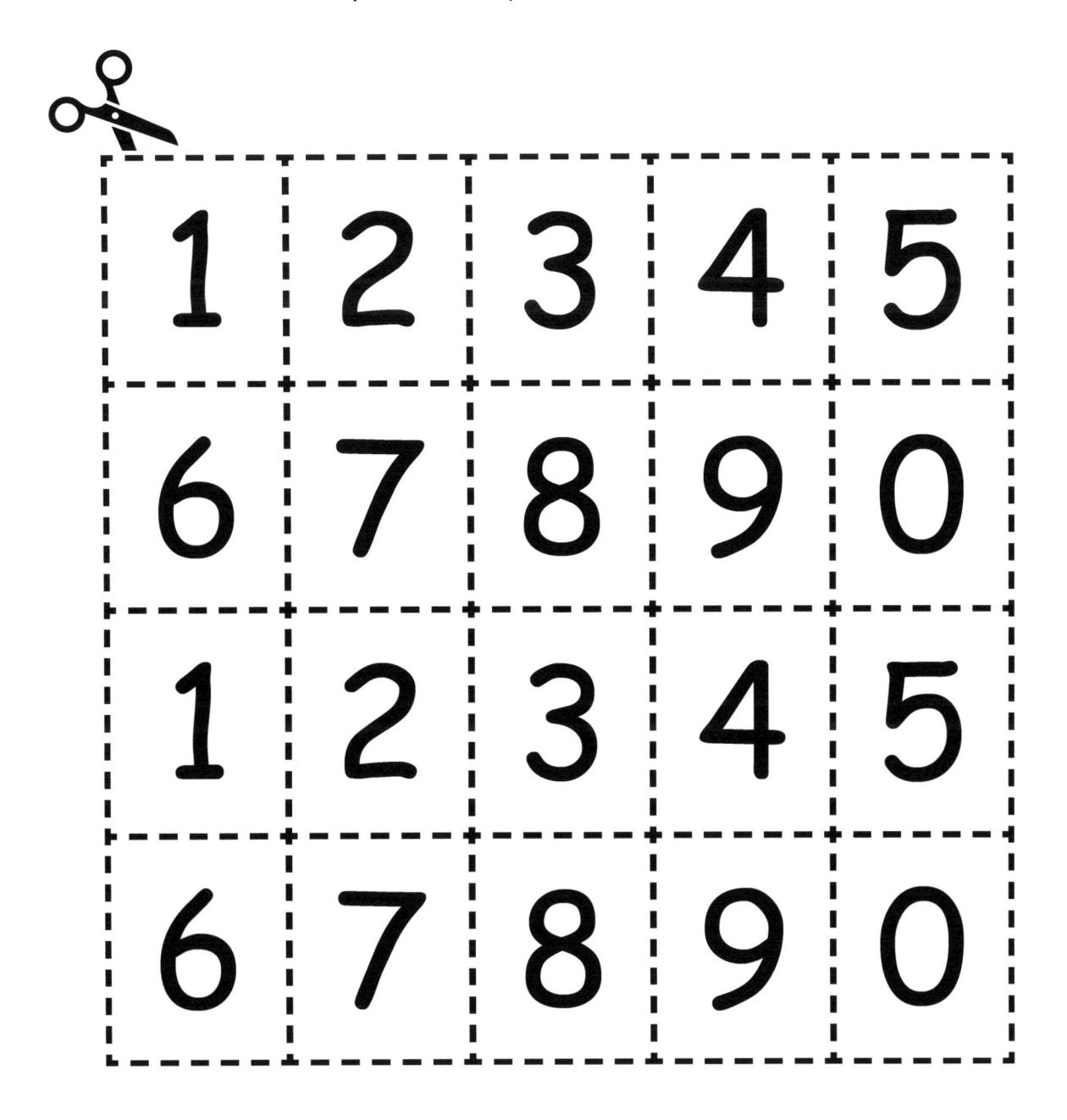

1	2	3	4	5
6	7	8	9	0
1	2	3	4	5
6	7	8	9	0

14.3 Two-Digit Subtraction Without Regrouping

Name: _____ Date: _____

Fact-Family Subtraction

Follow the directions on the next page. Then fill out the subtraction sentences in the middle of the fact-family triangle below.

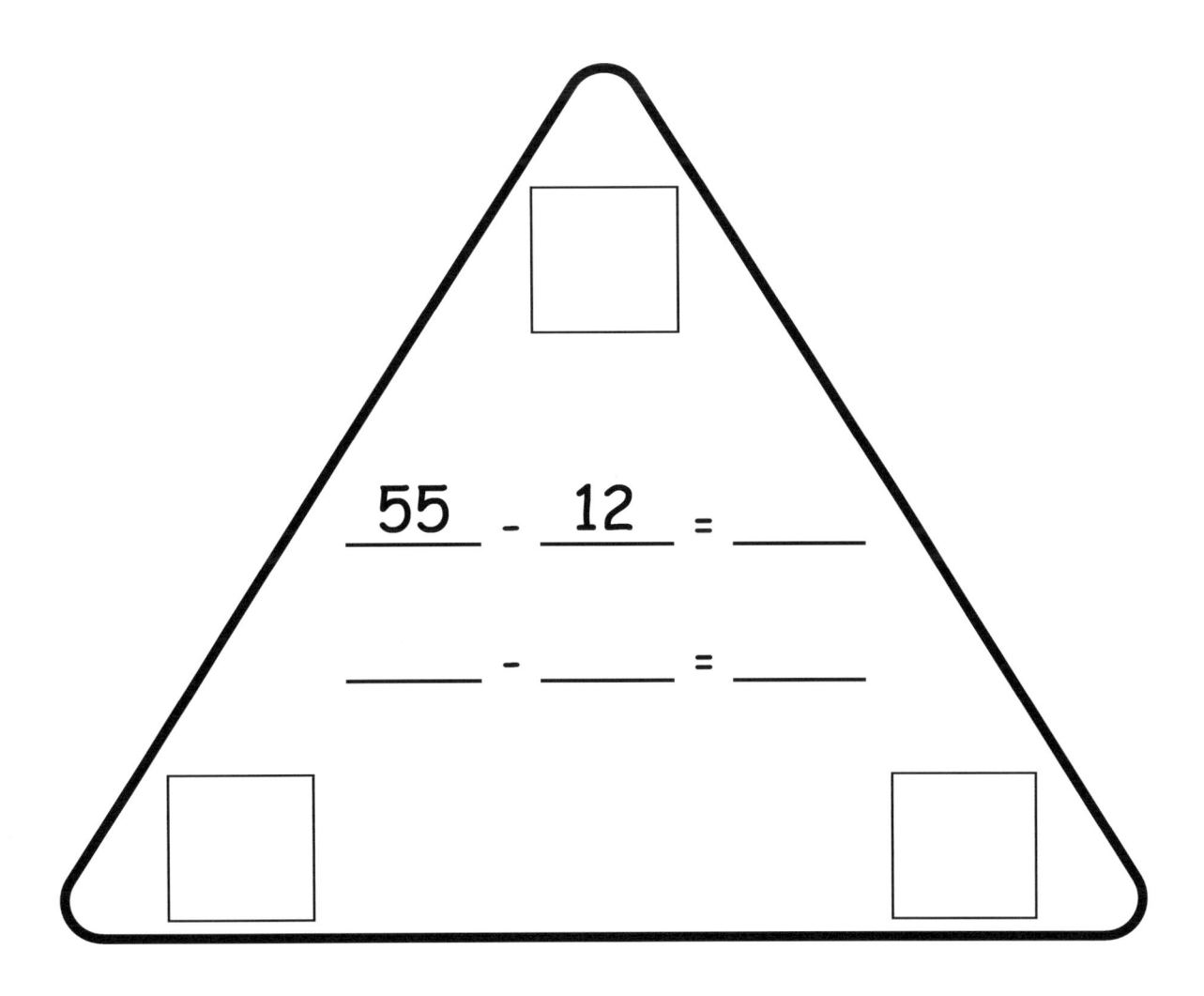

__55__ - __12__ = ____

____ - ____ = ____

15.1 Two-Digit Fact Families

324

Next page

Fact-Family Tiles

Where in the triangle do these numbers go?

1. Solve the first subtraction sentence.
2. Write the difference on the line.
3. Cut out the tiles. Put them on the triangle!

Hint: The whole goes at the top of the triangle. The parts go at the bottom of the triangle.

✂ | 55 | - | 12 | = | ___ |

15.1 Two-Digit Fact Families

Name: _____ Date: _____

Subtracting Page

Cut out the wreath cookie. Then, follow the directions in the lesson and use this page to help you subtract in parts.

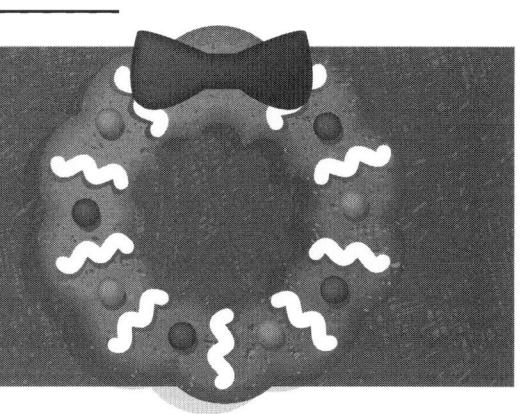

84 - 52 = ___

84 - ☐ = ☐

☐ - ☐ = ☐

15.3 Take Apart Tens to Subtract 328

Name: _____ Date: _____

Write a Subtraction Sentence

Cut out the numbers below. Then use them to write a subtraction sentence that fits each story problem. Glue down the numbers when you are done!

Example:

There were 822 birds in a tree. 410 birds flew away. How many birds are left in the tree?

$\boxed{822} - \boxed{410} = \boxed{412}$ birds

1. There were 828 berries on a bush. A squirrel ate 315 berries. How many berries are left on the bush?

   $\boxed{} - \boxed{} = \boxed{}$ berries

2. Kendra made 672 cookies. She gave 250 cookies away to her friends. How many cookies does Kendra have left?

   $\boxed{} - \boxed{} = \boxed{}$ cookies

3. There were 967 cans of fruit and vegetables at the store. 627 of the cans were fruit. How many cans were vegetables?

   $\boxed{} - \boxed{} = \boxed{}$ cans

16.4 Write a Subtraction Sentence

Next page

4. Heidi made 599 holiday cards. She gave away 346 cards. How many cards does Heidi have left?

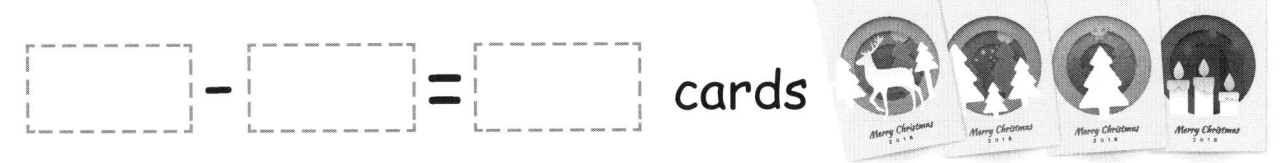

☐ − ☐ = ☐ cards

5. There were 775 brown and white horses at a ranch. 643 of the horses were brown. How many were white?

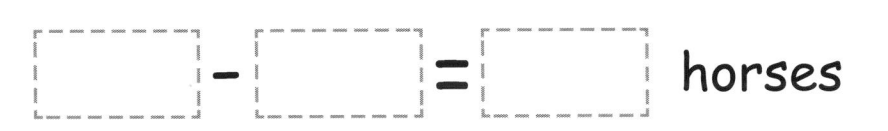

☐ − ☐ = ☐ horses

513	132	253	627	340
422	967	315	775	672
643	599	346	250	828

16.4 Write a Subtraction Sentence

332

Name: _____ Date: _____

Subtraction Page

Cut out the number cards below. Then, follow the directions in the lesson and use this page to help you subtract using the guess and check method.

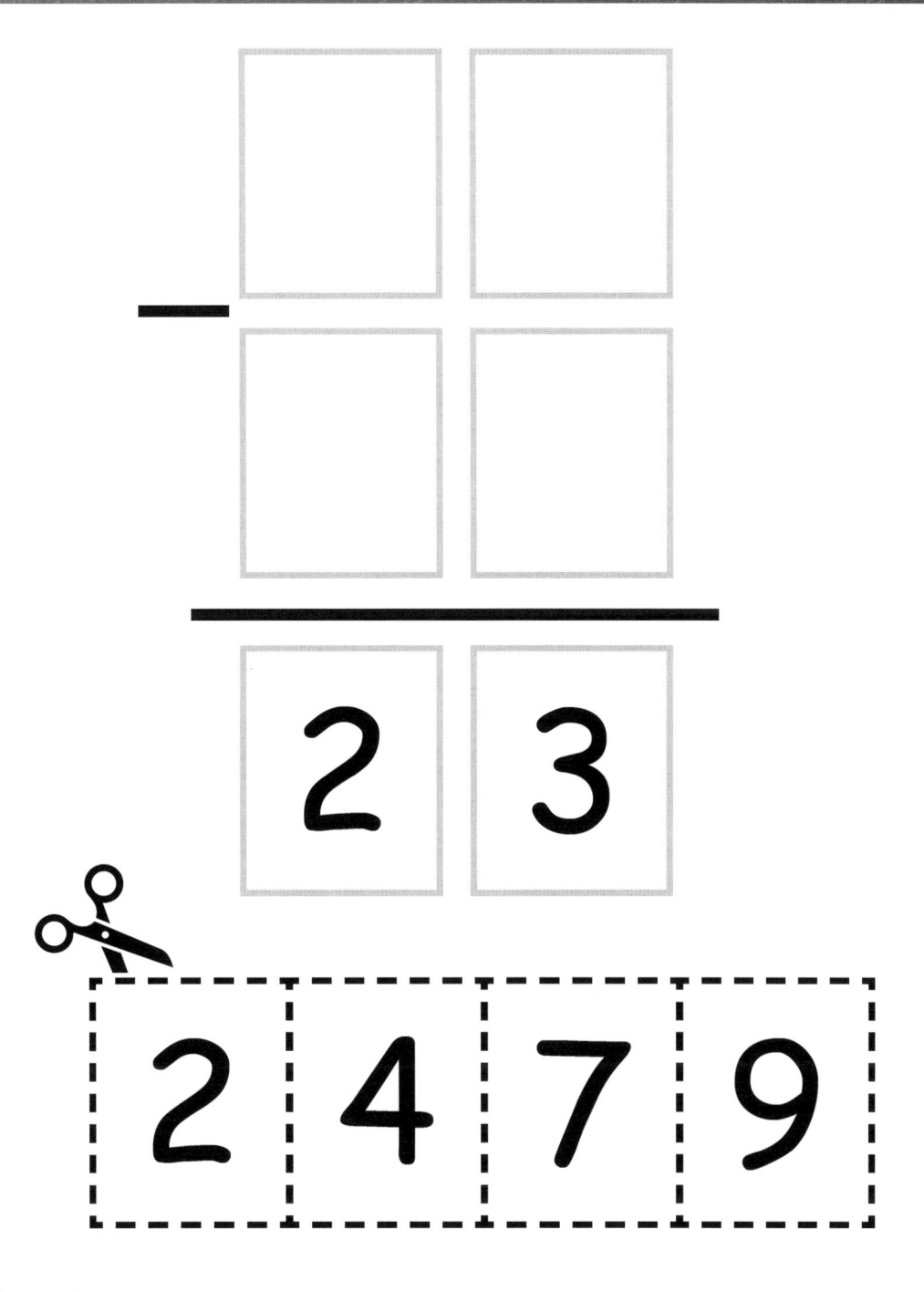

2 3

2 4 7 9

16.5 Find the Numbers 334

Extra Resources

The following pages are extra copies of tools you have learned to use in class. They may be helpful as you work through lessons.

Name: _____ Date: _____

Part-Part-Whole Chart

Use the chart below with your counters and walk through the steps given in the lesson.

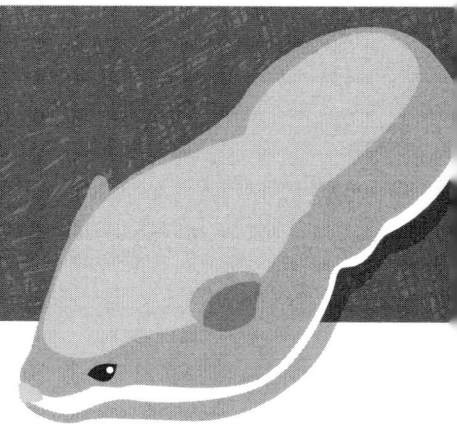

Part	Part
Whole	

Name: _____ Date: _____

Part-Part-Whole Chart

Use the chart below with your counters and walk through the steps given in the lesson.

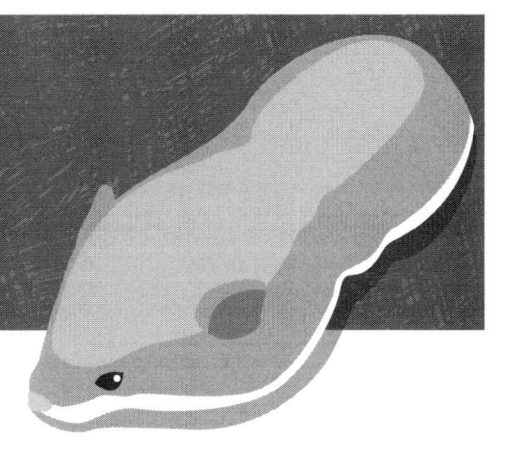

Part	Part
Whole	

Part-Part Whole Chart

Name: _____ Date: _____

Place-Value Chart
Use this place-value chart with your blocks to make numbers! Refer to the lesson for the numbers you need to make.

Tens	Ones

Tens Place-Value Chart

Name: _____ Date: _____

Place-Value Chart

Use this place-value chart with your blocks to make numbers! Refer to the lesson for the numbers you need to make.

Tens	Ones

Tens Place-Value Chart

Name: _____ Date: _____

Place-Value Charts
Use these two charts to compare numbers with your blocks!

10 100
1

Hundreds	Tens	Ones

Hundreds	Tens	Ones

Hundreds Place-Value Chart

Name: _____ Date: _____

Place-Value Charts
Use these two charts to compare numbers with your blocks!

Hundreds	Tens	Ones

Hundreds	Tens	Ones

Hundreds Place-Value Chart

Name: _____ Date: _____

Hundred Chart

Use this hundred chart with your counters to make number sequences!

100

1	2	3	4	5	6	7	8	9	10
11	12	13	14	15	16	17	18	19	20
21	22	23	24	25	26	27	28	29	30
31	32	33	34	35	36	37	38	39	40
41	42	43	44	45	46	47	48	49	50
51	52	53	54	55	56	57	58	59	60
61	62	63	64	65	66	67	68	69	70
71	72	73	74	75	76	77	78	79	80
81	82	83	84	85	86	87	88	89	90
91	92	93	94	95	96	97	98	99	100

Name: _____ Date: _____

Hundred Chart
Use this hundred chart with your counters to make number sequences!

1	2	3	4	5	6	7	8	9	10
11	12	13	14	15	16	17	18	19	20
21	22	23	24	25	26	27	28	29	30
31	32	33	34	35	36	37	38	39	40
41	42	43	44	45	46	47	48	49	50
51	52	53	54	55	56	57	58	59	60
61	62	63	64	65	66	67	68	69	70
71	72	73	74	75	76	77	78	79	80
81	82	83	84	85	86	87	88	89	90
91	92	93	94	95	96	97	98	99	100

Hundred Chart

Name: _____ Date: _____

Thousand Chart

Use the number patterns on this chart to count by 100s!

1000

10	20	30	40	50	60	70	80	90	100
110	120	130	140	150	160	170	180	190	200
210	220	230	240	250	260	270	280	290	300
310	320	330	340	350	360	370	380	390	400
410	420	430	440	450	460	470	480	490	500
510	520	530	540	550	560	570	580	590	600
610	620	630	640	650	660	670	680	690	700
710	720	730	740	750	760	770	780	790	800
810	820	830	840	850	860	870	880	890	900
910	920	930	940	950	960	970	980	990	1000

Name: _____   Date: _____

Thousand Chart
Use the number patterns on this chart to count by 100s!

1000

10	20	30	40	50	60	70	80	90	100
110	120	130	140	150	160	170	180	190	200
210	220	230	240	250	260	270	280	290	300
310	320	330	340	350	360	370	380	390	400
410	420	430	440	450	460	470	480	490	500
510	520	530	540	550	560	570	580	590	600
610	620	630	640	650	660	670	680	690	700
710	720	730	740	750	760	770	780	790	800
810	820	830	840	850	860	870	880	890	900
910	920	930	940	950	960	970	980	990	1000

Thousand Chart

Name: _____ Date: _____

Fact-Family Triangle

Follow along in the lesson to learn how to use this fact-family triangle to create related addition sentences.

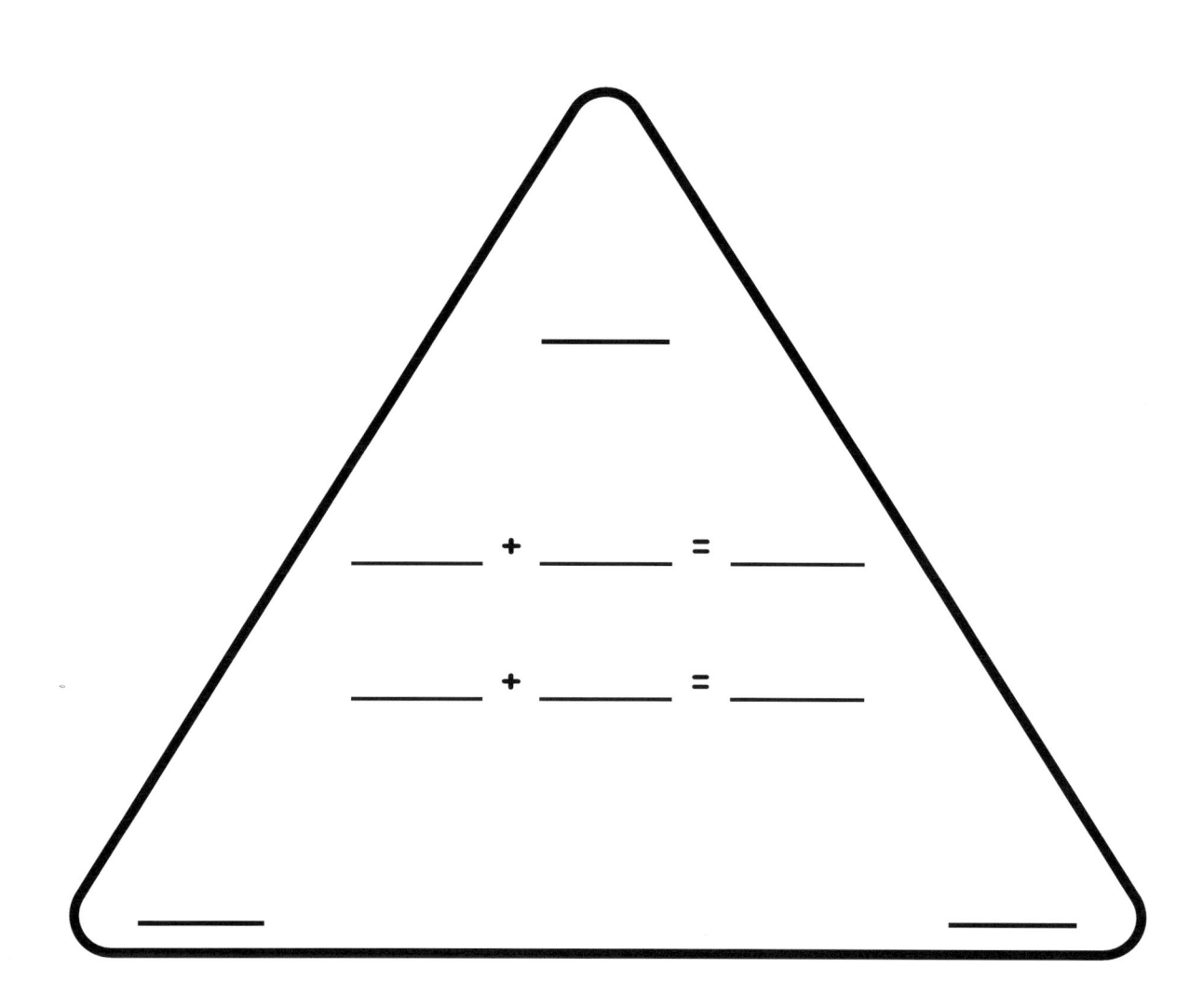

_____

____ + ____ = ____

____ + ____ = ____

____   ____

347   Fact-Family Triangle

Name: _____ Date: _____

Fact-Family Triangle

Follow along in the lesson to learn how to use this fact-family triangle to create related addition sentences.

_____

____ + ____ = ____

____ + ____ = ____

____   ____

Fact-Family Triangle

348